THE CHURCH AT WORSHIP: CASE STUDIES FROM CHRISTIAN HISTORY

Series Editors: LESTER RUTH, CARRIE STEENWYK, JOHN D. WITVLIET

Published·

Walking Where Jesus Walked: Worship in Fourth-Century Jerusalem
    Lester Ruth, Carrie Steenwyk, John D. Witvliet

Tasting Heaven on Earth: Worship in Sixth-Century Constantinople
    Walter D. Ray

*Longing for Jesus: Worship at a Black Holiness Church
in Mississippi, 1895–1913*
    Lester Ruth

*Lifting Hearts to the Lord: Worship with John Calvin in
Sixteenth-Century Geneva*
    Karin Maag

Forthcoming

*Loving God Intimately: Worship with the Anaheim Vineyard Fellowship,
1977–1983*
    Andy Park, Lester Ruth, and Cindy Rethmeier

*Joining Hearts and Voices: Worship with Isaac Watts in
Eighteenth-Century London*
    Christopher J. Ellis

*Leaning On the Word: Worship with Argentine Baptists in
the Mid-Twentieth Century*
    Lester Ruth and Eric Mathis

D1214918

Lifting Hearts

to the Lord

Worship with John Calvin in
Sixteenth-Century Geneva

KARIN MAAG

William B. Eerdmans Publishing Company
Grand Rapids, Michigan / Cambridge, U.K.

Published 2016 by
WM. B. EERDMANS PUBLISHING CO.
2140 Oak Industrial Drive N.E., Grand Rapids, Michigan 49505 /
P.O. Box 163, Cambridge CB3 9PU U.K.

Library of Congress Cataloging-in-Publication Data

Maag, Karin.
  Lifting hearts to the Lord : worship with John Calvin in sixteenth-century Geneva / Karin Maag.
    pages   cm. — (The church at worship : case studies from Christian history)
  Includes bibliographical references and index.
  ISBN 978-0-8028-7147-3 (pbk. : alk. paper)
  1. Public worship — Geneva (Republic) 2. Calvin, Jean, 1509-1564.
  3. Geneva (Republic) — Church history.   I. Title.
  BV15.M225   2016
  264'.042009494516 — dc23

                              2015025992

www.eerdmans.com

Contents

Series Introduction   ix

Suggestions for Complementary Reading   xii

Acknowledgments   xiii

PART ONE: LOCATING THE WORSHIPING COMMUNITY

The Context of the Worshiping Community: Sixteenth-Century Geneva   3

Timeline   6

Liturgical Landscape   13

Geographical Landscape   16

Cautions for Studying Geneva's Worship History   17

Significant Themes and Practices to Observe   19

PART TWO: EXPLORING THE WORSHIPING COMMUNITY

Describing the Community's Worship: John Calvin's Geneva, 1541-1564   25

Documenting the Community's Worship   33

People and Artifacts   33

    John Calvin in His Study   33

    Seventeenth-Century Pewter Communion Ewer   34

    Return of a Baptismal Party   35

Worship Setting and Space   36

    Geneva in 1548   36

    A Map of Geneva and Its Surroundings   37

    Saint Pierre Cathedral and Geneva   38

    A River-side View of Geneva in 1548   39

    A Street Map of Geneva's Old City   40

    A Seventeenth-Century Engraving of Saint Pierre   41

The Exterior of Saint Pierre Cathedral   42

The Interior of Saint Pierre Cathedral   43

The Interior of Saint Gervais Church before the 1903 Restoration   44

Paradis Church   45

Iconoclasm in Zurich   46

The Tables of the Law   47

Descriptions of Worship   48

Calvin Addresses Questions about the Lord's Supper (1561)   48

Calvin's Letters on Pastoral Leadership (1542)   50

Calvin Compares Catholic and Protestant Worship (1542)   53

Calvin Encourages Those Struggling over Differing Worship Practices (1554)   55

Calvin Writes about the Importance of Communal Worship (1554)   57

Calvin Writes about Baptism (1554)   58

Calvin Responds to an Attack on Images (1561)   59

Reactions to a Sermon Preached in Geneva by Guillaume Farel in 1553   61

A Catholic Perspective on Reformed Worship Practices (1556)   62

A Description of Household Worship Practices (1592)   66

Managing a Country Parish: A Country Pastor's Advice to His Successor (1567)   66

Orders of Service and Texts   73

The Form of Prayers and Church Singing (1542)   73

The Form for Administering Baptism (1542)   78

The Manner of Celebrating Holy Matrimony (1545)   82

Prayers from the 1542 Genevan Catechism   85

The Title Page of La Forme des Prieres et Chantz Ecclesiastiques *(1542)*   89

Genevan Psalm VIII from La Forme des Prieres *(1542)*   90

The Song of Simeon and the Lord's Prayer from La Forme des Prieres *(1542)*   91

The First Page of the Psalter at the Back of the 1567 Genevan Bible   92

Prayers and Creeds from the 1567 Bible Psalter   93

A Chart from the Psalter in the 1567 Genevan Bible   94

Sermons   96

Calvin's Sermon on the True Worship of God (1562)   96

Theology of Worship Documents   107

Calvin's Teaching on Baptism (1561)   107

Calvin's Teaching on Public Prayer (1560)   108

Calvin's Commentary on Psalm 9 and Psalm 50 (1557)   113

Calvin's Commentary on John 4 (1553)   122

Calvin's Commentary on 1 Corinthians 11 (1546)   125

Calvin's Commentary on Hebrews 13 (1549)   136

Calvin's Response to Arguments in Favor of the Worship of Images (1562?)   139

Calvin's Foreword to the Psalter (1545)   143

Polity Documents   148

Genevan Ecclesiastical Ordinances (1541)   148

Genevan Consistory Records   151

Genevan Council Minutes and Public Announcements   174

Extract of the Ordinance Established by the Small Council Regarding the Selection of Baptismal Names (1546)   181

Ordinances for the Supervision of Churches in the Country (1547)   182

Statutes of the Genevan Academy (1559)   185

Part Three: Assisting the Investigation

Why Study Geneva's Worship? Suggestions for Devotional Use   189

Why Study Geneva's Worship? Discussion Questions for Small Groups   192

Why Study Geneva's Worship? A Guide for Different Disciplines and Areas of Interest   195

Glossary of Names   198

Glossary of Terms   202

Suggestions for Further Study   204

Works Cited   206

Index   208

Series Introduction

The Church at Worship offers user-friendly documentary case studies in the history of Christian worship. The series features a wide variety of examples, both prominent and obscure, from a range of continents, centuries, and Christian traditions. Whereas many historical studies of worship survey developments over time, offering readers a changing panoramic view like that offered out of an airplane window, each volume in The Church at Worship zooms in close to the surface, lingering over worship practices in a single time and place and allowing readers to sense the texture of specific worship practices in unique Christian communities. To complement books that study "the forest" of liturgical history, these volumes study "trees in the forest."

Each volume opens by orienting readers to the larger contexts of each example through a map, a timeline of events, and a summary of significant aspects of worship in the relevant time period and region. This section also includes any necessary cautions for the study of the particular case, as well as significant themes or practices to watch for while reading.

Each volume continues by focusing on the practices of worship in the specific case. This section begins with an introduction that explains the nature of participation in worship for ordinary worshipers. Many studies of worship have focused almost exclusively on what clergy do, say, and think. In contrast, insofar as historical sources allow it, this series focuses on the nature of participation of the entire community.

Each volume next presents an anthology of primary sources, presenting material according to the following categories: people and artifacts, worship setting and space, descriptions of worship, orders of worship and texts, sermons, polity documents, and theology of worship documents. Each source is introduced briefly and is accompanied by a series of explanatory notes. Inclusion of these primary sources allows readers to have direct access to the primary material that historians draw upon for their summary descriptions and comparisons of practices. These sources are presented in ways that honor both academic rigor and accessibility. Our aim is to provide the best English editions of the resources possible, along with a complete set of citations that allow researchers to find quickly the best scholarly editions. At the same time, the introductory comments, explanatory sidebars, detailed glossaries, and devotional and small-group study questions make these volumes helpful not only for scholars and students but also for congregational study groups and a variety of other interested readers.

The presentation of sources attempts, insofar as it is possible, to take into account multiple disciplines of study related to worship. Worship is inevitably a multi-sensory experience, shaped by the sounds of words and music, the sight of symbols and spaces, the taste of bread and wine, and the fragrance of particular places and objects. Worship is also shaped by a variety of sources that never appear in the event itself: scriptural commands, theological treatises, and church polity rules or guidelines. In order to help readers sense this complex interplay, the volumes in this series provide a wide variety of texts and images. We particularly hope that this approach helps students of the history of preaching, architecture, and music, among others, to more deeply understand how their interests intersect with other disciplines.

Each volume concludes with suggestions for devotional use, study questions for congregational study groups, notes for students working in a variety of complementary disciplines, a glossary, suggestions for further study, works cited, and an index.

Students of Christian worship, church history, religious studies, and social or cultural history might use these case studies to complement the bird's-eye view offered by traditional textbook surveys.

Students in more specialized disciplines — including both liberal arts humanities (e.g., architectural or music history) and the subdisciplines of practical theology (e.g., evangelism, preaching, education, and pastoral care) — may use these volumes to discern how their own topic of interest interacts with worship practices. Liturgical music, church architecture, and preaching, for example, cannot be fully understood apart from a larger context of related practices.

This series is also written for congregational study groups, adult education classes, and personal study. It may be unconventional in some contexts to plan a congregational study group around original historical documents. But there is much to commend this approach. A reflective encounter with the texture of local practices in other times and places can be a profound act of discipleship. In the words of Andrew Walls, "Never before has the Church looked so much like the great multitude whom no one can number out of every nation and tribe and people and tongue. Never before, therefore, has there been so much potentiality for mutual enrichment and self-criticism, as God causes yet more light and truth to break forth from his word."[1]

This enrichment and self-criticism happens, in part, by comparing and contrasting the practices of another community with our own. As Rowan Williams explains, "Good history makes us think again about the definition of things we thought we understood pretty well, because it engages not just with what is familiar but with what is strange. It recognizes that 'the past is a foreign country' as well as being *our* past."[2] This is possible, in part, because

---

1. Andrew Walls, *The Missionary Movement in Christian History: Studies in the Transmission of Faith* (Maryknoll, N.Y.: Orbis Books, 1996), p. 15.

2. Rowan Williams, *Why Study the Past? The Quest for the Historical Church* (Grand Rapids: Wm. B. Eerdmans, 2005), p. 1.

of a theological conviction. As Williams points out, ". . . there is a sameness in the work of God. . . . We are not the first to walk this way; run your hand down the wood and the grain is still the same."[3] This approach turns on its head the minimalist perspective that "those who cannot remember the past are condemned to repeat it."[4] That oft-repeated truism implies that the goal of studying history is merely to avoid its mistakes. A more robust Christian sensibility is built around the conviction that the past is not just a comedy of errors but the arena in which God has acted graciously.

We pray that as you linger over this and other case studies in this series, you will be challenged and blessed through your encounter with one small part of the very large family of God. Near the end of his magisterial volume *A Secular Age,* Charles Taylor concludes, "None of us could ever grasp alone everything that is involved in our alienation from God and his action to bring us back. But there are a great many of us, scattered through history, who have had some powerful sense of some facet of this drama. Together we can live it more fully than any one of us could alone." What might this mean? For Taylor it means this: "Instead of reaching immediately for the weapons of polemic, we might better listen for a voice which we could never have assumed ourselves, whose tone might have been forever unknown to us if we hadn't *strained to understand it. . . .*"[5] We hope and pray that readers, eager to learn from worship communities across time and space, will indeed strain to understand what they find in these studies.

LESTER RUTH
Duke Divinity School

CARRIE STEENWYK
Calvin Institute of Christian Worship
Calvin College and Calvin Theological Seminary

JOHN D. WITVLIET
Calvin Institute of Christian Worship
Calvin College and Calvin Theological Seminary

3. Williams, *Why Study the Past?* p. 29.
4. George Santayana, *The Life of Reason* (New York: Scribner's, 1905), p. 284.
5. Charles Taylor, *A Secular Age* (Cambridge: Harvard University Press, 2007), p. 754.

Suggestions for Complementary Reading

For students of Christian worship wanting to survey the broader landscape, we recommend using the examples of these volumes alongside other books such as Geoffrey Wainwright and Karen B. Westerfield Tucker's *Oxford History of Christian Worship* (Oxford University Press, 2005); Gail Ramshaw's *Christian Worship: 100,000 Sundays of Symbols and Rituals* (Fortress Press, 2009); Marcel Metzger's *History of the Liturgy: The Major Stages,* translated by Madeleine Beaumont (Collegeville, MN: Liturgical Press, 1997); Frank C. Senn's *The People's Work: A Social History of the Liturgy* (Fortress Press, 2006) and *Christian Liturgy: Catholic and Evangelical* (Fortress Press, 1997); and James F. White's *Introduction to Christian Worship* (Abingdon Press, 2001), *A Brief History of Christian Worship* (Abingdon Press, 1993), and *Protestant Worship* (Westminster John Knox Press, 2006).

For those studying church history, volumes from this series might accompany volumes such as Mark Noll's *Turning Points: Decisive Moments in the History of Christianity* (Baker Academic, 2001) and Justo Gonzalez's *Church History: An Essential Guide* (Abingdon Press, 1996) and *The Story of Christianity,* vols. 1-2 (HarperOne, 1984 and 1985).

Students of religious studies might read these volumes alonside Robert A. Segal's *The Blackwell Companion to the Study of Religion* (Wiley-Blackwell, 2008) and John R. Hinnell's *The Routledge Companion to the Study of Religion* (Routledge, 2005).

History of music classes might explore the case studies of this series with Paul Westermeyer's *Te Deum: The Church and Music* (Augsburg Fortress Publishers, 1998) or Andrew Wilson-Dickson's *The Story of Christian Music: From Gregorian Chant to Black Gospel* (Augsburg Fortress Publishers, 2003).

History of preaching students might study the contextual examples provided in this series along with Hughes Oliphant Old's volumes of *The Reading and Preaching of the Scriptures in the Worship of the Christian Church* (Eerdmans, 1998-2007) or O. C. Edwards's *A History of Preaching* (Abingdon Press, 2004).

Courses on the Reformation and early modern Calvinism could combine study of this book with material in Philip Benedict, *Christ's Churches Purely Reformed: A Social History of Calvinism* (Yale University Press, 2002), Euan Cameron, *The European Reformation* (Oxford University Press, 2012), or Diarmaid MacCulloch, *The Reformation: A History* (Viking, 2004).

Acknowledgments

I am grateful to the many people who helped make this volume possible:

» to Lester Ruth, John Witvliet, and the Calvin Institute of Christian Worship for their encouragement and underwriting of this project;

» to Publications Manager Carrie Steenwyk, who patiently guided the volume from inception to completion and kept the volume editor on task and on track;

» to Calvin Institute of Christian Worship student assistants Rachel Adams, Calvin Brondyke, Samantha Brondyke Sweetman, Kyle Erffmeyer, Matt Gritter, Kent Hendricks, Shelley Veenstra Hendricks, Courtney Hexham, Rachel Klompmaker, Jana Kelder Koh, Brenda Janssen Kuyper, Anneke Leunk, Asher Mains, Becky Boender Ochsner, Kendra Pennings Kamp, Katie Roelofs, Katie Ritsema Roelofs, Eric Rottman, Annica Vander Linde Quakenbush, Bethany Meyer Vrieland, Tracie VerMerris Wiersma, Joanna Kooyenga Wigboldy, and Eric Zoodsma for their work in typing and copying documents;

» to Meeter Center student assistants Julia Bouwkamp, Matt Estel, Kristin Fidler, Jennifer Kuiper, and Michael Lynch for transcribing documents, working on timelines, locating sources, and helping to organize the glossaries and reading lists and going through the proofs;

» to Kate Miller and to Meeter Center volunteer Sue Poll, both of whom patiently spent hours reading back translations of documents from French to English, to verify that the translations were accurate and fluent. Any remaining infelicities of style are my own;

» to Meeter Center Curator Paul Fields and Program Coordinator Ryan Noppen, who hunted down references, scanned images, created maps, and provided deeply appreciated support at every turn — these fine colleagues make every project worthwhile;

» to my History Department colleagues at Calvin College, who listened to and gave insightful feedback on an early version of the introduction;

» to colleagues in Reformation studies worldwide, who continue to believe that this topic is an important one, and who value access to primary sources for their research and their teaching;

» to my church congregations in Canada, Scotland, Switzerland, and the United States (especially Woodlawn CRC in Grand Rapids, Trinity Episcopal Church in Statesboro, Georgia, and Church of Our Father in Hulls Cove, Maine), who have nurtured my faith and shown me how to worship in community in ways that are rooted in the rich inheritance of the church and that still speak to the concerns, joys, and challenges of twenty-first-century followers of Christ;

» to Urs and Tannis Maag — educators, models of integrity, and beloved parents;

» to the Lilly Endowment for financial support;

» and to Mary Hietbrink for assistance in the publication process.

PART ONE

LOCATING THE WORSHIPING COMMUNITY

The Context of the Worshiping Community: Sixteenth-Century Geneva

Twenty-first-century Geneva is a flourishing Swiss city, primarily known for its cutting-edge scientific research, its high-end jewelry and watch-making, and its many international headquarters, including the World Health Organization, the International Red Cross, and the World Council of Churches. Yet the tourists who visit the city often come as much to experience Geneva's past as its present. Among the biggest attractions for many visitors is Geneva's Protestant heritage that dates back to the 1500s, and its key impact on the Reformed faith, popularly known as Calvinism.

Yet even before the sixteenth century, Geneva played an important role in European history. First settled by an Indo-European people known as the Allobroges, Geneva was incorporated into the ancient Roman empire around 120 B.C., and flourished as a Roman town through the fifth century after Christ. Its prestige and standing grew in the Middle Ages, when the city became known for its quarterly fairs, attracting merchants and traders from Italy to the Netherlands.

Due to the political void that emerged after the fall of the ancient Roman empire, the bishop of Geneva grew in power both spiritually and politically, and the government of Geneva remained in the hands of its bishop until the first decades of the sixteenth century. Geneva's political situation was also shaped by the increasing influence of the neighboring Duchy of Savoy, which wanted to incorporate Geneva into its territory. By the fifteenth century, the Duke of Savoy had received papal permission to appoint the bishop of Geneva, thus drawing the city more firmly into the Savoyard orbit. At the same time, however, the city's leading merchants pushed successfully to gain greater control of local government. By the mid-1300s, for instance, the Genevan city leaders, known as syndics, had the right to administer and oversee justice in the city. Geneva's complex internal and external political realities decisively shaped the course of the Reformation in the first decades of the sixteenth century.[1]

Prior to the Reformation, Geneva, with a population of about 10,000 people, had been a Catholic city within the larger Catholic duchy of Savoy. After its earlier period of prosperity, the economy of Geneva was on a downward slope by the later fifteenth and early sixteenth century. The pattern of trade routes and major fairs had shifted west toward Lyon in France,

A duchy is a territory headed by a duke, one of several different kinds of nobles whose power was a blend of high social status, land ownership, and military might.

The people of Savoy were known as Savoyards. Savoyard was also the name of the dialect spoken in the region, a blend of Italian and French. Most Genevans understood both Savoyard and French.

The pre-Reformation political situation in Geneva was complex. Basically, the Genevan population headed by its most powerful inhabitants (the merchants) wanted more local power in their hands, and less power to their bishop, but the Genevans disagreed over which external political power (the Swiss, the French, or even the Duke of Savoy) was the best potential ally in helping the Genevans achieve greater independence from the bishop's control.

---

1. For more on the early history of Geneva, see Louis Binz, *A Brief History of Geneva,* trans. J. Gunn (Geneva: Chancellerie d'Etat, 1985), pp. 1-25.

and Geneva had become something of a backwater. The town had a merchant class but very few resident nobles, and much of the commercial activity went to supplying local markets.[2]

Geneva's formal adoption of the Reformation in 1536 was not particularly early, considering that Martin Luther's Ninety-Five Theses (usually understood as the starting point of the Reformation) were produced in 1517. Other neighboring cities, especially the Swiss towns of Zurich, Bern, and Basel, had all adopted the Reformation already in the 1520s, and crucially, all had chosen to follow the Reformed version of Protestantism under the leadership of Swiss Reformers, rather than the Lutheran path. This volume will examine how the Reformed Church in Geneva worshiped after the city officially accepted the Reformation in May 1536, in a public gathering of the *conseil général* or general council, bringing together all the men of the city who were entitled to vote. They raised their hands and swore "that all of us, unanimously, and with the help of God, want to live in this holy evangelical law and Word of God, as it is declared to us, wanting to leave aside all masses and other papal ceremonies and abuses, all images and idols, and live in unity and obedience to the law."[3]

To make sense of Reformation worship as practiced in Geneva from 1541 to 1564, one has to understand the pattern of Catholic worship that preceded the Genevan Reformation. Indeed, one of the biggest challenges facing the city's pastors in the first years following the Reformation was trying to get the Genevan population (who had grown up Catholic) to make the transition to Reformed worship without retaining or blending in any of their previously Catholic practices. The church leaders could not take support for the Reformation for granted, for although the male citizens of Geneva had voted publicly to adopt the Reformation, their decision may well have been based more on political factors than on any burning desire for (or even genuine understanding of) Protestant theology and practice.[4] Hence the implementation of Reformed worship in Geneva was as much an instructional process as a liturgical one, and the rich array of documents provides evidence of the give and take that occurred as the Genevans, visitors to the city, government leaders, and pastors all sought to come to terms with the dramatic changes that were taking place.

Geneva offers an exceptional case study for investigations of the theology and practice of worship in the Reformation era for two key reasons. First, Geneva has an extensive and well-preserved set of manuscripts and other archival materials from the sixteenth century, thanks to careful archivists and the small number of wars fought on Genevan territory since the sixteenth century. These factors have ensured the survival of primary source documents that are simply unavailable for many other places where the Reformation took hold. Second, because

Key points of difference between Lutheran and Swiss Reformed churches included the Lord's Supper (the Lutherans held to consubstantiation and the Real Presence of Christ in the elements, while the Swiss Reformed saw the sacrament as a memorial of Christ's sacrifice); baptism (Lutherans retained many more elements of traditional Catholic baptisms, such as anointing with oil and exorcising the power of Satan over the child); and worship (Lutherans sang hymns and retained more elements of the traditional Catholic liturgy. The Reformed of Zurich, in contrast, had no singing or music of any kind during their services, and adopted a very simple liturgy).

---

2. Geneva's political and economic situation at the time of the Reformation is effectively summarized by William Monter, *Calvin's Geneva* (Huntington, N.Y.: Krieger, 1975), pp. 1-59.

3. Amédée Roget, *Histoire du peuple de Genève, depuis la réforme jusqu'à l'escalade* ([Geneva]: Julien, 1870), Vol. I, p. 2.

4. For a helpful overview of the early Genevan Reformation, see William Naphy, *Calvin and the Consolidation of the Genevan Reformation* (Manchester: Manchester University Press, 1994), pp. 13-25.

the French Reformer John Calvin spent the major part of his adult life in Geneva and made the city one of the focal points for Reformed churches across Europe, later scholars interested in the history and theology of Calvin and Calvinism have produced extensive secondary sources that deal with worship and other aspects of religious life in Reformation Geneva.[5]

The time span of this volume extends from 1541, when Calvin returned to Geneva after his three-year exile in the German city of Strasbourg, to 1564, the year of Calvin's death. This period of over twenty years allows readers to examine various facets of worship in Reformed Geneva over the course of nearly one generation.

5. For an in-depth comparison of the changes in worship in Geneva before and after the Reformation, see Thomas Lambert, "Preaching, Praying, and Policing the Reform in Sixteenth-Century Geneva," Ph.D. dissertation, University of Wisconsin-Madison, 1998.

Timeline

What was happening in the world from 1500 to 1600?	What was happening in Christianity from 1500 to 1600?	What was happening in Geneva from 1500 to 1600?
1501: The Safavid dynasty begins in Persia, following the Shia branch of Islam.		
1506: After the victory of King Afonso I over his opponents, Catholicism becomes the state religion of the Kongo.		
1507: The Americas experience their first recorded smallpox epidemic on the island of Hispaniola.		
1509: Henry VIII accedes to the English throne.	**1509:** John Calvin is born in Noyon in northern France.	
1513: Machiavelli writes *The Prince*.		
	1516: Erasmus's edition of the New Testament in Greek is published.	
	1517: Martin Luther's Ninety-Five Theses against indulgences are made public.	
	1518: The Swiss Reformer Huldrych Zwingli begins his work as the people's priest in Zurich.	
1519: Charles V becomes the Holy Roman Emperor.	**1519:** Public debate takes place between Martin Luther and Catholic theologian Johannes Eck at Leipzig.	**1519:** The Genevan General Council votes for an alliance with Fribourg, its powerful Swiss neighbor. The Duke of Savoy, Charles II, opposes the alliance and occupies Geneva. One of the key proponents of the alliance and of greater freedom for Geneva vis-à-vis Savoy, Philibert Berthelier, is arrested and executed on the orders of the Bishop of Geneva.
1519-21: Under the leadership of Hernan Cortes, Spanish forces conquer the Aztec empire.		
1520: Suleiman the Magnificent begins his reign as the Ottoman Sultan.	**1520:** Martin Luther is excommunicated by Pope Leo X.	

What was happening in the world from 1500 to 1600?

1521: Ferdinand Magellan's expedition circumnavigates the globe, though Magellan himself dies in a skirmish in the Philippines earlier that year.

1524-25: Fueled by a combination of religious and political motivations, the German Peasants' War breaks out but is ultimately crushed by the forces of the German princes.

1526: Ottoman forces defeat the Hungarians at the battle of Mohács.

1526: The Mughal empire in India begins.

1527: Holy Roman Emperor Charles V's troops sack Rome.

1529: The Ottoman Turks invade Europe from the east and besiege Vienna.

1533: Under the leadership of Francisco Pizarro, Spanish forces conquer the Inca empire.

What was happening in Christianity from 1500 to 1600?

1521: Martin Luther appears before Emperor Charles V at the Diet of Worms and refuses to recant. On his way back to Wittenberg, Luther is secretly taken into protective custody by his prince, the Elector of Saxony.

1522: The Inquisition is established in the Netherlands.

1522: Luther's German translation of the New Testament is published.

1523: The first and second public debates on the Reformation take place in Zurich.

1524: The Mass is abolished in Zurich.

1524-29: The Zurich Bible is published.

1527: The Schleitheim articles are issued, outlining key beliefs of several German and Swiss Anabaptists.

1529: The Colloquy of Marburg brings together leading German and Swiss Reformers at the request of Prince Philip of Hesse. The Reformers split over their divergent understandings of Christ's presence in the Lord's Supper.

1529: Luther's Small Catechism and Great Catechism are published.

1530: The Lutheran Augsburg Confession is published.

1531: Huldrych Zwingli dies at the Battle of Kappel.

1531-32: The English church rejects the authority of the Pope and acknowledges King Henry VIII as supreme ruler over the English church.

What was happening in Geneva from 1500 to 1600?

1526: A new treaty of mutual alliance and protection is established between Geneva, Fribourg, and the powerful Swiss territory of Bern.

1532: French Reformer Guillaume Farel arrives in Geneva.

1533: Reformed preacher Antoine Froment gives the first public Protestant sermon in Geneva.

What was happening in the world from 1500 to 1600?

1534: French explorer Jacques Cartier claims territory in present-day Quebec for France.

1540: Francisco de Coronado of Spain becomes the first European to survey the Rio Grande River.

What was happening in Christianity from 1500 to 1600?

1534: In the Affair of the Placards, broadsheets denouncing the Catholic Mass are posted across Paris.

1535: The Anabaptist kingdom of Münster is defeated by a coalition of German princes, and its leaders are tortured and executed.

1536: The Inquisition is set up in Portugal.

1536: John Calvin publishes his first Latin edition of the *Institutes of the Christian Religion.*

1537: William Tyndale's translation of the Bible in English appears in print.

1538-41: Expelled from Geneva, Calvin settles in Strasbourg, where he pastors a French refugee church, teaches, publishes his commentary on Paul's letter to the Romans, and gets married.

1540: The Jesuit order (Society of Jesus) is formally established.

1540-41: The Colloquy of Regensburg brings together moderate Catholics and Protestants but reaches an impasse over divergent understandings of the Eucharist and of authority in the church.

What was happening in Geneva from 1500 to 1600?

1533: Pierre de la Baume, Bishop of Geneva, leaves the city for the last time.

1534: Geneva begins to strike its own coinage.

1535: The Mass is suspended in Geneva by the Council of Two Hundred.

1535: The *Hôpital général* is established in Geneva to serve as a central clearing-house for the care of the sick, orphans, widows, and the poor.

1536 (January): Called in to help protect Geneva from Savoyard pressure, the Bernese launch an all-out assault on the duchy of Savoy, conquering extensive sections of the territory and ensuring Geneva's external political safety for at least fifty years.

1536 (May): The Genevan General Council officially adopts the Reformed faith.

1536 (July): Calvin arrives in Geneva only intending a brief overnight stay, but is compelled by the Reformer Guillaume Farel to remain to help the Reformation take hold.

1538: Calvin, Farel, and fellow pastor Antoine Courault are banished from Geneva by the city government after conflicts between the pastors and the city leadership over the implementation of the Reformation and over the pastors' contention that the church should have the final say in cases of church discipline.

What was happening in the world from 1500 to 1600?

1541: In search of gold, Hernando de Soto of Spain becomes the first European to survey the Mississippi River.

1542: Francisco de Montejo of Spain subdues Mayan resistance in the Americas but is unable to conquer more of the Yucatán Peninsula.

1543: Copernicus publishes his *On the Revolutions of the Celestial Sphere,* setting forth his theory on the heliocentric system of the universe.

1545: Smallpox and typhus spread throughout the Americas, killing 1,300,000.

1546: Schmalkaldic War begins between the Holy Roman Emperor Charles V and the Protestant Schmalkaldic League.

1546: Francis I of France commissions the construction of the Louvre.

1547: Pushing back the Mongol forces, Ivan IV ("the Terrible") becomes the first Czar of Russia.

1547: Henry VIII of England dies and is succeeded by his son Edward VI, age nine.

1547: At age six, Mary, Queen of Scots, is betrothed to the future Francis II of France.

What was happening in Christianity from 1500 to 1600?

1541: Michelangelo finishes *The Last Judgment* fresco on the altar wall of the Sistine Chapel.

1543: For the first time, the Spanish Inquisition burns Protestants at the stake.

1545: The Council of Trent begins as the Catholic response to the Protestant Reformation.

1546: Martin Luther dies at the age of 63 in Eisleben, his birthplace.

1547: King Henri II establishes the Chambre Ardente in Paris, France, as a court to try heretics, increasing persecution against Protestants.

1549: Edward VI implements use of the Book of Common Prayer in all churches, fomenting a Catholic rebellion in the more religiously conservative northern and southern England.

What was happening in Geneva from 1500 to 1600?

1541: After shifts in political power, the Genevan magistrates invite John Calvin back from exile, and Calvin returns to Geneva after three years in Strasbourg.

1541-42: The Genevan Councils accept Calvin's Ecclesiastical Ordinances (1541) as law; Calvin's catechism (1542) and *Form of Prayers and Church Singing* (1542) help to consolidate the Reformed faith in Geneva.

1542: Meetings of the Consistory of Geneva and the Company of Pastors are established.

1543: Plague breaks out in Geneva.

1545-46: Refusing to give a reason, Calvin prevents Jean Trolliet from becoming a minister despite pressure from Genevan magistrates; from then on, Trolliet challenges Calvin's view on predestination.

1546: Riots against "French pastors" (particularly Calvin) arise as a result of disputes over church discipline between Calvin and powerful Genevan citizens.

1546: The onset of the Schmalkaldic War provokes fear in Geneva.

1547: Jacques Gruet is arrested and executed for a libelous attack on the French ministers.

1549: Calvin's wife, Idelette, dies after an extended illness.

What was happening in the world from 1500 to 1600?

1551: English settlers colonize Morocco.

1553: Catholic and Protestant princes form the League of Heidelberg to prevent the succession of Philip, the son of Charles V, as Holy Roman Emperor.

1555: Tobacco from the Americas is first introduced in Spain.

1555: French Huguenots arrive in present-day Rio de Janeiro in search of religious freedom; they establish France Antarctique, a colony that lasts twelve years.

1556: The worst earthquake ever recorded hits the Shanxi province in China, killing 830,000.

1557: Portuguese settle in Macao (China).

1557: Thousands in Europe die from an influenza epidemic.

1557: Spain declares bankruptcy (also in 1560, 1575, and 1596).

What was happening in Christianity from 1500 to 1600?

1549: St. Francis Xavier travels to Japan, founding a Jesuit mission.

1549: The *Consensus Tigurinus* (Zurich agreement on the sacraments) is issued, signed by the Zurich church and by John Calvin on behalf of the Genevan clergy.

1552: The Treaty of Passau temporarily allows Lutherans to exercise their faith in the Holy Roman Empire.

1553: Edward VI dies, and his half-sister Mary I becomes queen, re-establishing Catholicism in England.

1555: The Peace of Augsburg ends the religious wars between Catholics and Lutherans in the German states and officially allows both faiths to be practiced.

1558: Mary I dies, and her half-sister Elizabeth I becomes queen, re-establishing Protestantism in England.

1559: Under Pope Paul IV, the Catholic Church publishes its first *Index of Forbidden Books*.

What was happening in Geneva from 1500 to 1600?

1551: Geneva's magistrates banish Jérome Bolsec from the city for his criticism of Calvin's view of predestination.

1553: The civil authorities of Geneva arrest, put on trial, and burn Michael Servetus at the stake for his anti-Trinitarian views and publications.

1555: Following an abortive riot by Calvin's opponents, these men are forced into exile; Calvin's supporters gain power on Geneva's councils.

1555: Genevan pastors are dispatched to emerging Reformed congregations in France.

1559: The Genevan Academy is officially inaugurated, providing Latin-school and university-level education in Geneva. Calvin becomes a bourgeois of Geneva.

1559: Calvin publishes his final version of the *Institutes of the Christian Religion* in Latin.

What was happening in the world from 1500 to 1600?

1560: Francis II of France dies and widows Mary, Queen of Scots; Charles IX succeeds Francis as king.

1563: The first slave shipment from the Americas to England takes place.
1563: Outbreak of the plague in England kills 80,000.

1564: William Shakespeare, the English playwright, is born in Stratford-upon-Avon.
1564: Galileo Galilei, the Italian mathematician, physicist, and astronomer, is born in Pisa, Italy.

1568: The Eighty Years' War between Spain and the Netherlands starts.
1569: The crowns of Poland and Lithuania are unified.
1571: The Turkish fleet is defeated by European forces at the Battle of Lepanto.

What was happening in Christianity from 1500 to 1600?

1560: The Geneva Bible (in English) is published.

1561: The Belgic Confession is drafted by Guido de Brès.
1562: The forces of the Catholic Duc de Guise army massacre 1,200 French Huguenots at Vassy, leading to the First War of Religion in France.
1563: Under the authority of Frederick III of the Palatinate, Zacharius Ursinus and Caspar Olevianus compose the Reformed Heidelberg Catechism.
1563: The Council of Trent comes to a close, having tightened its church governance policies but reaffirmed traditional Catholic doctrines.
1563: The Thirty-Nine Articles, promulgating the doctrinal teachings of the Church of England, are issued.

1564: Pope Pius IV makes the Council of Trent's Profession of Faith normative for all Roman Catholics.

1566: The Catechism of the Council of Trent is published.
1566: The Wonderyear, which involves public preaching of the Reformed faith and image-breaking in many Catholic churches, takes place in the Netherlands.

1572: Catholics kill French Huguenots (Reformed Protestants), first in Paris and then in the rest of France, during the St. Bartholomew's Day massacre.

What was happening in Geneva from 1500 to 1600?

1564: John Calvin dies at the age of 55 and is buried in an unmarked grave.
1564: Théodore de Bèze is elected to be Calvin's replacement as moderator of the Company of Pastors.

1567-72: Geneva suffers from recurring plague epidemics.

What was happening in the world from 1500 to 1600?

1577-80: Sir Francis Drake and his crew circumnavigate the globe.

1580: Portugal is united to Spain (until 1640).

1581: Seven northern provinces of the Netherlands (the United Provinces) declare their independence from Philip II, king of Spain.

1588: The Spanish Armada's attempt to attack England by sea is defeated.

1589: Henri IV becomes king of France.

1592-98: With the assistance of Ming China, Korea resists and ultimately repels Japanese invasions.

1598: The Edict of Nantes is proclaimed in France, providing limited legal toleration for French Protestants and putting an end to over thirty years of intermittent civil war between Catholics and Protestants in the country.

1599: The Mali empire is defeated by Moroccan forces at the Battle of Jenné.

1600: The British East India Company is chartered.

What was happening in Christianity from 1500 to 1600?

1576-83: Elector Ludwig VI moves the Palatinate back to Lutheranism. After his death, the territory once again becomes Reformed.

1577: The Lutheran Formula of Concord is issued, bringing doctrinal agreement among Lutherans.

1600: Giordano Bruno is burned for heresy in Rome.

What was happening in Geneva from 1500 to 1600?

1586-87: The Duke of Savoy, Charles Emmanuel, blockades Geneva.

1589: Geneva launches military strikes against Savoyard territory. After a number of early victories, the Genevans are then pushed back by Savoy, and the war ends with a truce.

Liturgical Landscape

What liturgical worlds surrounded **Geneva** in the sixteenth century? If a Genevan worshiper looked around in 1545, what might she see?

John Calvin returned to Geneva in 1541 at the invitation of the city's magistrates, who had asked him to leave the city three years earlier due to conflicts between the pastors and government leaders over the direction of the church and oversight of church discipline. In the three-year interval between 1538 and 1541, Geneva had struggled, dealing with lesser-caliber pastors and receiving a strongly worded summons from Cardinal Jacopo Sadoleto to return to traditional Catholicism. Geneva's continued reliance on Calvin is evidenced by the decision of the Genevan city council to entrust to him the reply to the Catholic cardinal, asserting the validity of Geneva's continued commitment to Reformed Protestantism.

Yet in spite of his recall to the city and the implementation of edicts on worship in Geneva (the 1541 Ecclesiastical Ordinances), a Reformed liturgy (*La Forme des Prieres* — The Form of Prayers, 1542), and a new **catechism** (1541-42), getting the people of Geneva to change their liturgical habits and practices was an uphill struggle. Part of the problem, of course, was that Protestant liturgical practices were still in flux in these first decades of the Reformation.

A catechism is a summary of Christian doctrine used for instructional purposes and often in question-and-answer format.

Although Reformers across the theological spectrum agreed that a key component of Protestant liturgy was the use of the vernacular, some churches, especially in Lutheran areas, still tended to retain many more elements of the Latin pre-Reformation rituals, compared with the Reformed practice. For more on this subject, see, for instance, Frank Senn, "Luther's Liturgical Reforms" and "Word and Sacrament in Luther's Reformation" in his *Christian Liturgy: Catholic and Evangelical* (Minneapolis: Fortress Press, 1997), pp. 267-322; and Bryan Spinks, *Luther's Liturgical Criteria and His Reform of the Canon of the Mass* (Bramcote: Grove Books, 1982).

Meanwhile, Geneva's nearest Protestant neighbors, including the Swiss cities and territories of Bern and Zurich, had adopted a more wholesale liturgical reform, including having all parts of the service in the language of the people, whitewashing church interiors to remove any sign of images such as murals and frescoes, and even eliminating singing from worship services. For more on the changes in worship in the Reformed Swiss territories, especially Zurich, see Senn, *Christian Liturgy,* pp. 357-70, and Gottfried Locher, "In Spirit and in Truth: How Worship in Zurich Changed at the Reformation," in his *Zwingli's Thought: New Perspectives* (Leiden: Brill, 1981), pp. 1-30.

While there could be quite a bit of variation among the liturgical practices adopted by Protestant Reformers, there was general agreement that the seven Catholic sacraments (baptism, confirmation, communion, confession/penance, marriage, ordination, and extreme unction/last rites) should be reduced to only two, the only ones for which there was biblical warrant in Jesus' words in the New Testament — namely, baptism and communion.

Even then, however, the Reformers disagreed on the theology of these sacraments, and their theological disagreement took shape in their various liturgies for these sacramental celebrations. Theological and liturgical conflicts over baptism could include such fundamental issues as whether one should baptize infants, or only adults, who could personally testify to their faith and their desire for the sacrament; whether one should retain Catholic practices of anointing the baby with holy oil and exorcising the devil from the child; and whether emergency baptisms or private baptisms were ever allowable. Helpful studies on the sacrament of baptism in the Reformation era include Hughes Oliphant Old, *The Shaping of the Reformed Baptismal Rite in the Sixteenth Century* (Grand Rapids: Wm. B. Eerdmans, 1992), which in spite of its title offers an overview of Catholic, Lutheran, and Anabaptist baptismal rites as well; and Kent Burreson, "Water Surrounded by God's Word: The Diocese of Breslau as a Window into the Transformation of Baptism from the Medieval Period to the Reformation," in *Worship in Medieval and Early Modern Europe: Change and Continuity in Religious Practice,* ed. Karin Maag and John Witvliet (Notre Dame: University of Notre Dame Press, 2004), pp. 203-42.

Theological conflicts over the Lord's Supper could be even more intense. How often should the sacrament be celebrated? Weekly? Monthly? Quarterly? What kind of bread should be used — leavened or unleavened? Should only the pastor hand out the bread and wine, or could elders or deacons assist in the distribution? Should people come forward to receive the elements or remain in their seats? If they came forward, should they come in order of social precedence and hierarchy, with the most important men first, followed by all the other men, and then by all the women in the same order, or should a different approach be followed? For a detailed study of the subject, see Lee Palmer Wandel, *The Eucharist in the Reformation: Incarnation and Liturgy* (Cambridge: Cambridge University Press, 2006). This work does, however, leave out the practice of the Swiss churches.

Of all the various liturgical changes, the move from the Mass to the Lord's Supper would have been most evident and most radically different for the Genevan population. Those who kept abreast of religious controversies elsewhere may well have been aware of the 1534 French placard against the Mass, likely published in nearby Neuchâtel, but posted throughout France, including on the door of King Francis I's bedchamber. Attacks on the Mass and the theology of transubstantiation, whether written or oral, could also lead to acts of symbolic violence against images or elements of the Catholic liturgical practice. See Lee Palmer

Wandel, *Voracious Idols and Violent Hands: Iconoclasm in Reformation Zurich, Strasbourg, and Basel* (Cambridge: Cambridge University Press, 1995).

Hence the liturgical landscape was shaped not only by the decision to adopt specific worship practices that sought to reflect theological commitments, but also by the decision to reject other practices that were no longer considered acceptable. Through these decisions, the Reformers redefined what was sacred. For more on the understanding of sacredness in Reformation Geneva, see Christian Grosse, "Places of Sanctification: The Liturgical Sacrality of Genevan Reformed Churches, 1535-1566," in *Sacred Space in Early Modern Europe,* ed. Will Coster and Andrew Spicer (Cambridge: Cambridge University Press, 2005), pp. 60-80.

As the Genevans sought to come to terms with the changes in liturgical teachings and practices, their experience was part of the wider process of transformations in worship and liturgy that was happening at different speeds and with different end results across early modern Europe. As such, the Genevan experience is part of the larger picture and should not be understood in isolation from its broader context.

Geographical Landscape

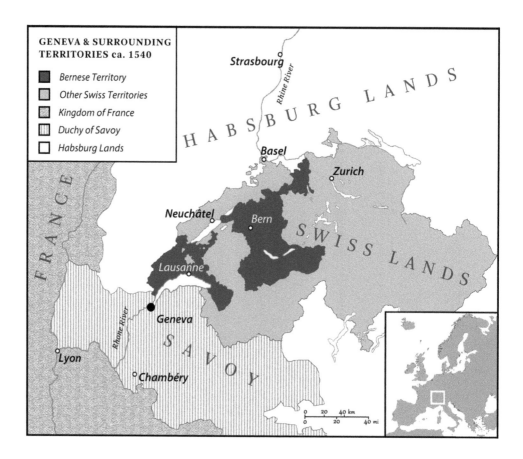

The city-state of Geneva was a tiny enclave with powerful neighbors — the Duchy of Savoy, the Swiss lands (especially the powerful and expansionist Canton of Bern), and France all sought to influence Genevan politics and religion.

Source: Image produced by Ryan Noppen, Meeter Center, Calvin College

Cautions for Studying Geneva's Worship History

The documents assembled in this collection offer a fascinating window into the beliefs and practices of Reformed Genevans at worship. However, as with all primary source analyses, readers should bear some fundamental points in mind before drawing conclusions.

- Instructions, ordinances, and regulations are prescriptive and not descriptive documents. In other words, we cannot assume that just because the ordinances say a given ritual or church service should take place at a given time or in a given way, the reality actually matched the regulation.

- **Consistory** cases, while fascinating, need to be analyzed very carefully for a number of reasons. First, although the minutes do at times provide the words spoken by those called before the Consistory, they are second-hand reports in that they were written down (more or less accurately) and perhaps filtered by the Consistory secretary. Second, the Consistory dealt with problem cases; it would be wrong to infer from these cases that the majority of Genevans had as little knowledge of the Reformed faith or were as ardent in retaining their Catholic practices as the minority who were called before the Consistory.

A consistory is an ecclesiastical council that oversees spiritual matters in Reformed churches. It is usually made up of pastors and elders who meet regularly to address faith and morality issues in the congregation.

- The eyewitness accounts of worship in Reformation Geneva included in this volume are all penned by outsiders. **Charles Perrot,** the pastor in Genthod and Moens, was a religious refugee from France, highly educated, and a former Catholic monk. He came from a very different world than his rural Genevan congregations. André Ryff was from Basel. His first language was Swiss German, not French, and he returned to Basel once his apprenticeship ended. Finally, the anonymous author of the *Passevent Parisien,* although reporting on what he had seen, was a French Catholic who framed his report within a strongly polemical text in which he sought to portray the Reformers in the worst light possible.

- Indeed, the polemical context of controversy between rival confessional groups makes it a challenging task to interpret the significance of worship changes as described and advocated or opposed in these various sources. How much were these changes underpinned by a reasoned theological argument, and how much were they simply the result of wanting to ensure a high degree of separation from previously Catholic practices?

- We have a strong selection of Calvin's teachings on worship, whether through his sermons, commentaries, or correspondence. It would be wrong to assume, however, that Calvin was the only Genevan pastor who taught on worship and liturgy. We lack sources from Calvin's fellow pastors, but that does not mean that Calvin's was the only voice that Genevans heard on the subject.

- The Genevan pastors were very concerned about any possibility of resurgent Catholicism, and hence they were very quick to condemn what they understood as "superstition." We should not take their assessment at face value, but rather try to understand what the Genevans who held to such practices thought they were doing.

- Many of the images and engravings of worship spaces and liturgical practices are not from the sixteenth century. Therefore, our inferences about liturgy and worship in Geneva based on these images have to be drawn very carefully.

Significant Themes and Practices to Observe

As you study and analyze these texts and images, watch for the following important topics and practices, organized thematically:

Piety

- After the Reformation, Genevans were expected to make all parts of their life conform to the Reformed faith. It was not enough for them to attend church on Sunday; instead, they were to live out their faith commitment in all aspects of their life, including their interactions with family and neighbors. See the first-person account by André Ryff in the primary sources, in which he described his experiences of household worship practices, including daily household prayers led by the mother of the family.
- Baptism ratified a child's participation in the covenant community that united God and his people. Baptisms, therefore, had to happen in the presence of a congregation during a regular church service.
- Infants who died before they could be baptized were not thought of as lost or damned, as God's covenant extended to his faithful people and their children. Thus, emergency baptisms by midwives were declared invalid.
- God was especially present to his people in the preaching of his Word and in the two sacraments, baptism and the Lord's Supper.

Time

- The Genevan church year was shaped by the quarterly celebrations of the Lord's Supper, at Christmas, at Easter, at Pentecost, and in September. Each Lord's Supper service was preceded by a Sunday of preparation during which special sermons were preached in the churches.
- To avoid any possible return to what they called "Papist superstition," the Genevan pastors strongly opposed any observance of Catholic feast days, whether these were associ-

Although Calvin noted that he would have preferred to celebrate the Lord's Supper more frequently (perhaps monthly or even weekly), the Genevan political authorities adopted the Swiss Reformed model of quarterly celebrations, in part to draw clear distinctions between Reformed and Catholic practice.

ated with the Virgin Mary, or with particular saints, or even with episodes of Christ's life, such as Epiphany.

- It was important for everyone to attend church services on Sunday. Everyone in the household had to attend at least one service, arrive on time, pay attention during the service, and not attempt to leave early, before the final benediction; pastors wanted to make sure parishioners understood that the whole worship service formed an integral unit and was important, not just the sermon or the celebration of the sacraments. For more on the times and schedules for church services on Sundays and during the week, see the Genevan Ecclesiastical Ordinances, specifically the introduction to the document (p. 148).

Place

- Because of its geographical location, Geneva ended up as a Protestant enclave, sharing its nearby border with Catholic Savoy. A Genevan could easily leave town early on a Sunday morning, go to Mass in Catholic Savoy, and be back well before dark. Being aware of this geographical set-up is key to understanding why the Genevan clergy were constantly concerned about the dangers of resurgent Catholicism.
- Geneva's three parish churches within the city were dramatically re-organized following the Reformation. The interior orientation of the church shifted from a focus on the high altar to a focus on the pulpit, and seating was configured accordingly. Men and boys sat separately from women and girls, and the schoolboys and the aged who were hard of hearing sat up front. Nursing mothers were excused from attendance, which helped cut down a bit on the noise level, because fewer infants were present.
- Geneva's churches were locked outside of service times, so that no one could go in to engage in traditional Catholic devotional rituals.

Prayer

- When the Consistory asked people appearing before it to "recite your prayers," the pastors and elders expected that people would respond by reciting by heart the Lord's Prayer, the Ten Commandments, and the Apostles' Creed, all in French.
- In the first years after the Reformation, many of those appearing before the Consistory responded to the request to recite their prayers by reciting the ones their parents had taught them: the Pater Noster and the Ave Maria, in Latin.

- To teach people how to pray, the Genevan catechism included a selection of prayers in French to be recited by families and individuals, at home and at work, at different times of the day.
- Prayers in Sunday and weekday church services were led by the pastor and usually included an extensive prayer bringing together adoration, thanksgiving, pleas for God's mercy, and the petitions of the church. In times of calamity, whether natural or human-made, the Genevan church held special services focusing on praying and Psalm-singing, asking for forgiveness, and calling on God for help.

Preaching

- Genevan pastors preached sequentially through books of the Bible, starting at chapter one, verse one, and working their way through to the end of the book. Each sermon usually focused on five or six verses at a time, so Calvin's sermon series on Job, for instance, involved 159 different sermons. The sequence of sermons on Job took over a year, from February 26, 1554, to March 20, 1555, when Calvin began his sermon series on Deuteronomy.
- Sermons usually took about an hour to preach; pastors kept note of passing time by using an hourglass.
- Genevans were expected to listen attentively, and, if asked by the Consistory, they were expected to recall the topic of a given sermon even days after it was preached.

Music

- Following Calvin's practice, which he developed in Strasbourg, Genevans sang in unison only unaccompanied Psalms and other key scriptural texts such as the Ten Commandments (in French) in church. The Psalm texts were versified by some of France's most able poets, including **Clément Marot.** For more on the experience of Genevans singing in church, especially in the first generation, see the account of Pastor Charles Perrot. His advice for his successor suggests that even up to the 1560s, in the Genevan countryside at least, Psalm-singing was hesitant and hardly enthusiastically adopted by congregations.
- Singing could be led by a chantre (cantor) or by a small group of schoolboys, who knew the Psalms better than others in the congregation because schoolboys had an hour of Psalm-singing during every school day.
- Singing Psalms in harmony was encouraged at home.

People

- Geneva was a city of merchants and artisans. The coming of the Reformation brought in numerous religious refugees, especially from France, often leading to tensions between the native Genevans and the new arrivals.
- The leading families of the city were particularly resentful of the greater economic power and prestige of some of these refugees and in many cases strongly objected to attempts by the new arrivals to shape the course of the Genevan Reformation.
- The entire Genevan pastorate was foreign-born during Calvin's lifetime. All had been born and grew up in France; none were native Genevans.

PART TWO

EXPLORING THE WORSHIPING COMMUNITY

Describing the Community's Worship:
John Calvin's Geneva, 1541-1564

When the Genevans voted in favor of the Reformation in May 1536, many of them were making a choice to break with Catholicism largely for political reasons, to help the city gain full independence from the rule of the Catholic bishop and from the Duke of Savoy, the city's overlord. Yet the Reformation meant dramatic changes for the city and its rural territory, not least in terms of its worship practices. What follows is a description of what worship life was like in Geneva during the two decades after 1541; the description is taken from Genevan church records, contemporary Genevan chronicles, and studies by historians of the Genevan Reformation.

In late May 1548, the Genevan Consistory, a body of pastors and elders charged with the oversight of the population's faith and behavior, met to investigate a disturbance that had taken place in church during a recent Sunday afternoon catechism service. According to the report of Pastor Michel Cop, he was conducting a baptism when an uproar ensued after he refused to give the baby boy the name Balthasar (as chosen by the family, because it was a clan name in the godfather's kin group), and baptized him John instead. The infant's father and other relatives and friends grew incensed, and accusations and threats flew back and forth about Pastor Cop's ministry and morals. Among other things, he was accused of having stolen a chalice from his monastery, of charging excessive interest on loans, and of buying manure when he should have been attending church services; more general comments were made about the nefarious influence of French religious refugees (like Cop) in Geneva. Yet the minister held his ground and knew that he had the weight of the law behind him, since the city had passed an ordinance in 1546 that barred certain names for babies, including Balthasar (one of the three wise men, according to Catholic legend). The Consistory called various witnesses to testify to what they had seen and heard in church that afternoon and ended up vindicating Pastor Cop's actions.[1]

> The catechism service followed the format of regular Genevan worship services, except that the pastor's sermon would focus on a different section of the catechism, Sunday by Sunday. The aim was to teach the key doctrines of the Reformed faith to make sure everyone understood clearly the fundamentals of their faith.

On the face of it, this account seems quite troubling: during what should have been one of the most holy moments of a person's Christian life, a pastor overruled a parent's choice of name, and a near-riot broke out. Yet this report, and the Consistory's careful investigation of what happened, opens up the lived experiences of Genevans at worship during the period. Thanks to the testimony of the witnesses, we know that catechism services in 1548

> Notice what these accusations tell you about pastors' roles in the early modern community: their regular salaries could allow them some measure of economic clout, which could assist, but also alienate, their community.

1. *Registres du consistoire de Genève au temps de Calvin,* Vol. IV (1548), ed. Robert Kingdon, Thomas Lambert, and Isabella Watt (Geneva: Droz, 2007), pp. 73-77 and 82.

were attended not only by children but by a cross-section of adults from the community: among the witnesses called to testify to what they had seen and heard during the service were a barber-surgeon, a bookseller, a tailor, a French nobleman, and two native Genevans. We learn that the 1541 Genevan ordinance stating that baptisms must take place during worship services (including catechism services) was being followed — no one seemed perturbed or surprised to have a child brought for the sacrament during what was otherwise a teaching service. The witnesses' testimony highlighted the active role of men in Genevan baptisms: the baby was accompanied by his father, grandfather, and godfather, as well as other male friends and relations, whose names appear as participants in the dispute. Finally, the eyewitness accounts underscore the powerful links between religious ritual and political clout: apart from threatening to take the baby elsewhere, even a hundred leagues away to have him baptized with the "right" name, the enraged family members (all of whom were from old Genevan families) blamed the fiasco on the undue influence of French refugees.[2]

Such eventful worship services are a matter of record. But outwardly, the city's decision in favor of Protestantism appeared firm and confident. Indeed, Geneva's magistrates quickly amended the motto of the city to reflect the change. Prior to the Reformation, Geneva's motto was *Post tenebras spero lucem* ("After darkness, I hope for light"). After 1536, the motto became distinctly more triumphant: *Post tenebras lux* ("After darkness, light"). Convinced

> Notice the continuing importance of godparents in the Genevan baptismal practice. Calvin himself was godfather to numerous infants. The practice was intended to help bring children up in the faith but also to build links of patronage and kinship across the community.

Crest and motto of Geneva on commemorative coin produced by Tolle Lege Press in 2009 to mark John Calvin's 500th anniversary.

Source: Meeter Center medal collection, Calvin College

2. For an analysis of this disrupted baptism, see W. G. Naphy, *Calvin and the Consolidation of the Genevan Reformation* (Manchester: Manchester University Press, 1994), p. 148. For more on the naming controversy in Geneva, see Karen Spierling, *Infant Baptism in Reformation Geneva: The Shaping of a Community, 1536-1564,* 2nd ed. (Louisville: Westminster John Knox, 2009), pp. 140-52.

Catholics who did not want to convert to the Protestant faith left the city, including most of the clergy and members of the religious orders.[3] In many ways, Geneva began its religious reformation with an ostensibly clean slate. Yet the reality, especially in terms of worship, was considerably more complicated.[4]

One of the first challenges for the new church was to produce vernacular (in this case, French) liturgies and instructions for properly Reformed worship. The task of drafting liturgies was made easier by making use of models from other Reformed cities' liturgies, especially those of **Strasbourg**, which had officially adopted the Reformation in 1529, and was where Calvin had spent his three-year exile from 1538 to 1541. The liturgies not only provided the words to be said by the pastor and congregation but also gave directions for the movement of people within the liturgical space as the sacraments were celebrated. Although the pastors had by far the biggest role in these rituals in terms of the number of words they had to say versus the amount uttered by laypeople, the texts themselves were made available to the general public in the printed collection of liturgical texts and Psalms produced in 1542, *La Forme des Prieres* [The Form of Prayers] (see p. 73). The new liturgy was thus accessible to anyone, lay or ordained, who was willing to pay the purchase price and was literate enough to follow the texts (which were written, of course, in the vernacular).[5]

Other key Reformed cities at the time included Zurich, Bern, Basel, and Lausanne.

However, providing the texts of the liturgies was not enough to help shape Genevans' worship and particularly their behavior at worship. One of the pastors' biggest concerns was to put an end to what they saw as Catholic superstitions. For his part, even as late as 1561, Calvin articulated his concerns about the dangers of not following proper procedures when administering the sacrament of baptism, and particularly opposed baptisms performed by laypeople and especially any attempt by women to perform baptisms.[6] To provide further instruction to the lay population about when, where, and how to worship in the newly Protestant context, the pastors and magistrates of Geneva came together in 1541 to produce ecclesiastical ordinances, which sought to regulate worship life in the city. A further hurdle for the authorities was to ensure appropriate Reformed worship in the rural territories under Genevan control.[7] In the eyes of the Genevan pastors and magistrates, the rural inhabitants needed even more direction and oversight than the city-dwellers to ensure conformity to Reformed beliefs and practices. By 1547, the ordinances for worship in the countryside,

---

3. For more on the departure of Geneva's Catholic clergy, see Thomas Lambert, "Preaching, Praying, and Policing the Reform in Sixteenth-Century Geneva," Ph.D. dissertation, University of Wisconsin-Madison, 1998, pp. 199-203.

4. For a very clear and concise overview of the changes in worship in Geneva, see Robert M. Kingdon, "The Genevan Revolution in Public Worship," *Princeton Seminary Bulletin* 20, no. 3 (1999): 264-80.

5. See Bard Thompson's introduction to his section on Calvin and the *Forme des prières* in his *Liturgies of the Western Church* (Reprint: Cleveland: Collins, 1979), pp. 185-96.

6. Spierling, *Infant Baptism*, pp. 67-83.

7. For a discussion of the complex geographical and political forces that shaped Geneva's territories, see Naphy, *Calvin and the Consolidation of the Genevan Reformation*, pp. 16-35.

prepared by the pastors and approved by the magistrates, had been enacted. Comparing the ecclesiastical ordinances of 1541 and the regulations for countryside churches of 1547 is instructive: the later document moves quickly to fines to ensure the compliance of the rural inhabitants.

Yet throughout the period under discussion, the Genevan government struggled to ensure that community members did in fact worship according to the ordinances: the numerous reiterations of worship-related rules in council minutes and public announcements show how hard it was to get the population in the city and the countryside to adopt these new religious practices. For instance, on December 15, 1544, the pastor of Cologny, one of the villages in the Genevan countryside, appeared before the city council to complain that his parishioners were not attending church and that he had to go door to door to get them to come. He also asked for a watchman to call people to the services and for a bell for the church building. The very next day, the council summoned the people of Cologny, warned them solemnly to attend church, made provisions for a church bell, and organized the hiring of a watchman to summon people to church.[8] Clearly, in spite of the pastor's individual efforts, his flock was less than enthusiastic about the opportunity to gather for worship, and the authority of the government, coupled with auditory reminders, had to be called into play to get them to comply.

Formal liturgies and ordinances aside, the Genevan pastors led by Calvin (see p. 33) clearly realized that the faithful needed more direct instruction on how to worship as Reformed Christians and on what true worship really was. This instruction was conveyed through biblical commentaries and sermons and through catechetical teachings. Beginning in 1542, Calvin's Genevan catechism included a section of prayers at the end of the volume, which were to be said throughout the day: when rising from bed, before and after meals, before starting one's schoolwork, and before going to sleep at night. These prayers served two purposes: they replaced the traditional Catholic prayers that pre-Reformation Genevans were taught to recite at similar times of day, and they taught each successive generation how to pray to God, always acknowledging divine sovereignty on the one hand and human frailty and sin on the other. While the schedule of prayer was modeled on Catholic tradition, these prayers were distinctively non-Catholic in that none of them were addressed to a saint. In the Catholic tradition, saints, and especially the Virgin Mary, had served as crucial intercessors who relayed the believer's prayers to God. One of the crucial innovations of the Reformed prayer liturgy was to make Jesus Christ the sole intercessor.[9]

For more advanced audiences in Geneva and elsewhere, Calvin in his *Institutes of the*

Unlike in much of the western world today, the Genevan church and state worked together to ensure that everyone living in the Genevan territory followed the same religious practices and held to the same beliefs — those who did not want to accept the Reformed faith could choose to leave and find a more confessionally-congenial community elsewhere, or could remain and conform, at least outwardly. The same approach to making use of government power to ensure religious conformity held true in Lutheran, Anglican, and Catholic communities.

---

8. *Registres du consistoire de Genève au temps de Calvin,* ed. R. Kingdon, T. Lambert, and I. Watt (Geneva: Droz, 2001), Vol. III, pp. 11-12.

9. For more on prayer in Reformation Geneva, see Lambert, "Preaching, Praying, and Policing the Reform in Sixteenth-Century Geneva," pp. 402-8 and pp. 453-69.

Christian Religion included sections on the true worship of God and on how the Reformed were to avoid the faulty beliefs and practices of the Catholic Church when it came to worship. He also addressed specific aspects of Catholic worship that he considered particularly likely to mislead the faithful, as in his 1562 letter to an unknown recipient rejecting Catholic arguments in favor of images in worship.[10] Many of his other letters addressed a range of worship-related questions, several of these stemming from Reformed Christians living as minorities among Christians of different denominations. These letters highlight Calvin's pastoral skills but also his firm commitment to Reformed principles, especially faithfulness to the teachings of Scripture.

Another way of teaching the foundations of Christian belief and using this teaching effectively in worship was to make use of the Psalms, which Calvin considered the songbook of the church. Calvin began the task of versifying the Psalms during his exile in Strasbourg (1538-41). This task continued somewhat more successfully when he returned to Geneva, with the versifications done by the French poet Clément Marot and Calvin's colleague **Theodore Beza,** and the music written by Louis Bourgeois and Pierre Davantès. The complete psalter was either made available as a stand-alone book or included with Bibles, as in the case of the 1567 psalter bound with the Bible published in Geneva in the same year. The use of the Psalms in worship was so consistent that both psalters and church buildings included charts indicating which Psalm or part of a Psalm should be sung at which service. This careful structure ensured that all Psalms were sung over a succession of weekday and Sunday services over the course of seventeen weeks and was reminiscent of the equally careful practices of monastic worship in which the Psalms were chanted in turn over the course of the various offices of the day. Although Calvin highlighted the importance of the Book of Psalms, the Genevan church also set other key biblical and non-biblical creedal texts to music, such as the Song of Simeon, the Lord's Prayer, and the Apostles' Creed.[11]

The work of providing written and oral instruction on how to worship as Reformed Christians in Geneva after 1541 was accompanied by a reshaping of the liturgical space since the traditional Catholic arrangement of church interiors was inconsistent with the new theology and the new liturgy. Most fundamentally, the Reformed teachings on the majesty and sovereignty of God left no place for images in churches, especially as these were seen as contravening the Second Commandment: "Thou shalt have no graven image." The Catholic distinction between veneration and adoration was largely lost on Reformed leaders, and as a result, churches in Reformed areas went through more-or-less violent processes of image removal.[12] In Geneva, all the images that could be removed were taken down, with

In a monastery or nunnery, the monks and nuns gathered for eight times of prayer daily: matins, lauds, prime, terce, sext, none, vespers, and compline. Each of these services would feature psalms and responses, whether recited or chanted.

To Catholics, veneration meant honoring those people who had lived holy lives and whom the Catholic Church had named as saints. Adoration was reserved for the triune God: the Father, Jesus Christ, and the Holy Spirit.

10. For more on Calvin's view of images and their place in worship, see Randall Zachman, *Image and Word in the Theology of John Calvin* (Notre Dame: University of Notre Dame Press, 2007), pp. 373-77.

11. John D. Witvliet, "The Spirituality of the Psalter: Metrical Psalms in Liturgy and Life in Calvin's Geneva," *Calvin Theological Journal* 32, no. 2 (1997): 273-97. The Song of Simeon can be found in Luke 2:29-32.

12. For more on the process of iconoclasm in Swiss and south German cities, see Lee Palmer Wandel,

the exception of those in the stained-glass windows, as the risk of misplaced worship of an image in a window seemed low and the cost of replacing glass was very high.[13] Instead of images, the Reformed used texts to draw worshipers' eyes and instruct them, as in the case of the Ten Commandments tablet put up in 1689 in the rural church of Satigny.

To highlight the key features of Reformed worship, the liturgical space was reoriented. Where the Catholic worship space had focused on the Mass and thus on the high altar (and side chapels in larger churches and cathedrals), Reformed worship was centered on the preaching of the Word and hence focused on the pulpit. Seating was installed since congregations were expected to sit and listen to sermons at every service, and these sermons usually ran for about an hour. The seating was oriented around the pulpit, which was topped by a sounding board, to help make the sermons more audible to the congregations. Seating was divided up according to gender and age, with the women sitting toward the front and the men behind them. Special seating was reserved for members of the city government, underscoring the significance of Geneva as a state church.[14] The statutes of the Genevan Academy, established in 1559, indicate that the schoolboys were to be seated in the very front, under the eyes of the congregation, and were to be led to church and supervised there by their teachers. In Geneva, no new churches were built; instead, previously Catholic spaces were turned into Reformed places of worship. For purposes of comparison, it is instructive to consider what kind of worship space might be created by Reformed communities who constructed their own places of worship. The best contemporary example for this study is the Temple de Paradis, built in Lyon in 1564 and destroyed three years later during the French Wars of Religion (see p. 45).

Already by the 1540s, therefore, the Genevans had access to a wide range of texts and restructured liturgical spaces to guide their transition from Catholic to Reformed worship. Yet it would be simplistic to therefore conclude that this transition was largely straightforward and trouble-free. Indeed, the mention of fines in the document regulating worship in the Genevan countryside points to the authorities' awareness that in some quarters, the change had to be enforced rather than simply encouraged. Given the amount of opposition facing Calvin and his colleagues both inside and outside Geneva, especially during the first decades of the Reformation, it is hardly surprising that the new forms of worship were among the most contested aspects of the Reformation, at least in the early years. Calvin himself acknowledged the struggles he faced in trying to get the Genevans to change their practices, and noted how quickly a certain way of doing things, be it the frequency of communion services or even the flow of the liturgy, became fixed.

Voracious Idols and Violent Hands: Iconoclasm in Reformation Zurich, Strasbourg, and Basel (Cambridge: Cambridge University Press, 1995).

13. Kingdon, "The Genevan Revolution in Public Worship," pp. 269-70.

14. Lambert, "Preaching, Praying, and Policing the Reform in Sixteenth-Century Geneva," pp. 332-36. Lambert notes that the pattern of separating men and women in church probably had its roots in pre-Reformation Catholic practice. See also pp. 122-23 for his description of the separation of men and women at Mass.

One of the best ways to appreciate how the changes in worship were perceived by the inhabitants of the city and territory of Geneva is to analyze firsthand accounts. One such document is the set of notes left by Pastor Charles Perrot to his successor in the rural parishes of Genthod and Moens in 1567. Although the date of composition falls just outside the time span of this volume, Perrot's recollections of leading worship in these rural communities from 1564 to 1567 is invaluable, as he provides an unparalleled insight into the patterns of worship in the Genevan countryside. However, one should read and analyze his text carefully, bearing in mind that he was an educated, exiled French pastor overseeing his often-recalcitrant flock, and not a native Genevan rural inhabitant. Another first-person account of worship practices in Geneva, this time in the city and within a private home, comes from André Ryff from the Swiss city of Basel, who recalled his experiences as an apprentice to a grocer in Geneva from 1560 to 1563. Accounts of familial worship are few and far between, making Ryff's testimony all the more valuable.

Finally, an eyewitness account of a different sort sheds light on how opponents of Geneva's Reformation may have perceived the changes in worship. Published anonymously in 1566, the strongly Catholic *Passevent Parisien* provided an overview of Genevan worship practices, which the author claimed to have seen with his own eyes during a covert eighteen-month stay in Reformed Protestant areas. This detailed account of regular worship services, baptisms, celebrations of the Lord's Supper, marriages, and funerals is invaluable because it both outlines what the author saw and points out how these worship practices differed from traditional Catholic ones. Although it is a polemical text (most of the work deals with the purported moral failings and sexual wrongdoing of the leading Reformers), the account of worship practices is reliable in that it fits with the liturgies and ordinances as laid out in previous documents.

Polemical texts were writings designed to attack one's opponents and defend one's own position. Attack ads would be a modern equivalent.

Apart from firsthand accounts, other insights into the practice of worship in Reformed Geneva can be gained through a study of images and artifacts from the period. For instance, the International Museum of the Reformation in Geneva has preserved exemplars of the pewter wine ewers used in communion, albeit from the seventeenth century (see p. 34). These vessels held large quantities of wine that was then poured out into cups before being distributed to the faithful. These ewers or pots are similar to the ones described in the account of the *Passevent Parisien*. Images of marriage ceremonies in church are very rare, though there is a seventeenth-century engraving of a wedding procession outside **Saint Pierre Cathedral.** Although there are no surviving images of baptisms in Reformed Geneva, a later image of the return home of a baptismal party helps readers understand who attended the baptism, who played leading roles in the baptism, and who stayed home and why (see p. 35).

Another route into the lived experiences of Genevans at worship comes from analyzing extracts of the registers of the Genevan Small Council (the city's governing group of magistrates), of the Company of Pastors, and of the Genevan Consistory. In the 1540s and 1550s, there were many recorded instances of complaints about the content of pastors' sermons and about their critical approach toward their flocks. In May 1546, the Small Council records noted the outburst of Pastor **Reymond Chauvet,** who apparently spoke out against those leaving church early during a service he was leading by exclaiming "May evil, plague, war, and famine strike you!" Not surprisingly, members of his congregation lodged a complaint with the city government.[15] For their part, the Company of Pastors' weekly meetings brought together the clergy of the city and the countryside. The pastors addressed the concerns of the church, including any controversies surrounding their sermons. In 1553, the records preserve the account of the very diverse reactions to a sermon preached by **Guillaume Farel,** who was visiting Geneva from his home base of Neuchâtel at the time. In this instance, opinions were divided between those who were offended by Farel's message and those who felt that his interpretation of Scripture and application to the Genevan context were entirely in order.

As for the Consistory, which met weekly to deal with disciplinary issues in the city, it was chaired by a syndic (one of Geneva's four top city officials), and its elders were appointed by the city government. Its mandate included problems that today might be addressed by the police or social services, or by trained psychologists and family counselors. These problems could include family violence, suicide attempts, marital strife, and intergenerational conflicts. Some Genevans came to the Consistory's attention because of worship-related issues, ranging from continuing Catholic practices to non-attendance at church or fairly serious misunderstandings about Reformed rites and beliefs. It is interesting to note the dates of these encounters: they become much more sporadic after about 1545, suggesting either that Genevans began to conform more readily to the new ways of worshiping or that the Consistory moved on to other issues of concern. It is certainly clear that once a generational shift took place and the majority of Genevans had grown up Reformed, far fewer cases of continued Catholic beliefs and practices appeared in the Consistory records.

By 1545, a Catholic visitor to a Reformed church in Calvin's Geneva could not fail to be struck by the dramatic transformation of the worship space and of the pattern of worship when compared with traditional Catholic practices.[16] Everything — from the language of worship, to the use of congregational Psalm-singing, to the rearrangement of church interiors to accommodate the strong focus on the sermon — marked a break from previous worship patterns. Yet the story of worship in Reformation Geneva was not merely a top-down one: inhabitants and visitors actively responded to the changes, some supporting the new practices and others hankering for the older forms. The wide range of sources available allows us to hear a cross-section of Genevan responses, as they sought to lift their voices to the Lord.

---

15. Lambert, "Preaching, Praying, and Policing the Reform in Sixteenth-Century Geneva," p. 368.

16. For a helpful overview, see John D. Witvliet, "Introduction," in *Worship in Medieval and Early Modern Europe: Change and Continuity in Religious Practice,* ed. Karin Maag and John D. Witvliet (Notre Dame: University of Notre Dame Press, 2004), pp. 1-14.

Documenting the Community's Worship

PEOPLE AND ARTIFACTS

John Calvin in His Study

This seventeenth-century Dutch engraving depicts Calvin in his study, surrounded by all his books. This image appeared in the opening pages of the 1667 edition of Calvin's works published in the Netherlands by Johannes Jacob Schipper. It is interesting to note that very few portraits of Calvin were done in his lifetime. He seems to have been particularly keen on discouraging any attempt to make himself the central focus of the Reformed movement.

Source: H. Henry Meeter Center for Calvin Studies, Calvin College

Seventeenth-Century

Pewter Communion Ewer

Large containers like this one held the wine for the quarterly celebrations of the Lord's Supper. In Roman Catholic celebrations of the Mass, the laity receiving the sacrament would receive only the Host (consecrated wafers). But during Genevan celebrations of the Lord's Supper, the members of the congregation would receive both the bread and the wine. The Genevan practice involved the laity coming forward, first the men and then the women, and sitting in groups around specially set-up tables near the pulpit. The minister would hand out the bread and the wine, which was served in a common cup from which everyone drank in turn. The ewers were used to refill the cup as needed. Notice the crest of Geneva on the ewer: what would be the rationale for including that crest?

Source: Eglise protestante de Genève, on loan to the International Museum of the Reformation. Image supplied by the Museum.

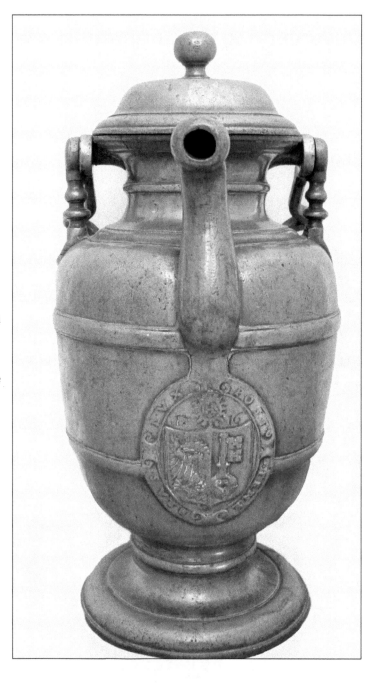

Return of a Baptismal Party

This engraving is by the well-known French Protestant artist Abraham Bosse (c. 1604-1676). Bosse created over 1600 different engravings, including scientific illustrations, scenes featuring household interiors, religious images, and scenes of daily life. He taught in the French royal academy of painting and sculpture, and wrote one of the earliest French works on engraving. During Bosse's career, French Protestants were sufficiently tolerated in France to be able to hold relatively prominent positions, though Bosse, like other Protestant artists, put his talents to work in the service of both Catholic and Protestant patrons.

This image portrays the return of family members from a church baptism back to the mother's bedside, and depicts the standard practice among both Catholics and Protestants at the time: new mothers, who were still recovering from giving birth, did not attend the baptism of their children. In Reformation Geneva, the father was required to be present at the baptism to promise to bring the child up in the Christian faith, but this requirement went against traditional Catholic practice, in which only the godparents brought the baby to baptism. Theologically, the baptismal ritual revolved around God's covenantal promises expressed in the sacrament and the promises made by those presenting the child. The promises had to be made before baptism could be administered.

Source: A. Bosse, *Returning from a Christening,* 17th century. Image supplied by the International Museum of the Reformation, Geneva.

Worship Setting and Space

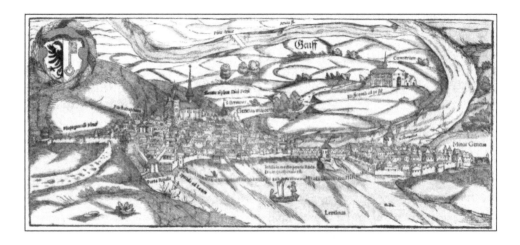

Geneva in 1548

The first "authentic" view of the city, this engraving was originally published in **Sebastian Mün-ster's** *Cosmographia* (Basel, 1550). The image shows the two parts of Geneva, which were linked by a bridge fortified with a watchtower known as the *Tour de l'Ile* or Island Tower. A renowned Hebrew scholar and cartographer, Münster taught at the University of Basel from 1529 until his death in 1552. Calvin made use of Münster's Hebrew Bible edition in his commentaries and lectures on the Old Testament. Münster published his *Biblia Hebraica* in 1534/35. His Bible included both the Hebrew text of the Old Testament and a new Latin translation as well as an extensive commentary and scholarly apparatus drawn from the best of rabbinic scholarship.

Source: H. R. M. Deutsch, View of Geneva, 1548. Image supplied by the International Museum of the Reformation, Geneva.

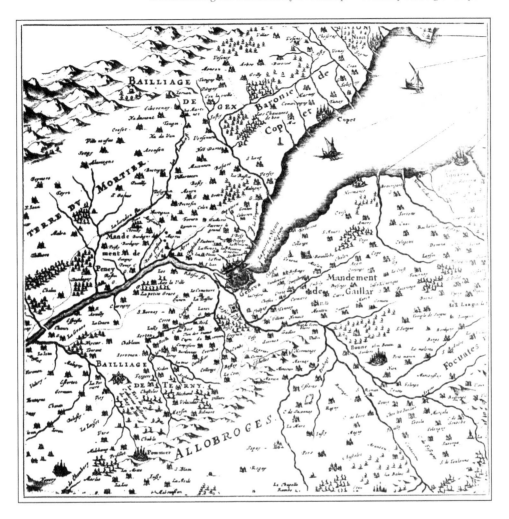

A Map of Geneva and Its Surroundings

This 1619 engraving helps us understand Geneva's geographic situation. One of the city's key features was its relative lack of a rural territory under its direct control: Geneva's neighbors (some allies, such as the powerful territory of Bern, and some enemies, such as the Duchy of Savoy) were close at hand. Geneva's position at the very end of the lake of Geneva, at the mouth of the Rhône and Arve rivers, was crucial. While the lake and the rivers allowed for communications and transport of merchandise, they also highlighted potential vulnerabilities in the city's defenses. Genevans put chains across the rivers and the end of the lake to prevent any water-based attacks.

Source: Geneva's surroundings, based on the map by Jacques Goulart, 1619, in Emile Doumergue's *La Genève Calviniste* (Lausanne: Bridel, 1905), X.

Saint Pierre Cathedral and Geneva

This view of the city clearly shows the predominant role played by the cathedral, both in terms of its size in comparison to all the other city buildings and in terms of its location at the top of the hill. This image also highlights the city's defensive walls in their seventeenth-century form, designed to repel attacks more successfully than the older-style flat or rounded walls of medieval fortifications. This new star-shaped wall made it more difficult for enemy troops to launch a direct frontal assault without encountering defensive firing from the bastions that stuck out from the walls and eliminated dead zones in which attackers could take shelter.

Source: Emile Doumergue, *La Genève Calviniste* (Lausanne: Bridel, 1905), pp. 28-29.

A River-side View of Geneva in 1548

This view of Geneva is taken from the river side, rather than the lake side, as in the image of Geneva in 1548. Once again, Saint Pierre Cathedral stands out in the cityscape. Although the author of the book in which this engraving appeared is listed as Isaac Spon, his name in fact was Jacques Spon. He was a medical doctor with a deep interest in antiquities who lived from 1647 to 1685. Spon was a convinced Protestant who left France even before the revocation of the Edict of Nantes, which had given limited legal recognition to French Protestants. His history of Geneva was published in French in 1680 and translated into English seven years later.

Source: Isaac [Jacques] Spon, *The History of the City and State of Geneva from Its First Foundation to This Present Time* (London: Bernard White, 1687). Image supplied by the Meeter Center Rare Book Collection.

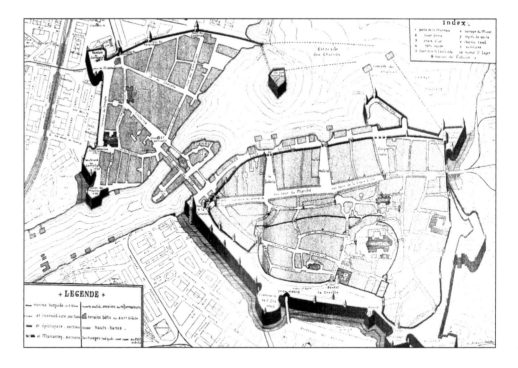

A Street Map of Geneva's Old City

This street map of Geneva offers a bird's-eye view of Geneva in Calvin's day. The merchants, traders, and artisans lived and worked in the lower city or on the far side of the river, while the upper city was the administrative and religious center of the city, where pastors and professors had their homes. Estimates of the population of Geneva in the 1540s and 1550s range from 10,000 to 13,000 people, but by 1560, the population had virtually doubled due to the arrival of numerous Protestants fleeing Catholic pressures elsewhere in Europe. Given that all the buildings that lay outside the city walls had been razed already by the 1530s, the surge in population meant that living space was at a premium in the city.

Source: Emile Doumergue, *La Genève Calviniste* (Lausanne: Bridel, 1905), pp. 636-37.

Veüe du Frontispice du Temple de Sainct Pierre etlecircuit de
la place ou est represente un conuoy de nopces.

A Seventeenth-Century Engraving of Saint Pierre

This engraving by François Diodati (1647-1690) shows the medieval façade of Saint Pierre Cathedral (c. 1680). This view is likely closer to what the building would have looked like in Calvin's day. The people outside the church are part of a wedding procession. The door next to the cathedral leads to the **cloister** where, on May 21, 1536, the principles of the Reformation were voted on as binding for the city. In Calvin's day a traditional wedding practice was for the bride and groom to be accompanied by friends and relatives on their way to and from church. The Genevan Consistory was particularly interested in ensuring that these processions were carried out with due solemnity, and investigated cases where musicians accompanied them.

A cloister is a sheltered, enclosed space bordered by a walkway, often in a monastery or nunnery.

Source: F. Diodati, *Wedding Procession in Front of St-Pierre Cathedral,* c. 1680. Engraving from the Musée historique de la Réformation, exhibited in the International Museum of the Reformation, Geneva, and supplied by the Museum.

The Exterior of Saint Pierre Cathedral

The architecture of Saint Pierre Cathedral has changed considerably since Calvin's day, given the number of major renovations the cathedral has undergone. The earliest archaeological evidence for a church building on this site dates to the fourth century A.D. By 1160, the first prince-bishop of Geneva, Arducius de Faucigny, ordered the construction of a cathedral on the site. The cathedral combined elements of Romanesque and Gothic architecture and was completed in 1250. Since then, the exterior has changed several times due to later additions and renovations, including the neo-classical front portico added in the mid-eighteenth century, and the spire added in 1895.

Source: M. A. van den Berg, W. J. Eradus, and Sjaak Verboom, *Van Noyon tot Genève: tien woonplaatsen van Calvijn in beeld* (Bunnik: De Banier, 2009), p. 186.

 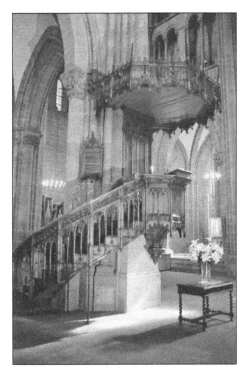

The Interior of Saint Pierre Cathedral

These two images show different aspects of the cathedral's interior. Like the exterior, the interior of the cathedral has undergone several significant changes over the centuries. Among the most important changes that took place at the Reformation were the installation of a pulpit with a sounding board in the middle of the sanctuary and the introduction of benches for the congregation so that they could sit and listen to the sermons. Prior to the Reformation, those attending Mass would stand or kneel during worship, though they could bring their own stools if they felt the need. Although these two images do not really show it, the other main change that happened at the Reformation was the disappearance of the numerous side chapels that had been a prominent feature of the pre-Reformation cathedral in favor of a single focus on the pulpit, from which the Scriptures were expounded during each Reformed worship service.

Source: M. A. van den Berg, W. J. Eradus, and Sjaak Verboom, *Van Noyon tot Genève: tien woonplaatsen van Calvijn in beeld* (Bunnik: De Banier, 2009), p. 187.

The Interior of Saint Gervais Church before the 1903 Restoration

There are very few scenes of Genevan church interiors with congregations present, especially from the early modern era. Although this engraving is from the nineteenth century, several features of this Genevan church interior date back to the sixteenth century, including the orientation of all the seating, with the focus on the pulpit. **Saint Gervais Church** was one of Geneva's three main churches following the consolidations of the Reformation, along with Saint Pierre Cathedral and the **Temple de la Madeleine.** A church building had been erected on this site already by the fourth century. By the tenth century, a Romanesque church had been built. The church was damaged by fire in 1345 and completely rebuilt in 1436. Saint Gervais was located on the far side of the Rhone River and served as the parish church for that part of the city.

Source: Emile Doumergue, *La Genève Calviniste* (Lausanne: Bridel, 1905), p. 39.

Paradis Church

Here is a rare surviving image of a sixteenth-century Reformed church interior, with a congregation present, though this image is from Lyon in southeastern France, not from Geneva. The architect and artist Jean Perrissin depicted the interior of the Temple de Paradis, a French Reformed church that was newly built in 1564 and destroyed in 1567. This worship space differed from the Genevan Reformed churches in that the Genevans made use of the pre-existing Catholic church buildings rather than constructing new structures. The Temple de Paradis offers an insight into how a Reformed community might choose to organize its church interior. The semicircular set-up of the benches underscored the focus on the pulpit, and the addition of a balcony allowed for a greater number of worshipers in the space.

Source: Olivier Fatio, *Understanding the Reformation* (Geneva: International Museum of the Reformation, 2005), p. 28.

Iconoclasm in Zurich

The Zurich Reformed pastor and theologian **Heinrich Bullinger** completed his monumental *History of the Reformation* in 1567, though the work was not published until 1838. Bullinger chronicled many of the key events of the Reformation in Zurich, including the destruction of religious images that had adorned Zurich's Catholic churches prior to the Reformation. In this set of two images, men are removing images from the walls of a church and burning the images outside. This destruction of religious images, known as **iconoclasm,** took place not only in Zurich but in other Swiss cities, and later on in other parts of Europe where the Reformed faith took hold, most notably in the Netherlands. In some communities the destruction was the result of mob violence, while in other areas the process was organized and overseen by the community's political leaders.

Iconoclasm took place in Geneva as well, mainly between 1530 and 1535. Begun originally by Reformed soldiers from Bern stationed in Geneva, acts of iconoclasm then surfaced sporadically, culminating in wholesale destruction of statues, crucifixes, and altars in Genevan churches and chapels in 1534 and 1535.

Source: L. Vischer et al., eds., *Histoire du Christianisme en Suisse: une perspective œcuménique* (Geneva: Labor et Fides, 1995), p. 108.

The Tables of the Law

These tables, dated 1689 and signed "Jacobus N.," were likely created by a French refugee named Jacques Nicol from Marsillargues in the Gard, who died in the village of Peissy (close to Satigny) in 1727. They are a good example of what might have been put up on the walls of churches to replace the religious images removed by the iconoclasts. Note the coat of arms at the top of the image, indicating the close alignment of church and state. The inscription below provided not only the text of the Ten Commandments but also the summary of the Law and the greatest commandment, as described in Matthew 22. The Ten Commandments were one of three fundamental texts that all Genevans were to know by heart; the others were the Lord's Prayer and the Apostles' Creed.

Source: Olivier Fatio, *Understanding the Reformation* (Geneva: International Museum of the Reformation, 2005), p. 30.

DESCRIPTIONS OF WORSHIP

Calvin Addresses Questions about the Lord's Supper (1561)

Very little is known about the circumstances under which Calvin wrote this text, though it seems that he was writing to a group of people who were leading a Reformed community outside of Geneva. Calvin's focus in this text was on practices that he had wanted to put in place in Geneva, particularly surrounding confession and the celebration of the Lord's Supper. Evident in paragraph two is Calvin's willingness to adapt his practices, and his constant emphasis on making sure people understood what they were told: he preferred not to continue a practice, even if it had spiritual meaning, if the words were lost in the process.

In this instance, writing in 1561, Calvin was looking back over his career in Geneva and honestly admitting that he had not succeeded in every aspect of liturgical change that he had planned. His awareness of the need to bear with the relative lack of openness of congregations to extensive and ongoing liturgical innovations is clear and worth noting.

For the prayer of confession in Calvin's liturgy, see p. 73.

All of us recognize that it is extremely useful to add to the public confession some sort of promise that might rouse sinners to a hope of forgiveness and reconciliation. From the beginning I wanted to introduce this custom, but certain people feared that its novelty would give offense. I yielded too readily and the subject was dropped. As things are now, it would not be opportune to make the change here, because too many people begin to stand up even before the confession has ended. This makes us all the more hopeful that your people will become accustomed to both while you are still open to change.

Calvin seems to be lamenting a lost opportunity here. What had he hoped to put in place, and why was the change never made?

In administering the Lord's Supper I have sometimes used Paul's words, but I preferred to stop doing this because the words could not be repeated to each individual without a long delay; and if numbers of people went across during the recitation, scarcely one in ten understood what I wanted understood, and no one grasped the entire meaning.

We are very pleased that the Lord's Supper is being celebrated every month, provided that this more frequent observance does not produce carelessness. When a considerable part of the congregation stays away from Communion, the church somehow becomes fragmented. Nonetheless, we think it is better for a congregation to be invited [to take Communion] every month than only four times a year, as usually happens here.

When I first came here, the Lord's Supper was observed only three times a year, and seven whole months intervened between the observance at Pentecost and at the Birthday of Christ. A monthly observance pleased me, but I could not persuade the people, and it seemed better to bear with their weakness than to continue arguing stubbornly. I took care to have it recorded in the public records, however, that our way was wrong, so that correcting it might be easier for future generations.

Many weighty reasons force me to feel that the sick should not be denied access to the Lord's Supper. I see that this can lead to a headlong fall into many abuses which need to be countered sensibly and carefully, for unless there is a real communion there will be a wrongful turning away from Christ's sacred institution. Relatives, friends, and neighbors should gather, therefore, so that the elements may be distributed as Christ commanded. There should then be the canon, combined with an explanation of the mysterious sacrament, but there should be nothing different from the ordinary procedure of the church.

To carry the sacrament here and there indiscriminately is very dangerous. It is difficult to guard against a situation in which some people are led to seek the sacrament out of superstition, others from ambition, and others for empty show. The situation calls for judgment and discrimination. The sacrament should only be given to the sick whose lives are in great danger. It is preposterous for the bread to be brought from the church as if it were sacred, and for it to be carried in a procession is intolerable.

Farewell, distinguished men, brothers cherished from my heart. May the Lord protect you, guide you, and bless you forever.

Geneva. August 12, 1561

What does Calvin mean by "carelessness" in this context?

A fascinating instance of Calvin's awareness of future generations and the dangers of enshrining practices "because our predecessors did it this way."

Calvin was therefore disallowing private Communion, with only the pastor and the sick person present.

Calvin was implicitly critiquing the Catholic practice of bringing Communion to the sick in solemn procession.

Source: John Calvin, "To a Question about Certain Rites of the Church," in *Calvin's Ecclesiastical Advice,* trans. Mary Beaty and Benjamin Farley (Louisville, Ky.: Westminster John Knox Press, 1991), pp. 95-97. This translation is based on the Latin text published in the nineteenth-century collected edition of Calvin's works: *Joannis Calvini Opera Quae Supersunt Omnia,* ed. W. Baum, E. Cunitz, and E. Reuss (Braunschweig: Schwetschke and Son, 1872), Vol. X, cols. 213-214. The Latin text in the *Opera* is taken from the first edition of John Calvin's *Epistolae et Responsa* (Geneva: Pierre de Saint-André, 1575), p. 329.

Calvin's Letters on Pastoral Leadership (1542)

One of the key components of community worship was the leadership provided by the pastor. This letter highlights some of the challenges faced by the Genevan church in the constant search for men to serve in ordained ministry. In this case, though a candidate came forward, his attitude and preparation left so much to be desired that the Company of Pastors turned him down. Assuming the Genevan report is accurate, imagine what this man's leadership of worship might have been like if he had been allowed to pursue ordination.

May the grace and peace of God our Father through our Lord Jesus Christ be and remain always upon you through his Holy Spirit.

Beloved brothers, we would prefer to write something to you to give you greater comfort, for if someone else would sadden you, we would be the first to work to help you rejoice. But right now we have to take another approach than we would prefer. However, since we hope that none of you will believe our intention to be other than to edify, comfort, and confirm you in our Lord, we will not make any further apologies at this point regarding the content of this letter, so that you will not be upset if this letter gives you more cause for concern than for rejoicing. We also know that it is a terrible thing to condemn a man who is both well-respected and fairly well-known. But when you hear the reasons that have led us to do so, we have no doubt that you will be very satisfied.

In short, we want to give you some information about the **Carmelite** who preached during this past **Lent** — this information is not favorable. Our critique is not based on any desire to discredit him. Even though we do have justification to do this, we have no desire to do so, nor is it our common practice. But once we explain our reasons, you will fully understand. Since he has returned to you disappointed about our welcome, as he informed some people, we are aware that he may make many complaints about us to you, if only to justify his slide back into the chasm from which the Lord had freed him. Hence we can also imagine how upset you might be with us, if you were not fully informed about the whole matter. Since we are linked to each other because of the bonds with which the Lord has knit us together, and since we would be blameworthy before God if we did not try to prevent all the scandals that the devil tries to foster to divide us and detract from the unity which the Lord has put between us, we have thought it best to simply tell you the story of his welcome and reception. We will contrast that with his behavior, to let you evaluate the grounds for his displeasure with us. Our account will be delivered as if before God, whom we call as witness, asking him to show forth the full truth of the matter, and to confound those who would turn to lies and calumnies.

A few days after he arrived, having already spoken with him one-on-one in a friendly and humane fashion, we called him before us to know what he wanted. After he told us that he

Carmelites were members of the Catholic religious order of the Brothers of the Blessed Virgin Mary of Mount Carmel, founded in the late 12th or early 13th century.

In sixteenth-century Europe, Lent was a time for penance, reflection, and deepening one's faith.

had come to serve the Church of God, we asked him not to be upset that we had not already given him access to the pulpit on the first day. In the same way, we asked him to bear with us if we waited a bit longer, and we explained the reasons that kept us from rushing into things. First, our Lord has given us a written rule, that we cannot contravene, namely that we may not receive any man into the ministry without first having properly and carefully approved him. This rule has to be kept in its entirety if we want to have good order and procedures in the church. We warned him to consider God's injunction in favor of excellence in ministry, an injunction that would be trampled underfoot if we rashly received a man without following the legitimate practice. Second, we pointed out to him the consequences that could ensue if we were to admit him so hastily, namely that others would want to follow suit, and in such a fashion we would land in a worse confusion than even in the past, by giving one person a pass and denying it to another. Such inequality would be a mortal blow to God's Church. Third, we told him that even if we were willing to go against our good conscience and transgress God's commandment on his behalf, we would still not be able to do so, because our written ecclesiastical ordinances teach us the opposite lesson. These ordinances must be kept, given that we charged the population to submit to these. Fourth, we showed him that a slower process would be to his benefit, because he would then have the time to understand how challenging and difficult it is to be a pastor, and could take advice about what he should do. He could also learn our approach and ways, so as to adapt to these, to avoid scandalizing the people, who are weak and fragile: the least cultured are sometimes the hardest to satisfy. However, we made it clear to him that our intent was not to make him wait a long time in suspense and have him pointlessly wait, but rather to consider quickly and as soon as possible, how to use him in God's service. At that point we asked him to bear with us for just a little longer while waiting for things to be done according to God's order, and that in the meantime, he could deal with us privately as his brothers, offering to help him and satisfy him in all things handed to us by the Lord.

We felt that our response had been so reasonable that he should have accepted it at face value. Furthermore, we spoke as amiably as he could have asked, and we are sure that any God-fearing man with a good conscience would have been very satisfied. Furthermore, even an ill-intentioned man, if he had a modicum of honesty and was not overconfident, would be embarrassed to object. However, our monk's only response was to demand that we approve him immediately, in spite of all the reasons to the contrary that we had presented. He had two grounds, the first being that he currently had a guide who could lead him safely from danger and provide him with a horse and with funds, and that this opportunity would not last. His second was that if he had to go back to France, it would be better to go as soon as possible, before news of his travel here would spread. His answer clearly showed that he knew nothing of the church, or of ministry, and that he was lacking both in intelligence and in courage and zeal. However, after we asked him to leave the room, we spoke together, and

While Reformed churches had much simpler regulations than the lengthy Catholic canon law, this passage demonstrates Calvin's commitment to good order — an area of expertise known as "church polity."

This candidate for ministry assumed that prior practice in preaching should be given more weight than any vetting the Company of Pastors might carry out.

then gave him another very gentle and gracious response, asking him to forgive us if we failed to fulfill his request, given that our consciences were bound by God's Word, and that our earlier statements to him were explained and confirmed both by the testimony of Scripture and by examples from the early church. We also gave him advice that would have worked to lead him to a better frame of mind if he had not already been too far astray. To keep him from feeling that we were not giving him sufficient respect, we pointed out that we had done the same for others of the same quality, and that they had gladly subjected themselves to this process.

However, instead of accepting this, he answered sharply that if we thought we had the Spirit of God, he too was not lacking it, and he showed that he did not take seriously anything we had said. We answered him that first God's Word on this subject was so clear that our consciences were sufficiently at rest. And even if the issue were doubtful or if we had any qualms about it, our task was to do nothing against our understanding of God's will. However, the matter was so clear that there was no need to debate it further. Furthermore, he should consider his position to be more questionable than ours, because he was focusing only on himself while for our part we were only aiming to follow God's law. He also responded that if he had come before Lent, he would have been willing to be examined, but since he had preached in a church so close by, we should consider that as approval. We replied that in France, as Solomon said, people are so famished that even bitter things seem sweet, for the poor people are so starved of true doctrine, that when someone gives them even a small sample, even a half-measure, the people are so overjoyed that they have no capacity to evaluate it. As for his boast of having preached there, we told him not to be so swollen-headed, and that we knew how weak his preaching had been. However, we emphasized that we were not criticizing him, and that we were not so cold-hearted as to fail to support those who perform weakly in such danger, but that we wanted him to assess himself accurately, to avoid vain arrogance and instead to understand why he had reason to humble himself. In the end, we tried again to mollify him and encourage him, but for his part, he only seemed to get irritated.

The next day, he was in a tavern where numerous people were gathered, including about ten pastors from the region. After the conversation touched on several matters, without him being provoked or having any reason to do so, as if he was everyone's overseer, he stated that there were no learned men here, and he said even more outrageous things than we are reporting. As truth always comes to light over time, we have since been told that from his first day in the city, he never stopped maligning first one person, then another, then everyone, even to the point of saying that he found no enjoyment nor was he edified by our sermons and lectures. However, he was so bold as to come eat with us. We are well aware of the reasons for his behavior, namely that the poor man is so desirous of glory that he attacks everyone, and yet we fail to see what he has to be so proud of. For if we could see into the depths of his being, it would be clear that there is nothing there but hot air. He knows a little less Latin than a boy of eight should. He is as ignorant as a hypocrite about Scripture, and yet he is so drunk with ambition that he can hardly stand on his feet. We will leave aside several of his attempted actions. If he had had enough time, he would certainly have had no qualms at disrupting our church. . . . He cannot deny that he has slandered our preaching, although it is hard to see how he could give any kind of accurate assessment of it, even if he knew how to do so. For although he came to our sermons a few times for form's sake, he spent his time apart, reading a book, perhaps out of fear of being seen to listen in order to learn, thus showing his insane ambition, in that he was so afraid that his reputation would diminish that he did not deign to honor God's Word by actually paying attention to it. . . .

This vignette shows that mere attendance at church services and sermons did not necessarily correlate with paying attention.

Source: Letters of John Calvin in *Joannis Calvini Opera quae supersunt omnia,* ed. W. Baum, E. Cunitz, and E. Reuss (Braunschweig: Schwetschke and Son, 1873), Vol. XI, cols. 396-403. Translated by Karin Maag. The original letter from Calvin to the church of Lyon in May 1542 is from Bibliothèque publique et universitaire, Geneva, Cod. 145, fol. 131. Reprinted in *Lettres de Jean Calvin: recueillies pour la première fois et publiées d'après les manuscrits originaux,* ed. Jules Bonnet (Paris: Meyrueis, 1854), Vol. I, p. 57.

Calvin Compares Catholic and Protestant Worship (1542)

In this letter Calvin contrasts Catholic and Reformed worship, highlighting what he sees as the flaws in Catholic worship. In the process he summarizes much of what he said at much greater length in his Scripture commentaries. The plague that Calvin mentions in the first paragraph below was a less virulent recurrence of the Black Death, which re-emerged every fifteen to twenty years throughout the sixteenth century.

Reverend sir, we admit that your point in your letters is very true, namely that the plague that is at work in our city is a scourge sent by God, and we confess that he is justifiably punishing and chastising us for our faults and wrongdoing. Furthermore, we have no doubt that he is using this means to urge us to examine our consciences, to induce us and bring us to repentance. Therefore we are happy to accept what you say, namely that it is time for us to turn to God, to ask and obtain forgiveness and mercy from him. . . .

However, we should bear in mind that God is particularly concerned about his glory, and that he hates and principally detests idolatry and superstitions through which he is dishonored, and that he is more seriously offended by this than by anything else. Think a bit about your common practice. There people worship stone and wood, they invoke the dead, and trust in vain things. They try to serve God by baseless and insane ceremonies not found in his Word. There the doctrine of truth is buried, and if someone wants to revive it, he is cruelly persecuted. . . .

Calvin turns the tables on the priest's argument. What forms of idolatry and superstition does Calvin see in Catholic worship?

The fundamental starting point of Christianity is to adore God rightly. However, we have learned that the way we were worshiping was wrong and perverse, because it was not done in spirit and in truth (John 4) but in external ceremonies and even in superstitious fashion. For we were not worshiping God alone, but stones, wood, paintings, reliquaries of the dead, and other such things instead. Right worship is tied to the right invocation of God. And how do people invoke God throughout the Papacy but with doubt and mistrust, since no one knows the role of Jesus Christ, who serves as our advocate and intercessor so that our requests will be granted? (Rom. 8; 1 Tim. 2; 1 John 2; Heb. 4). And then what were the public prayers other than murmurs or senseless howling? Third, how blasphemous to attribute the virtue of the sole mediator to saints, seeking to obtain grace through them and their merits. . . . What shall we say about the sacraments, whose use had been completely turned around from what Jesus Christ our Lord taught? How many crazy ceremonies were added to baptism by human beings without God's authority? Even worse, the true and pure institution of our Lord was almost abolished by such a shambles. In any event, it seems people placed more value on the **chrism** than on the water of baptism. And today, you seem to almost believe that our baptism is worthless, because we have only retained what the Lord commanded, and what the Apostles held and observed. As for the Lord's Supper, it was even more profaned. Our Lord left it to us as a sign, so that through it we could be sure that our souls are fed by his body and his blood, so that we are made participants in all his goods, especially in his suffering and death. To ensure this, the sacrament should have been distributed according to his command, all the while declaring the benefit and the fruit of the mystery. In contrast, the sacrament was transformed into a sacrifice, to engineer a new reconciliation with God, this time through the work of a man, not only for the living, but also for the dead. In making use of the sacrament, the priest separated himself from the church. Everything was done and said in an unknown language, like when magicians recite their spells. When it came to Easter communion, people only received half the sacrament, being barred from the chalice against the express command of the master. There was no reason to consent to these sacrileges. Now, however, we are being accused of having destroyed this holy sacrament. But in fact we have restored it in its entirety, where previously it was corrupt and polluted in many ways.

Similarly, when you urge us to submit to God to appease his anger, you propose means that are more likely to provoke and fan his fury even further. First, you would like us to make an oblation of the precious body and blood of our Lord Jesus. We are well aware that this practice is customary for you, but to know whether it is a work pleasing to God, one has to find out if it is according to his will. Yet he does not tell us to offer his body, but that we should receive it (Matt. 26; Mark; Luke; Paul). Take, he said, and eat. Instead of receiving the body of Jesus Christ, if we want to convince God that we are offering him a sacrifice, where will we find the grounds for approval of our fantasy? We ask you to give due consideration to our reasoning. You advise us to have a priest offer the body of Jesus Christ, so that we may obtain grace. We reply that he did not give his sacrament for this purpose, but for us to receive it, so that we may participate in his unique and eternal sacrifice that he alone offered, according to his office (Heb. 7, 8, 9, 10). . . . You then refer to the beautiful general processions. But

Chrism refers to the practice of anointing with holy oil.

Calvin regularly critiques worship held in Latin. After reading over this letter, articulate in your own words why he was so firmly opposed to this practice.

what are these for, except to appease God through great pomp and ceremonies? You tell us that your intention is for these processions to be carried out with devotion. But what devotion is it to put one's trust in candles and torches, in colorful and sumptuous decorations, in images, and in reliquaries? As history has shown, this has always been the pagans' practice. But if such practices are suitable for Christianity, we need to know how. We have no disagreement over the need to gather to pray to God. But we ask: what is the point of these general processions apart from the pomp of decorations, lights, relics, and other such things? All of this smells of judaizing or is more appropriate for pagans than for Christians. It is true that there is shouting and singing, but it is all done in an unknown language, thus going against the clear command of the Holy Spirit (1 Cor. 14), who wants community prayers to be done in the common tongue, so that the unlearned and ignorant can participate and can say amen at the end. You then exhort us to invoke the virgin Mary and the saints, among whom you particularly list Saint Peter as our patron saint. But God calls us to himself alone, prohibiting us from seeking help elsewhere, and rightly so. For the fundamental part of his glory stems from our calling upon him alone in the name of Jesus Christ. Even if this reason did not apply, there are so many calls in Scripture to turn back to God with prayers and invocations in times of plague, war, and famine (Isa. 44:55; Jer. 3; Hosea 2). Nothing is ever said about invoking saints. Thus it would be reckless on our part to follow what you say, and turn away from all of the doctrine of God. . . .

Calvin is using the term "judaizing" pejoratively to refer to Jewish practices as followed by Christians.

Source: Letters of John Calvin in *Joannis Calvini Opera quae supersunt omnia,* ed. W. Baum, E. Cunitz, and E. Reuss (Braunschweig: Schwetschke and Son, 1873), Vol. XI, cols. 483-89. Translated by Karin Maag. The original undated letter from Calvin to an unnamed Catholic priest is from Bibliothèque publique et universitaire, Geneva, Cod. 107a, fol. 365. Reprinted in *Lettres de Jean Calvin: recueillies pour la première fois et publiées d'après les manuscrits originaux,* ed. Jules Bonnet (Paris: Meyrueis, 1854), Vol. I, p. 68.

Calvin Encourages Those Struggling over Differing Worship Practices (1554)

This letter displays Calvin's pastoral care and his strategic good sense: he understood that separating oneself from other Christians over differing worship practices when one is in the minority or living as a refugee in someone else's community is a bad plan. Wesel was a Lutheran city. Calvin would in all likelihood have been much less flexible if the Reformed Christians were living among a majority Catholic population.

Note that the letter comes from the Genevan Company of Pastors rather than from Calvin on his own — why might sending a group letter have been more effective than a personal one?

May the love of God our Father and the grace of our Lord Jesus Christ be always with you through the work of the Holy Spirit.

Beloved brothers, we praise God that in the face of the troubles that hold sway today over all the world, he gave you a shelter where you can serve and adore him in freedom. Not only that, but he also gave you the means to gather in his name, to practice hearing his Word, to call on him in common accord, and to make a pure confession of your faith. This is no small grace, given the horrendous confusion we see everywhere. But you must take advantage of this, and be all the more fervent in glorifying the one who granted you such a gift in order to have it bear fruit. As for the form of celebration of the sacraments, you have good reason to hold certain doubts and concerns. For there is nothing better than to keep to the pure simplicity we received from God's Son, whose ordinance should be our sole guide, to which also the Apostles' practice fully conformed. And in fact as soon as one deviates from it even slightly, this human mixture can only lead to corruption. But it seems to us that your situation is different from that of the pastors and all the people of the place. If the pastors were doing their duty, they would work to remove the excesses that fail to edify, and even in fact obscure the lucidity of Scripture. For their part, the rulers too should address the matter. One should therefore condemn the fault of those who feed on this paltry rubbish that is like a residue of papal superstitions, which we should try to eliminate from popular memory as far as we can. But because you are only private individuals, you not only can but must bear with and endure weaknesses of this kind that you have no authority to fix. We do not think that having lit candles and bread stamped with images at the Lord's Supper are indifferent matters that we should consent to and approve, but we should accommodate ourselves to these accepted practices when we lack the authority to amend them. If the issue was whether we would agree to receive such ceremonies here, we would be forced to resist to the end, and to maintain continuously the purity of the church that has been entrusted to us, a purity which it already possesses. But if we were to go somewhere where different forms held sway, none of us would separate ourselves from the body of the church over an abhorrence for candles or **chasubles,** and in so doing deprive ourselves from participating in the Lord's Supper. We have to avoid creating stumbling-blocks for those still enmeshed in such weaknesses, who may feel you are rejecting them over minor matters. And we would be very unhappy if the French church that could be established there was broken apart because of our unwillingness to go along with a few ceremonies that do not impinge on the essence of the faith. For as we have said, it is perfectly acceptable for the children of God to accommodate themselves to many things of which they disapprove. What is crucial is to know how far such freedom should extend. Thus we uphold this firm principle that we should bear with one another in all ceremonies that do not impinge on our confession of faith, so that the unity of the church is not lost by excessive rigor or intransigence on our part. It is true that you should try by all means to retain as much restraint as possible. Hence it would be good to politely ask those who are in authority not to compel you in all circumstances to do as they do. Yet we do not advise you to give up on having a Christian church in this place solely because of ceremonial differences. The main thing is not to weaken in confessing your faith and that you fully commit to upholding doctrine. True, you must avoid contentions and not only behave with restraint but also declare that your intention is not to lessen the effect of the Sacraments but rather to highlight the

Reformed Christians persistently critiqued Lutherans for retaining too much Catholic ritual in their worship.

A chasuble is a liturgical vestment worn by clergy during church services in the Catholic, Anglican/Episcopalian, and Lutheran traditions.

spiritual gifts God gives us through them. But when you confess that in the Lord's Supper we are made true participants in the body and blood of Jesus Christ and that our souls feed on him, make sure you rule out the errors which some there may hold to. At the very least do not hide what God has taught to us, when you are asked. . . .

<hr>

Source: Letters of John Calvin in *Joannis Calvini Opera quae supersunt omnia,* ed. W. Baum, E. Cunitz, and E. Reuss (Braunschweig: Schwetschke and Son, 1876), Vol. XV, cols. 78-80. Translated by Karin Maag. The original source is a letter from Calvin and the pastors of Geneva to the brothers of Wesel, 13 March 1554. Manuscript source: Bibliothèque publique et universitaire, Geneva, Cod. 197a, fol. 271. Reprinted in *Lettres de Jean Calvin: recueillies pour la première fois et publiées d'après les manuscrits originaux,* ed. Jules Bonnet (Paris: Meyrueis, 1854), Vol. I, p. 418.

Calvin Writes about the Importance of Communal Worship (1554)

Throughout his life, Calvin focused on the situation of Reformed believers in France. By the mid-1550s, communities of French Reformed Christians had come into being, albeit often covertly, to avoid detection and persecution from the French Catholic authorities. Notice how much emphasis Calvin put on gathering together for worship — to him, the encouragement and edification that came from communal worship were much greater than could be attained when worshiping on one's own or in individual households.

May the love of God our Father and the grace of our Lord Jesus Christ be always with you through the work of the Holy Spirit.

Beloved lords and brothers, we praise our loving God because he has once again strengthened you, so that you can find courage and energy to work in his service, not only as individuals, but also all together. In fact, we need to encourage each other in this way, because of our weakness and of so many obstacles that slow us down in doing our duty. It is true that gathering to pray to God and hear his Word is not the be all and end all, but it is such a vital help, given that on our own, we are much too sluggish. Therefore, my brothers, keep this goal in mind when you gather together: to fortify yourselves in the faith of the Gospel and grow in all holiness of life. But in any event do not deprive yourselves of this blessing: of calling on God together with one heart and of receiving the fruit of good doctrine and exhortation to help you continue on the right path. For though each of you can and should also pray to God in secret, having withdrawn in private, and can read at home, still God is pleased by our sacrifice when we gather together to pray to him as if from one mouth, and to dedicate with all solemnity our souls and our bodies to him. It would be wonderful if we could do this in public, but when human malice and tyranny cut us off from such freedom, we must at least still praise our God in the company of his people, as taught by Scripture. To this end, little flocks gather here and there, until the whole body of the church is gathered together in the Kingdom of

Heaven. I know very well that you cannot gather together without great fear and doubt. I also know that you are being watched by enemies. But the fear of persecution must not keep us from seeking the food of life and from being led by our good shepherd. Entrust yourselves to him, therefore, and take heart. For he will show you that he cares for his poor sheep, and that his true charge is to save them as from the jaws of wolves. Even in the face of real danger, we should not be too afraid to leave the fold. . . .

Source: Letters of John Calvin in *Joannis Calvini Opera quae supersunt omnia,* ed. W. Baum, E. Cunitz, and E. Reuss (Braunschweig: Schwetschke and Son, 1876) ,Vol. XV, cols. 222-23. Translated by Karin Maag. The original source is a letter from John Calvin to the faithful of the Poitou (France), 3 September 1554. Manuscript source: Bibliothèque publique et universitaire, Geneva, Cod. 107, fol. 54. Reprinted in *Lettres de Jean Calvin: recueillies pour la première fois et publiées d'après les manuscrits originaux,* ed. Jules Bonnet (Paris: Meyrueis, 1854), Vol. I, p. 431.

Calvin Writes about Baptism (1554)

For Reformed individuals and churches facing persecution, baptism presented a particular challenge. If no Reformed pastor was available, should one delay the baptism, perhaps indefinitely, or was it better to have the child baptized, even if the person leading the service was a Catholic priest? Calvin rejected this last option, even though Reformed churches did recognize the validity of Catholic Trinitarian baptisms performed by ordained Catholic priests. What if a Reformed pastor was available, but there was no formally constituted Reformed congregation? Was a private baptism allowable? Here too, Calvin said no. The covenantal reality of Reformed baptism meant that even if there was no formally constituted church, a body of believers was to gather, to hear and bear witness to the promises made.

Regarding the request of our beloved brother Mr. Jean Paule for our advice, we felt the best would be to give him a written answer, so that those involved in the case would be all the more certain about this.

If a man living under the tyranny of the Pope, abstaining from the idolatries and contamination that are in force there, now desires also to offer his children to God in all purity, and have them baptized according to the clear rule of the Gospel, his zeal is holy and praiseworthy. For in fact it is a sign of great poverty when one takes the treasured gift of God, namely one's children, and defiles it immediately by contact with the superstitions that men have jumbled into holy baptism. But above all one should note that since this sacrament is the solemn entry into the Church of God, or a testimony of the heavenly citizenship in which all those whom God adopts as his children are enrolled, one can only administer baptism in the presence of the faithful. Not that one needs to have a public place of worship, but there must be a gathered flock that is a church community, and the one doing the baptism must be acknowledged as a pastor. For if one were to baptize a child in secret and without witnesses, that would in no way match the ordinance instituted by Jesus Christ, nor the practice of the Apostles. Therefore it is essential that the child be baptized within a community that continues to keep clear of the contamination of the Papacy.

When those whom we have been told about will have the means and the desire to gather together in God's name, even if they are not numerous, but a small group, we pray that God will strengthen them in this good zeal which he has given them, to dedicate themselves and their descendants to God our Father and to our redeemer Jesus Christ. And when we know that they have done so, we will seek out an appropriate and apt man to fill this office [of pastor] as is our duty.

11 October 1554
John Calvin, in the name of all his brothers

Source: Letters of John Calvin in *Joannis Calvini Opera quae supersunt omnia,* ed. W. Baum, E. Cunitz, and E. Reuss (Braunschweig: Schwetschke and Son, 1876), Vol. XV, 265-66. Translated by Karin Maag. The original source is a letter from John Calvin to Gianpaolo Alciati, 11 October 1554. Manuscript source: Bibliothèque publique et universitaire, Geneva, Cod. 145, fol. 115. Reprinted in *Lettres de Jean Calvin: recueillies pour la première fois et publiées d'après les manuscrits originaux,* ed. Jules Bonnet (Paris: Meyrueis, 1854), Vol. I, p. 445.

Calvin Responds to an Attack on Images (1561)

While Calvin spoke out strongly in other letters and writings about what he saw as idolatry in Catholic worship, he was careful in practice to restrain people from taking action to attack Catholic religious images, especially in communities where the Reformed were in the minority. Calvin was also always conscious of the need to proceed with legitimacy, allowing only the regularly appointed political authorities to take action and condemning any free-for-all. In this instance, Calvin strongly rejected the conduct of a French pastor in Sauve, who had galvanized his community to destroy Catholic religious images.

What was Calvin's reasoning in this letter? Assess his arguments: was he being inconsistent, given his often-voiced objection to these very same images?

Dear lords and brothers, if each person carefully practiced the rule given to us by the Holy Spirit through the mouth of Saint Paul, to proceed with due care and all modesty, to prevent others from seizing the opportunity they are looking for, you would not be facing such anxiety. You would not be constantly afraid to see the poor churches in your area laid to ruin, and we would not have to struggle to advise you and exhort you to repair the scandal that has already taken place and to prevent such actions from taking place in the future. We are talking about the irresponsible exploit that took place in Sauve, to burn the idols and knock down a cross. We are stunned that the one who is supposed to restrain others and keep them in line

In all likelihood, the target was not simply a cross but a crucifix. Reformed Christians particularly objected to crucifixes, where the body of Christ was displayed on the cross and was often venerated by the faithful.

was so foolhardy himself. For according to what we have heard, not only did he agree to this (which is already bad enough) but he incited the people to it, acting as the leading rebel. But had he forgotten himself, overcome by thoughtless fervor, at least he should have admitted his fault and shown remorse, especially when he was warned and exhorted about it. But to insist that he acted in all things in good conscience is intolerable obstinacy. If he wants us to believe this, he needs to prove that he is grounded in the Word of God in this matter. But we know the opposite to be true. For God never commanded people to lay idols low apart from any held privately in one's home. Those to whom God gives authority are also allowed to remove idols from public places. For there are good reasons why the people of Israel were told: "When you come into the land which God is giving to you and you possess it, then, etc." Therefore, let that firebrand show us his title to the land where he carried out his burnings. Since God did not authorize him to do so, the "good conscience" he refers to is nothing other than the good intention of the Papists. In speaking in this way, we have not become supporters of idols and would to God that all of them were abolished from the earth, even at the cost of our lives. But since obedience is worth more than any sacrifice, we have to consider what is permissible for us and keep to these boundaries. For to try to do more than we are called

Why was the example of Daniel in Babylon so effective in this context?

to do is to be like a runaway horse. We believe that Daniel and his companions, and Ezekiel, and many others were just as zealous as this poor man who takes pride in his presumption, but while they were captives in Babylon, they limited themselves to rejecting idolatry without usurping power that was not theirs. It is more than time that this poor man who forgot himself lowers his gaze, but it is incredible that he was so stupid as to neglect to consider what an opening he gave to evil men who want to ruin everything. But the height of his pride and audacity is that he is digging in his heels and does not want to follow wise counsel. Since this is the situation, dear brothers, we ask you to have pity on the poor churches and not expose them to slaughter by your actions. We ask that you disavow his act and openly declare to the people who were misled that you have disassociated yourselves from the one who was the prime leader of this deed, and that he has been cut off from your company because of his rebellion. If he had submitted himself and was willing to see reason, we could handle him more gently. But now since he is belligerent, he cannot be excused without violating and casting out all good order. . . .

Source: Letters of John Calvin in *Joannis Calvini Opera quae supersunt omnia,* ed. W. Baum, E. Cunitz, and E. Reuss (Braunschweig: Schwetschke and Son, 1878), Vol. XVIII, cols. 580-81. Translated by Karin Maag. The original source is a letter from John Calvin to the Consistory of Sauve, France, written June/July 1561. Manuscript source: Bibliothèque publique et universitaire, Geneva, Cod. 107a, fol. 340. Reprinted in *Lettres de Jean Calvin: recueillies pour la première fois et publiées d'après les manuscrits originaux,* ed. Jules Bonnet (Paris: Meyrueis, 1854), Vol. II, p. 415.

Reactions to a Sermon Preached in Geneva by Guillaume Farel in 1553

Guillaume Farel had been one of the earliest preachers who brought the message of the Reformation to Geneva. After he and Calvin were exiled by the Genevan government in 1538 because of the controversy between church and state regarding oversight of church discipline and worship, Farel went to the neighboring city of Neuchâtel, where he became the chief pastor. He regularly returned to Geneva and was often asked to preach. In 1553, Geneva was very divided, with the supporters of John Calvin (many of them recently arrived religious refugees from France) advocating more rigorous church discipline on the one side, and local Genevans who objected to what they saw as the pastors' undue influence in Genevans' lives on the other. In this fraught atmosphere, any statements made in public that could be construed as favoring one side or the other tended to lead to conflict. This document comes from the records of the Genevan Company of Pastors, in other words, from men who were Farel's professional colleagues. Bear this information in mind as you analyze this text.

On Wednesday, November 1, [. . .] Master Guillaume Farel, having arrived in the city, preached a sermon in which he exhorted and vehemently criticized young people. Some of these young people were offended by his sermon, including even a number who were not present when he preached. They lodged a complaint, alleging that he had called all of them atheists. M. Guillaume Farel had already returned to Neuchâtel. At this point, information was gathered regarding the said Farel.

On Saturday, the 11th of the same month, the said Master Guillaume Farel, having been alerted that such agitation had surfaced about him, returned to the city and was ordered by Messieurs [the magistrates] not to preach until his case had been looked into.

On the following Monday, Master John Calvin, M. Abel Poupin, M. Jacques Bernard, and M. Matthieu Malesien appeared before Messieurs on behalf of all the pastors to point out the affront caused to the said M. Guillaume. And M. **Pierre Viret** accompanied them.

On the same day, a fair number of the citizens of the city appeared before Messieurs regarding the matter of the said M. Guillaume Farel, in opposition to those who had complained about him. They stated that the plaintiffs were unjustified in making their complaint in the name of all the citizens, and that for their part, they who were citizens had never agreed to this complaint and did not agree with it at all. Instead, they held the said Farel to be a true servant of God, and found his sermon to be holy and good, and they had benefitted and learned a great deal from the exhortations he had made to them.

Based on all this, Messieurs ordered that the said M. Guillaume Farel be acknowledged as a true pastor, as he has always been, and stated that he had faithfully preached and carried out his duties. Many also called him father, because he brought them into the family of our Lord, and because he was the first to establish the church here. Messieurs wrote letters to Messieurs of Neuchâtel following all this and [declared] that the said Master Guillaume, after having preached as usual, would leave whenever he wanted to, at the expense of this city, and

Note that the Genevan church seemed to be happy to offer Farel the privilege of the pulpit, even after his departure from the city. His status as the man who had helped bring Geneva to Protestantism gave him a large measure of authority, though, as seen in this report, not everyone felt so positively about his message.

This controversy provides strong evidence to show that sermons mattered to people at the time: their content was discussed, and debates could and did erupt over what the preacher had said in the pulpit.

accompanied by a herald. All this was done to the great consolation of the children of God and to the confusion of the wicked.

Source: Reactions to a sermon preached by Guillaume Farel in Geneva in 1553 in *Registres de la Compagnie des Pasteurs de Genève au temps de Calvin*, ed. R. Kingdon and J.-F. Bergier (Geneva: Droz, 1964), Volume II, p. 53. Translated by Karin Maag. The original manuscript of the Registers of the Company of Pastors for this period is held by the Archives d'état de Genève, Registres de la compagnie des pasteurs de Genève, Vol. B2.

A Catholic Perspective on Reformed Worship Practices (1556)

This anonymous work is a Catholic anti-Reformed polemical work that alleges serious moral failings of the Reformed church leaders in Geneva and surrounding areas, including John Calvin, Theodore Beza, and Pierre Viret. While hardly reliable as an account of the behavior of these leaders, the text does offer some interesting and accurate descriptions of worship in Geneva and Lausanne, from the perspective of an outsider, a Catholic, who was constantly comparing what he saw in these Reformed communities to what he was used to in Catholic churches. In the introduction, the anonymous author notes that he spent eighteen months in Protestant lands and that he is recounting "what I saw with my eyes and heard with my ears." The work is written in dialogue form, in which Passevent, returning from his travels in Protestant areas, recounts his experiences and answers the questions of Pasquin.

p. 3: *Passevent:* Regarding their clothing, the preachers, or would-be preachers, dress just like our attorneys and lawyers, apart from the square cap. These men are held to be worthy for the church. All the others dress like our merchants, and are held to be as worthy as lay men.

pp. 11-12: *Passevent:* After the sermon, the preacher or the deacon of the place, standing up, with his head uncovered, reads four or five prayers already prepared by Calvin and others, more texts than in our baptisms. Everyone sits wherever they want. And even if there is more than one child, they only once say "I baptize you" and then throw a handful of water on the face of the child that they have taken from the arms of the midwife. In their baptisms, they only have one godfather or one godmother who carries the child in front. After that comes the midwife carrying a pitcher full of water and a napkin to dry the hands of the preacher or deacon. Then the men and the women file in, two at a time, as if a single man or a single woman could procreate! This shows their folly and their ignorance about the institution of godfathers and godmothers. What is worse, they do not worry if their children die without baptism, something that tells you, in short, just how they consider the fundamentals of the Christian faith. Some wait [to hold a baptism] until Sunday, others only wait until the end of a sermon, and others hold it at three in the afternoon, which just shows their division and discord.

Controversies over baptism were numerous in the Reformation era. The Reformed rejected the Catholic idea that unbaptized babies who died would never get to Heaven, and instead asserted that the children of faithful and believing parents were included in God's covenant, and so would also get to Heaven even if they died before baptism.

Given the high rate of infant mortality, Catholics did not wait any length of time before baptizing their babies – the Reformed insistence on having baptisms take place during regularly-scheduled church services with a congregation present, even if that meant waiting, was bewildering to Catholics.

pp. 26-28: *Pasquin:* Please tell me the state of their churches and how they behave in these places.

Passevent: Inside, it is just like a college or a school. It is full of benches, and in the middle there is a pulpit for the preacher. In front of it, the low benches are for the women and small children, and further around the higher benches are for the men, with no distinctions of rank. Almost all the stained-glass windows are already destroyed, and thick dust up to the ankles is everywhere.

Pasquin: Do they utter certain prayers or petitions together or individually? And how do they pray? Do they have any images of the crucifix, of the Virgin Mary, or of any saints there, on which they can fix their gaze?

Passevent: You ask whether they pray together or alone. They do not. As soon as they come into church, each person chooses a spot and sits down, as in a school, and there they wait until the preacher goes into the pulpit. As soon as the preacher appears, they all kneel down except for him. He stands with his head uncovered and his hands folded together to pray. He prays a prayer he makes up out of his own mind, ending it with the *Pater Noster*, but no *Ave Maria*, and does the whole thing in French, and the people quietly answer *So be it*. And twice a week (only in the cities), they sing a Psalm or part of a Psalm before the sermon. Everyone sings together: men, women, girls, and children, all of them sitting down. And if anyone prays when he comes into church, people point their fingers at him and mock him, and hold him to be a Papist and an idolater. In the same way, if he is accused of having [books of] hours, or rosaries, or images in his house, or if he observes feast days, he is immediately called before the Consistory to be punished for this.

Pasquin: Tell me whether they preach in each church, for I have been told by reputable people that convents and the abbey have been destroyed and ruined. And what have they done with the ornaments and images that were in those churches?

Passevent: They care about as much for church buildings as they do for any other building. They feel that two churches in a city is plenty and they use the others as stables, granaries, slaughterhouses, or for even worse purposes. And the wooden images have been burned, and the stone ones have been used as building materials. Those that remain are vandalized or headless. And the church buildings themselves are slowly decaying and falling apart, because they say that the faithful believers are God's Church, and even if the walls were each to fall down, one after the other, it is all the same to them, so long as the revenues keep coming in to their lordships and their church fornicators [reference to the pastors] receive their pensions.

pp. 70-71: *Pasquin:* Now tell me about their way of getting married.

Compare this description to the church interior in Lyon (see p. 45). Does Passevent's description seem accurate?

Why might stained-glass windows be destroyed?

Remember that this text is not a genuine conversation: the questions are set up by the author in such a way as to highlight the dramatic differences between Reformed and Catholic worship practices.

"So be it" is the translation of *Amen*.

Why might some Christians object to prayers made up out of one's own mind?

Passevent's main claim about the Reformed pastors was that they were serial adulterers.

A satrap was a high-ranking government official of ancient Persia. Why might Passevent have used this term to refer to Calvin's role in Geneva?

Given the lack of descriptions of church ceremonies and religious practices in Geneva, this description is ethnographically invaluable. Notice how wedding ceremonies were incorporated into regular worship services.

Catholic funerals were often elaborate processions including clergy. A funeral Mass would also have been customary in a Catholic context.

A reliquary is a specially made container for sacred objects or actual physical parts of holy persons.

Passevent: Those who want to do things according to the will of Calvin, the great **Satrap** of Geneva, do as follows: the husband-to-be, with his guests, each with a sprig of rosemary or flowers in hand, go to find the fiancée at her home. He waits for her there, with his guests. She dresses according to the customs of those parts. In other words, if she is a widow, she covers her head, and if she is a virgin, she wears her hair down, with a crown of flowers on her head. Both widows and virgins wear these flowers. She is accompanied by her women friends, each with a bouquet in hand or at their breast. Everyone then goes to the sermon at the sound of the bell. The men go first, two by two, as the advance guard, followed by the fiancé holding the bride-to-be by her hand, for fear of losing her, and at the end come the women two by two as the rear guard. They come in this order to the door of the church (which they call the temple) and then each person takes a seat, waiting for the preacher to start. After the sermon, the husband-to-be takes his fiancée once again by the hand and brings her before the door of the choir or to the steps where the high altar used to be. There the minister, or the deacon in his absence, standing with his head bare and facing the people, joins the couple by ceremonies that are as long or longer than ours, claiming that he only does what he is doing to ratify the promise (in the presence of their church) that the couple previously made together. Then, following the same order as before, they go back to the husband's home, and after the meal, everyone goes away to leave the couple to discuss their private affairs, and thus the marriage and wedding are consummated in this fashion. Those who do not worry much about Calvin and his companions follow the same process but add the accompaniment of a Swiss drum or other instruments on the way to and from church, and after the meal they dance or play games in the house, though secretly, because of the risk of being called before the Consistory.

pp. 72-73: *Pasquin:* Please tell me how they conduct their funerals after someone dies.

Passevent: You are asking me about one of the most pitiable practices in all of human nature, for as soon as the man or woman dies, those of the household prepare the body as they wish, and then alert their relatives and neighbors to accompany them. They also alert the church service bell-ringers, whose task it is to carry the bodies and bury the deceased and dig graves in the appointed place as follows. The two bearers described above carry the deceased on their shoulders, as we might carry a **reliquary**. The body is covered with a sheet or a cloth and is followed by the men in pairs and then the women, also two by two. Some laugh while others cry, and then they go throw the body in the pit without saying anything and do no other ceremony, just as one might for a dog or a horse. Then everyone who participated in the procession goes back to the home of the deceased and at the door, each person says to the closest relatives, "God preserve your life," and they respond, "And yours too." And if anyone is so bold as to utter a prayer or give a charitable gift for the soul of the deceased, they are in danger of being called to the Consistory and held to be a Papist and idolater.

p. 74: *Pasquin:* Continue the description I asked you concerning their Lord's Supper.

Passevent: Three or four times a year, according to the wishes of the lords and princes, two tables are set up in the church, and each is covered with a tablecloth. On the left hand at the end there is a pile of communion wafers, and on the other end on the right are three or four cups or glasses. Under the table there are several pewter pots, filled either with white or red wine — it does not matter. And after the sermon the preacher comes down from the pulpit and goes to stand at one end of the table by the communion wafers, and standing with his head bare he places a piece of the wafer in the hand of each person, saying, "Remember that Jesus Christ died for you." Then each person eats the piece of wafer and walks over to the other end of the table where they take their drink from the hand of one of the lords or another person delegated for this purpose, without saying anything. The sergeants at arms, their heads uncovered, pour out more to drink and supply more communion wafers if needed. At the same time, someone else standing in the pulpit, with his head bare, reads in the vernacular from the Gospel of Saint John from the start of the thirteenth chapter. He continues until each person has taken his piece, both men and women, each at their own table, as well as the children and girls aged at least eight to ten years old. And after everyone has had this snack, they all go have a meal if they have one, or go look for one otherwise.

Passevent clearly found nothing holy nor worthy of respect in this ritual.

Pasquin: But how is it that they call it the Lord's Supper, since they do it before going to eat, since you told me they have this snack before going to their dinners? I would like to know if they take the Supper fasting, due to the reverence that they may have and feel for it.

Fasting before partaking of the sacrament of Communion was a standard Catholic practice.

Passevent: You are much more scrupulous and concerned than they are. Indeed I asked this to one of them once, whether the Lord's Supper was done fasting, and he replied very sharply that Jesus Christ celebrated his Supper with his Apostles after a meal, and therefore they would do better to have it after dinner, to drink as much and eat as many of the wafers, and have a roast lamb, following the example of Jesus Christ.

This exchange illustrates how much importance the Reformed placed on following the biblical text and on the Lord's Supper as a remembrance of Christ's Last Supper, rather than a re-enactment of Christ's sacrifice.

Source: *Passevent Parisien* (1556). Translated from the French by Karin Maag using the 1875 Paris edition (with no author given; it may have been written by **Antoine Cathelan** or **Artus Désiré**): *Passevent Parisien respondant à Pasquin Romain. De la vie de ceux qui sont allez demourer à Genève, et se disent vivre selon la réformation de l'Évangile: faict en forme de Dialogue* (Paris: Isidore Liseux, 1875); reprint of the third edition of at least five, all published in 1556: *Passevent Parisien, respondant à Pasquin Romain. De la vie de ceux qui sont allez demourer à Geneve, ou au pais jadis de Savoye, et maintenant souz les princes de Berne, et se disent vivre selon la réformation de l'Evangile* (Paris: Widow of N. Buffet, 1556).

A Description of Household Worship Practices (1592)

André Ryff, a boy from Basel, described his life in Geneva in the home of a grocer, where Ryff did his apprenticeship. After recalling the beatings he received from his master for mistakes he made, Ryff described household worship practices.

In spite of this [referring to the beatings], I never complained, because I liked my life with my master, and I felt that I would benefit from this apprenticeship. Furthermore, the strictness of Master Jean was matched by the kindness of his wife, and I thank God especially for having guided me to their house, because the household was run with perfect discipline and good order. Each morning and again every evening, Master Jean, his wife, his brother-in-law, and the whole household knelt down in the main room, and there the mistress prayed in a very loud voice, reverently thanking God for his gracious gifts and his blessings, and praying to him with fervor, asking him to grant us his Spirit, his protection, his blessing, and his mercy. Later on, my master gave me the charge of leading the prayer after he had taught it a bit to me. I believe that in this way I developed a sincere religious zeal. Incidentally, I should say that it is the custom for the Genevan ministers to visit every house every three months. They gather together the inhabitants of about six or eight households, young and old together, to ask them questions, examine them, have them give an account of their faith, and catechize them before they partake in the Lord's Supper, which is only celebrated every three months. In view of this, my master taught me himself, so that I was able to answer satisfactorily the questions set by the reverend pastors, and this was a means of edification for me, which causes me to rejoice, praying almighty God that he keep me in this faith by his grace, as I professed it, and as it is contained in our Basel confession. And may he also grant me a blessed end in Jesus Christ, our only Savior and Redeemer. Amen.

This text provides an important eye-witness account of the active role of women in household worship.

Notice that the oversight of pastors extended to apprentices who were not even from Geneva: all those living in Geneva, whatever their place of origin, were expected to take an active part in Genevan Reformed religious life.

Source: André Ryff, "Memories of a boy from Basel," 1560-63, translated by Karin Maag from the French text presented by Adolphe Gautier, "Un jeune Bâlois à Genève au XVIe siècle," in *Mémoires et documents publiés par la société d'histoire et d'archéologie de Genève* 17 (1872): 412-16. Gautier translated the text from Ryff's original autobiography, written in German, and first published in a critical edition by H. Heusler-Ryhiner in *Beiträge zur vaterländischen Geschichte, herausgegeben von der historischen Gesellschaft in Basel* 9 (1870). Ryff wrote his autobiography in 1592, covering the story of his life only up to his marriage in 1574.

Managing a Country Parish. A Country Pastor's Advice to His Successor (1567)

This engaging set of reflections was prepared by Pastor Charles Perrot as advice to the man who was to succeed him in his rural charge, which included several different parishes. Perrot was promoted to a city post and later taught in the Genevan Academy. Perrot gives a candid view of the challenges facing pastors in the rural territories of Geneva, even thirty years after the Reformation had been officially adopted.

I must not forget, at the beginning of this memoir, to bid all those who read it, and especially those of my brethren who succeed me in this charge, to take it all in good part, to regard what I have to say with tolerance . . . and to adopt (at their discretion) anything in it which may help in the edification of the flock. . . . I would not wish it to be thought that I want to constrain anyone to follow my judgment, which is not founded on as much experience as I would have liked. Each person has to make out as best he can, and this is as it should be, provided that no innovations or changes are introduced without good reason. For my part, I learned a lot from my predecessors. . . . Indeed, I am indebted to them for most of what follows here. . . .

What do these prefatory remarks tell you about Perrot's character and approach to ministry?

Charles Perrot

Concerning the order of the sermon

Every Sunday morning between the September celebration of the Lord's Supper and Easter, the Minister enters the temple as soon as the tolling of the church bell has stopped, which will probably be at about eight o'clock. He waits for a little while until the people have finished arriving, especially those who can help with the singing. If there is a wedding or a **christening,** the custom is that the master and mistress of every family must be present, together with their servants and those of their children who take communion. In practice one is often obliged to let them off, provided that they do not miss the catechizing which comes afterwards; one has also to let off nursing mothers, provided they do not turn this into a prescriptive right, and provided that they at least make an effort to come to the catechism class.

When the Genevan texts speak of the "sermon," they actually mean the whole of the worship service itself (which was focused around the sermon). When they use the word "temple," they mean the church building.

Why might nursing mothers be excused from church attendance?

At the sermon the following Psalms are sung: 1, 3, 15, 24, 42, 119 Aleph and Beth, 129, 130, 128, and sometimes the Ten Commandments. Each Psalm is divided into two halves, one for the beginning and one for the end of the service. At the Lord's Supper the whole of Psalm 23 is sung at the beginning, and the whole of Simeon's canticle at the end, before the closing prayers and the Grace. In the prayers, we never use the paraphrase of the Lord's Prayer.

In other words, the congregation recited the Lord's Prayer rather than singing the paraphrase.

I decided that I would not sing at those services where there wasn't another man present to help in the singing, but I did sing with another man even if there were no women or girls to join in. Some people know the Psalms very imperfectly, or can just about repeat after the others, which usually means only Pierre Chapusi, Godmar, Jeanne from Monet's house, the Defosses woman, and the Gervaise woman's daughter, together with anyone who happens to have come over from Geneva. It was my practice to time the service to last until the last grain

What does Perrot's practice regarding Psalm singing tell you about the level of participation of the congregation in the service? What picture is emerging of congregational singing at these services, and does this picture surprise you in any way? Why or why not?

of sand had trickled into the bottom of the hourglass, but then to bring it to an end as rapidly as I could, because people watched out for this, and were irritated if it was done otherwise.

What one should do on Sundays after the service

Based on this paragraph, what can you infer about the relationship between the rural churches and the Genevan Consistory? How might the effectiveness of church discipline in the rural churches be affected by these procedures?

After the service the minister remains behind a little with the two elders to make a note of any absences, sick people to visit, or scandalous ones to call to account. Those who have failed to attend the sermon, or who have committed some other fault, are then called upon and warned by the minister in the presence of the elders in a manner appropriate to the particular case and to the persons involved. If you think it will be good for the offender, you may refer the matter to the Consistory in Geneva, which will then summon the offender to appear there. Also, if there is a really clear allegation of blasphemy, drunkenness, adultery, and if the charge, as far as you can judge, is well-founded and the offense proven, you should refer it to the Consistory in the city, because it is there that the safeguard on the Lord's Supper is upheld, not in the village. It is also the duty of the minister to seek out those who have already been forbidden to attend the Supper to take heed of their position, and to predispose them to go back to the said Consistory to apply for reinstatement. It is not permissible for the minister to take it upon himself to readmit them, as I have discovered by personal experience. If there was any quarrel or bad feeling which those involved were willing to make up in front of the minister, I used not to send the matter to the city, provided the matter was entirely clear and no great harm had been done.

Preaching services during the week

Pastor Perrot's pragmatism shines through this document, here and elsewhere. See if you can find other instances of his awareness of the challenges facing his rural flock in relation to church attendance and faith practice.

At the end of a catechism class, people can be called to respond, and also at sermons preached on weekdays. My practice was to preach on Thursdays, at least from the first Thursday in October to the last Thursday in March, or thereabouts. For the people simply have to work in the fields most of the time. Such sermons (prayers included) should not run beyond the hourglass, if at all possible. They should be attended at the very least by one leading member of each household in the village of Moin, that is to say, by the husband or the wife.

When I had some announcement to make to the parishioners, I used to make it at the end of the prayers, in order to catch the masters of the households, because after the Benediction they made their escape so quickly. I could not abide the way they hung around in the graveyard after the service making a noise, but since this was the time they chose for settling their business deals, I kept quiet about it, at least when they behaved decorously enough. I would advise the minister not to take his text from those parts of the Scriptures which are difficult to understand out of context because they are all connected with the other passages, as is the case with the Epistles of St. Paul, for the people here rarely carry over anything they have learned from one sermon to the next; I think they profit more from the catechizing.

Concerning the order to be observed in catechizing

I used to run these classes for about one hour and a half after the sermon. I used to set about it, every Sunday, by singing through the Ten Commandments with the men, and the women or girls, one table of the law at the beginning and the other at the end. Except during the extreme cold of winter I used to take each of the two tables separately, concluding with a brief general confession and a prayer. . . . Afterwards I would read out the Creed, and the Lord's Prayer, but I have never yet entered into any teaching on the sacraments with the people here. What is more, I used to explain everything in as brief and simple a way as I could, over three or four consecutive Sundays, for there are questions and doctrines in the catechism which one cannot readily teach people, for fear of confusing them. This being so, in order to do as little harm as possible, my practice used to be to take each article word-for-word as it is in the catechism, paraphrase its content in a couple of lines at most, and then to get all the boys and girls, the menservants and the maidservants, one after another, to recite it twice, out loud. It was above all the children and the servants who were supposed to attend the catechizing. After I had asked them to do this, we came to the final prayer, and those children at whom I pointed had to recite "Our Father . . ." or "I believe . . ." or "Hear, O Israel . . . ," just as it is done in Geneva. I made sure that they got it more or less right, allowing them to get away with a good deal of inaccuracy provided that the substance was not corrupted — but one had to watch out. After that we sang the Commandments, either the whole lot, or (if we had sung the first table earlier) the second table only, and finished with the Blessing, just as they do at the weekday services in the city. In summer, when the catechizing was done after dinner, I used to take the little children, at the bottom end of the church, or sitting outside it, in the open air and try to get them to say nicely the words of "Our Father . . ." and "I believe . . ." and to teach them something about the Commandments.

Concerning the interrogations which should occur before Easter Communion

During the four or five Sundays before Easter I used to announce that everyone should turn up at the temple at the catechism hour, and that instead of holding a catechism class I would question people individually, asking them to think carefully about the state of their faith, without using any set form of words of prayer, although occasionally I would use a short

Was Perrot realistic or patronizing about his congregation's abilities? See if you can find any other evidence in the text to help you decide.

Once again, Perrot was teaching the three basic texts: the Lord's Prayer, the Apostles' Creed, and the Ten Commandments.

Although the Lord's Supper was celebrated quarterly, the Easter Communion carried a lot of weight given that the Catholic practice of lay people receiving the consecrated Host once a year took place at Easter.

prayer when they came in and when they left. I used to call them together in this place and at the catechism hour because in the village of Moin it proved impossible conveniently to get them to assemble, house by house, during the week. In Magny, however, I was able to get people together once or twice, on a weekday, in the house of Tombeti the tailor. I used to begin by getting one or more individuals from the row of men to recite the Lord's Prayer, the Creed, or the Commandments, choosing especially those who seemed the most likely to be ignorant. And I would counsel all those who did not have too poor a memory to learn the Commandments by heart, and I would try to help them to do so before they came to the Lord's Supper. At the very least I would try to get them to recite the Summary, and I used to give some of them a bit of a fright, in order to gain at least something. The women came next, after the men. And if the whole session lasted an hour and a half, that was enough for one occasion, for there was still to come the catechism class which the interrogations had displaced, and which could not last more than another three-quarters of an hour. As for the form of the interrogation, I used to follow rather freely the one in the catechism, or indeed to use a form of questioning I had worked out specially. Those who answered reasonably well were received at Communion, and those who genuinely had good intentions were tolerated also. Those to whom all of this meant nothing at all were warned that they must not present themselves in so ignorant a state. However, the minister should not refuse to admit to Communion anyone who presents himself, except those he has earlier decided to report to the Consistory in the city.

It is also to be noted that in order to get people to answer properly (in the interrogations) you have to put the question to them several times over, and also to take care not to vary the wording from one year to the next, if you can. It is the duty of the elders to get the people assembled.

Baptisms

At baptisms I used to see that the father and the godfather were both standing side by side and that these two (and only these two) were involved when it came to making the promise to do their Christian duty. Because from time to time the women will push in if you don't watch out. I always refused to confer names which were too outlandish, and sometimes instead of "Vincende," for example, I would say "Suzanne," using liberty for the sake of edification. I wrote the godfather's name down, and I recorded the day of the baptism. I did not readily agree to the postponement of baptism on the pretext that godparents were being sought, and I used to warn that there was danger in thus undervaluing the role of the parents. When they invited me to the christening party, I used sometimes to go, out of friendliness, or for some other good reason, but usually I did not attend.

Perrot was referring to the summary of the law as written in Deuteronomy 6:4.

This evidence of flexibility in catechizing was very common: pastors from across Europe tended to try to develop what they saw as the most effective way to teach the basics of the faith to their congregations.

Again, what can you infer about the relationship between the rural churches and the "mother church" in Geneva based on these rules?

Getting fathers to attend baptisms was challenging, since that had not been part of Catholic practice.

See later documents on allowable names and on the controversies that arose as a result. How might the father have reacted to Perrot's change?

Marriages

At a wedding — and I performed only one — one must not tolerate the appearance of a bride with an insufficiently modest headdress. The **banns** must be read on the three Sundays before the wedding, just before the main sermon. If the announcement concerned a wedding in another parish, I used to record in Latin as is customary: "Proclamatum Tridominico nomine intercedente Car. Perrottus." If it was for my parish, one of the parties being from another parish, a similar attestation, signed by the representative of the civil power, had to be provided by the minister there. If the parties had slept together before marriage, and this matter had come before the Consistory, one had to get them to acknowledge this before one married them, or one wrote a little note to this effect on the copy of the banns one sent to the minister of the other parish to alert him to the fact that he had to secure this admission from them, so that no one should remain under the shadow of scandal or be encouraged to act as they had done.

The banns were the announcement of the names of the prospective bride and groom, read from the pulpit over the course of several weeks, so those with objections could let the pastors know.

Based on Perrot's comments, how serious an offense was it to have sexual intercourse before marriage?

Visitation of the sick

When I visited the sick, I used either to cheer them up with exhortation or to offer them consolation, whichever I judged to be the more appropriate in the light of their condition, and then I would pray, and try to get them to pray also, and to make them (in true repentance and faith) embrace the remission of their sins in the death and passion of our Lord Jesus Christ. I would question them on a number of points, as far as their condition permitted, and I would exhort them that if by chance any rancor or ill-feeling existed between themselves and anyone else, they should put it aside in a spirit of reconciliation.

Do not wait to be summoned to the bedside, especially in Genthod or in Malagny. And be sure to mention the sick in your prayers during church services, as they do in Geneva.

Notice the very Protestant emphasis on trusting in Christ, rather than in the intercession of saints or of the Virgin Mary.

Bearing in mind that Pastor Perrot was providing advice to his successor, it does sound as though he wanted his successor to learn from his mistakes.

Catechism class at Genthod

When I took the catechism class at Genthod, I would come down from the pulpit, the little children all being there, and I would sit down on a bench and start to get each of them to recite in turn "Our help cometh from the Lord, who has made heaven and earth . . . ," and then I would teach them how to pray. All their little ones would recite "Our Father" — one should correct their pronunciation. Then in the same way I would ask those who knew it to recite the Creed, or the Ten Commandments. Once that was done, I would go on to explain to them what the Lord's Prayer and the Creed and the Commandments were all about, but I would do

The reference here is to Psalm 121.

so in a much simpler and more straightforward way than at Moin. But just as in Moin, here too the older boys and girls were expected to be able to answer questions. So far, I have not managed to go any further than this with instruction. I have also tried to teach the older ones, a line at a time, to recite "Lift up your hearts." All this can go on for about half an hour or more. I used to conclude with a brief prayer.

Form of interrogation before Communion

Q. What is necessary if one is to be properly prepared for coming to the Supper?

A. It is necessary to have true faith and repentance.

Q. What is repentance?

A. Repentance is renouncing our own desires so that the Spirit of God can dwell in us.

Q. What is faith?

A. Faith is a firm assurance that God, for love of his Son Jesus Christ, extends his grace towards us.

Q. How can we have that assurance?

A. Through the power of the Holy Spirit, in the preaching of the Gospel.

Q. What is the Gospel?

A. Good news.

Q. What does it contain?

A. The letter of the grace of God in Jesus Christ his Son, of which baptism and the Lord's Supper are the two seals.

Q. What does the word "baptism" mean?

A. Washing.

Q. What does the word "Supper" mean?

A. A meal.

Q. What does baptism signify to us?

A. That we are washed in the blood of Jesus Christ through the power of the Holy Spirit.

Q. What does the Supper signify to us?

A. That our souls are nourished by the body and blood of our Lord Jesus through the power of the Holy Spirit, in hope of everlasting life.

Pastor Perrot's questions were fairly basic: what fundamentals did he expect his parishioners to know?

Source: Charles Perrot, "Managing a country parish" (1567), in *Calvinism in Europe, 1540-1610: A Collection of Documents,* trans. and ed. A. Duke, G. Lewis, and A. Pettegree (Manchester: Manchester University Press, 1992), pp. 49-56. The original document is a manuscript held by the Archives d'état de Genève, EC [Etat Civil] Genthod 1, pp. 1-16.

Orders of Service and Texts

The Form of Prayers and Church Singing Together with the Way to Administer the Sacraments and Consecrate Marriage, Following the Practice of the Ancient Church (1542)

One of the most important ways to shape worship and ensure uniformity was to create liturgies, written texts that provided the framework for worship. Even today, most church services follow a regular structure of prayers, readings, songs, and preaching — this sequence, repeated week by week, is a liturgy, even if the words change at each service. Highly structured liturgies, like the ones from Geneva, were vital in helping both clergy and laypeople make the transition from Catholic to Reformed worship.

The Form of Church Prayers

On weekdays, the pastor gives an invocation to prayer as he sees fit, tying it to the season and the subject of his sermon. For Sunday mornings, the following form is generally used.

Our help is in the Name of God, who made Heaven and earth. Amen.

My brothers, may each of you present yourselves before the Face of the Lord, confessing your faults and sins, following my words in your hearts.

Lord God, eternal and almighty Father, we confess and admit openly before your holy Majesty, that we are poor sinners, who were conceived and born in iniquity and sin, inclined to evil, useless in doing good, and that because of our sin, we endlessly and ceaselessly break your holy commandments. In doing so, we draw down ruin and damnation on

Notice that not every part of the liturgy is prescribed, and pastors are free to pray extemporaneously, at least during weekday services.

The phrase "born in iniquity and sin, inclined to evil" refers to the doctrine of original sin, a significant theological theme in Western Christianity especially influenced by Augustine.

73

ourselves, according to your righteous judgment. Yet, Lord, we inwardly despise ourselves for having offended you, and we condemn ourselves and our vices with true repentance, pleading for your grace to come to our aid in our distress. O loving God and Father, full of compassion, have mercy upon us in the name of your Son Jesus Christ, our Lord. By wiping away our sins and stains, free us and make the gifts of your Holy Spirit grow in us daily, so that as we wholeheartedly confess our evildoing, we may be filled with remorse, which leads us to true repentance. May this repentance help us to learn to struggle against all sins and produce in us fruits of justice and innocence that are pleasing to you, through the same Jesus Christ, etc.

This being done, the congregation sings a Psalm, and then the pastor begins to pray once again, asking God for the grace of his Holy Spirit, so that God's Word may be faithfully explained to the honor of his Name and for the edification of the church, and that the Word be received with appropriate humility and obedience. The form of the prayer is left to the pastor's discretion.

At the end of the sermon, following his invocation, the pastor begins as follows:

Almighty God, heavenly Father, you promised to grant the petitions which we make in the Name of your beloved Son Jesus Christ, our Lord (John 16:23), and we are taught by his doctrine and that of the Apostles to gather in his Name. He promised that he will be there in our midst (Matt. 28:20) and that he will intercede for us before you, to request and obtain all things which we agree on here on earth. First of all, you have told us to pray for those whom you have set over us, our superiors and rulers (1 Tim. 2:2), and then for all your people's needs, and even for the needs of all men. Therefore, trusting in your holy doctrine and promises, and since we are gathered here before your Face and in the Name of your Son, our Lord Jesus, we beseech you, our loving God and Father, in the name of our only Savior and Mediator, to forgive our sins freely through your infinite mercy. Please draw and raise up our thoughts and desires to you, so that we may petition and call on you with all our heart, and according to your good pleasure and will, which is the only true foundation.

   Therefore, we pray to you, heavenly Father, for all princes and lords, your servants, to whom you have entrusted the administration of your justice, and especially for the lords of this city. Please give them your Spirit (Ps. 51:12), the only good and truly essential gift, and increase it in them daily that they may truly acknowledge in faith Jesus Christ your Son our Lord as King of kings and Lord over all lords (1 Tim. 6:15; Rev. 17:14; 19:16; Matt. 28:18). Since you gave him all power in Heaven and on earth, may they seek to serve him and to exalt his reign in their territories, leading and governing their subjects, who are the creatures of your hands, and the sheep of your pasture, according to your good pleasure. Both here and throughout the world, dwelling in true peace and tranquility, may we serve you in all holiness and equity,

---

Marginal notes:

This instruction (or rubric) helped to establish the Reformed practice of the prayer for illumination, an explicit calling upon the Holy Spirit to illumine the preaching and the hearing of the Word of God.

Obviously, the pastor did not read out this set of biblical references in the midst of his prayer. What was the point of including them, and what can that tell you about the ways this text might be used?

and, being freed and delivered from the fear of our enemies, may we praise you our whole life long. Amen.

Our true Father and Savior, we also pray for all those whom you have ordained as pastors for your faithful, to whom you have given the charge of caring for souls and expounding your holy Gospel. Please direct them and lead them by your Holy Spirit, so that they may be found to be faithful and loyal ministers of your glory. May they always pursue the goal of finding and bringing back all the poor, lost, and wandering flock to our Lord Jesus Christ, the chief Pastor and Prince of Bishops (1 Pet. 5:4). Day by day, may the faithful benefit and grow in all justice and holiness in him. Furthermore, please deliver all the churches from the mouth of ravening wolves and from all mercenaries, who only look to their own ambition or benefit, and not to the praise of your holy Name alone, and to the salvation of your flock.

Then, loving God and merciful Father, we pray to you for all people, for since you want to be acknowledged as the Savior of the whole world through the redemption of your Son Jesus Christ, may those who still do not know him, who are stuck in darkness and imprisoned by error and ignorance, be brought to the straight path of salvation through the inward light of your Holy Spirit and the preaching of your Gospel. This salvation is to know you as the only true God, and to know the one whom you have sent, Jesus Christ (John 17:3). May those whom you have already touched with your grace and enlightened by the knowledge of your Word (Eph. 1:18) grow daily in all goodness, being strengthened by your spiritual blessings, so that we may all adore you with one heart and one mouth, giving praise and honor to your Christ, our Master, King, and Law-Giver.

In the same way, O God of all comfort, we bring before you all those whom you have touched and chastised through crosses and tribulations, whether through poverty, or imprisonment, or sickness, or banishment, or other bodily calamity or spiritual affliction. We ask that you help them to see and feel your fatherly care, which chastises them for their improvement, so that they may turn to you with their whole heart, and, being converted, that they may receive full consolation and be delivered from all their ills.

Finally, O God and Father, grant also to us, who are gathered here in the Name of your Son Jesus because of his Word (and of his Holy Supper) [parenthesis added only on Communion days], the ability to see clearly and honestly our natural state of perdition, and our deserved condemnation, only deepened daily by our desperate and disordered lives. Seeing and hearing that there is nothing good in us and that our flesh and blood cannot enter into the inheritance of your Kingdom, may we put our whole trust and confidence in your dear Son Jesus, our Lord, the only Savior and Redeemer. As he makes his dwelling in us, crush our old Adam and renew a better life within us, so that your holy and worthy Name may be exalted and glorified everywhere and in all places. With all creatures, may we be truly and fully obedient to you, just as your angels and heavenly messengers only ask to fulfill your commands, so that your will be done without any opposition. May all turn to serve and please you, giving up

The progression of this prayer from petitions "for all princes and Lords" to "those whom you have ordained as pastors" to "all people" to those suffering under "crosses and tribulations" to "those gathered here" follows the example of several early church intercessory prayers.

their own will and all their fleshly desires. In this way, may you have lordship and dominion over all of us, and may we learn daily more and more how to submit to and serve your Majesty. May you be King and Lord over all, leading your people by the scepter of your Word, and by the power of your Spirit, defeating your enemies by the power of your truth and justice.

And therefore may all powers and principalities that challenge your glory be daily destroyed and abolished, until your coming Kingdom is revealed, when you will appear as judge. May we who walk in the love and awe of your Name be fed by your goodness, and please grant us everything necessary and expedient to eat our bread in peace. As we see that you care for us, may we acknowledge you all the more as our Father, expecting all good things from your hand, removing and jettisoning our trust in creatures to put it fully in you and in your goodness. And because during this mortal life we are poor and fragile sinners, who constantly fail and wander from the right way, please forgive us for our faults which lead us to be condemned in your sight. By this remission, you free us from the burden of eternal death under which we labor. Therefore, please turn your wrath away from us and do not ascribe to us the evil that is within us, just as, according to your commandment, we forget the harm done to us, and instead of seeking vengeance, we do good to our enemies. Finally, please sustain us in the future by your goodness, so that we do not stumble because of the weakness of our flesh. And because we are so weak by ourselves that we could not even stand firm for a minute, and furthermore we are constantly surrounded and attacked by so many enemies, including the Devil, the world, sin, and our own flesh, who constantly make war against us, please strengthen us by your Holy Spirit and equip us with your grace. Then we will be able to constantly resist all temptations and persevere in this spiritual fight, until we gain the full victory and finally triumph in your Kingdom with our Captain and Protector, our Lord Jesus Christ.

At the end a Psalm is sung, after which the pastor sends out the congregation, saying,

The Lord bless you and keep you. The Lord lift up his face to shine upon you and be gracious unto you. The Lord turn his face towards you and keep you in good prosperity. Go in peace, and may the Spirit of God lead you to eternal life. Amen.

[After 1545, the editions of the Form of Prayers included the following:] *On days when the Lord's Supper is celebrated, the following is added to the above:*

And as our Lord Jesus not only offered his body and blood to you on the cross in atonement for our sins but also wants to give these to us as food for eternal life, grant us this grace to receive from him such a great benefit and gift with pure hearts and ardent zeal. With genuine Faith, we receive his body and blood, and receive him completely, just as he being true God

Read this paragraph carefully — does it sound familiar? It is in fact a paraphrase of the Lord's Prayer.

This benediction (blessing) is drawn from Aaron's blessing of the people of Israel, recorded in Numbers 6:24-26.

and true man is truly the holy bread of Heaven that gives us life. Therefore we no longer live for ourselves and according to our nature, which is entirely corrupt and vicious, but rather he lives in us, to lead us to holy, blessed, and eternal life. In this way we will truly participate in the new and eternal Testament, namely, the covenant of grace, being sure and convinced that your good pleasure is to be our loving Father for all eternity. You do not ascribe our faults to us, and you give all that is both physically and spiritually necessary to us as your children and beloved heirs. So we will ceaselessly praise and glorify you and magnify your Name in our deeds and our words. Therefore, gracious Father, help us today to celebrate the memory and blessed recollection of your beloved Son, to learn from it, and to proclaim the benefit obtained from his death, so that being once again built up and strengthened in faith and in all good, we may more and more trustingly call you our Father, and glory in you.

After having celebrated the Supper, the following thanksgiving or a similar one is said:

Heavenly Father, we praise and thank you forever for giving such a gift to us poor sinners, to have drawn us into communion with your Son, Jesus Christ our Lord, having delivered him to death for our sake, and giving him to us in flesh and food of eternal life. Now please also grant us this gift, to make sure that we may never forget these things, but rather have them imprinted in our hearts so that we may grow and increase diligently in faith, which finds its outlet in all good works. In the process, may we order and direct all our life to praise your glory and edify our neighbor, through the same Jesus Christ your Son, who in the unity of the Holy Spirit, lives and reigns eternally with you, O God. Amen.

The blessing given at the close of the service, according to our Lord's command: Num. 6:

The Lord bless you and keep you. The Lord make his face to shine upon you and be gracious unto you. The Lord lift up his countenance upon you and keep you in good prosperity. Go in peace, and may the Spirit of God lead you to eternal life. Amen.

> Note the emphasis on both forgiveness of sins and "being built up and strengthened" in faith and life, twin emphases which recur throughout Calvin's teaching on both baptism and the Lord's Supper.

> Note the reference to all three persons of God's triune being in the conclusion of this prayer — an echo of many early church prayers.

Source: "The Form of Prayers and Church Singing," translated by Karin Maag from the French, *La Forme des Prieres et Chantz Ecclesiastiques avec la maniere d'administrer les Sacremens, et consacrer le Mariage: selon la coustume de l'Eglise ancienne,* published in the nineteenth-century collected edition of Calvin's works: *Joannis Calvini Opera Quae Supersunt Omnia,* ed. W. Baum, E. Cunitz, and E. Reuss (Braunschweig: Schwetschke and Son, 1867), Vol. VI, cols. 173-80. The editors of the *Opera* established their version by comparing the original 1542 edition of *La Forme des Prieres* ([Geneva: Jean Girard], 1542) with later editions published in 1545, 1547, 1559, 1562, 1563, and 1566. There are interesting differences between this 1542 version and a 1545 version published in Strasbourg. Both versions can be found in Bard Thompson, *Liturgies of the Western Church* (Philadelphia: Fortress Press, 1961), pp. 197-210.

Baptism

The Lord's Supper and baptism were the only two sacraments the Reformed Church retained from the set of seven sacraments of the Roman Catholic Church. Above all, Reformed baptisms stressed the centrality of God's covenant with his people — the children of faithful believers were part of the household of God. Calvin and other Reformed leaders wanted to distinguish their baptismal liturgy and practice from Catholic practices but were also particularly keen to distance themselves from the Anabaptist view, which rejected infant baptism in favor of adult or believer's baptism. This liturgy dates from 1542, a year after Calvin's return to Geneva from his three-year exile in Strasbourg.

The Form for Administering Baptism (1542)

The preaching of the Word was an integral part of the baptism service. It took a lot of effort on the part of the pastors to prevent family members from arriving late or leaving early in an attempt to skip all but the baptism they had come for.

It is to be noted that children should be brought for baptism either on Sunday, at the Catechism service, or on other days at sermon time, so that because baptism signifies that the child is solemnly received into the church, the baptism should be done in the presence of the congregation.

The child should be presented at the end of the sermon. Then the minister begins by saying,

Our help is in the name of God, who made Heaven and earth. Amen.

Do you present this child to be baptized?

Answer:

Yes.

The Minister:

Why might it have been important to place the baptism after the sermon, rather than earlier on in the service?

Our Lord shows us the poverty and misery in which we are all born, by telling us that we must be reborn (John 3:3). For if our nature must be renewed in order to enter into the Kingdom of God, that is a sign that our nature is totally perverse and damned. Thus in this way he warns us to humble and despise ourselves, and hence prepares us to want and need his grace, through which all the perversity and condemnation of our original nature can be erased. For we are not able to receive this grace unless we are first emptied of all confidence in our own virtue, wisdom, and righteousness, until we reach the point of condemning all that is in us.

The term "regeneration" here is nearly synonymous with sanctification.

However, once he has shown us our misery, he comforts us in the same way by his mercy, promising to renew us through his Holy Spirit to new life, which is just like an entrance into his Kingdom for us. This regeneration is in two parts. First, that we deny ourselves, not relying upon our own judgment, desire, and will, but making our understanding and our heart subject to the wisdom and justice of God, mortifying ourselves and our flesh. Second, that we follow the light of God, to please him and obey his good will, as he shows us in his Word, and as he leads and directs us in this way by his Spirit. Achieving these two aims is reached through our Lord Jesus, whose death and passion are so powerful that through our participation in his passion and death it is as if we are dead to sin, so that our fleshly desires are put to death. Similarly, through the power of his resurrection, we rise to new life which comes from God, in that his Spirit leads and guides us to accomplish in us the works that are pleasing to him. However, the first and central point of our salvation is that through his mercy he remits and forgives all our sins, and does not hold them against us, but he erases any memory of them, so that they are not taken into account against us in his Judgment. All of these graces are granted to us when he is pleased to incorporate us into his Church through baptism. For in this sacrament he testifies to us that our sins are forgiven. And for this reason, he has ordained that water be the sign to show us that just as through this element bodily filth is cleaned off, so he wants to wash and purify our souls, so that they be free from all stains. Furthermore, in baptism he shows us our renewal, which lies, as has been said, in the mortification of our flesh and in the spiritual life that he produces and calls forth in us.

Thus we receive a double measure of grace and blessing from our God in baptism, so long as we do not destroy the benefit of this sacrament by our ingratitude. In baptism we have a clear testimony that God wants to be a gracious Father to us, not holding our sins and offenses against us. Second, that he will help us by his Holy Spirit, so that we may fight against the Devil, sin, and the desires of our flesh until we triumph over them, to live in the freedom of his Reign, namely, the Reign of justice.

What are the implications of the first sentence of this paragraph? Can baptized people, therefore, fall away from God?

Therefore, since these two things are accomplished in us by the grace of Jesus Christ, it follows that the truth and essence of baptism flows from him. For we do not have any other washing except through his blood, and we do not have any other renewal except through his death and resurrection. But just as he transmits his riches and blessings to us through his Word, in the same way he issues them to us through his sacraments.

Note the profound importance given to the preaching and hearing of Scripture.

Yet our gracious God is not satisfied only with having adopted us as his children and having received us into the communion of his Church, and still wants to extend his goodness even further over us, by promising that he will be our God and the God of our descendants, through a thousand generations (Gen. 17:7 and following). Even though the children of the faithful are part of Adam's corrupt race, yet by virtue of this covenant he still continues to accept them, numbering them among his children. For this reason, from the beginning in his Church he wanted children to receive the sign of circumcision, through which he displayed back then everything that is now visible to us in baptism. And as he commanded that they be circumcised, so he acknowledged them as his children, and said he was their God, just as he was the God of their fathers.

The parallels between circumcision and baptism were a feature of almost every Reformed presentation of baptism and helped make the Reformed argument in favor of infant baptism against the Anabaptists' view.

Now therefore, since our Lord Jesus came to earth not to diminish the grace of God his Father but to spread the covenant of salvation throughout the world, a covenant which was at the time limited to the Jewish people, there is no doubt that our children are heirs of the life that he promised to us. For this reason, Saint Paul said (1 Cor. 7:14) that God sanctifies infants even in their mother's womb, so as to separate and distinguish them from the children of pagans and unbelievers. Hence our Lord Jesus Christ received the children that were brought to him, as it is written in the nineteenth chapter of Saint Matthew: People brought them to him, etc.

Since he declared that the Kingdom of Heaven belonged to them, and that he blessed them and entrusted them to God his Father, he amply teaches us that we should not exclude them from his Church. Thus, following this rule, we will receive this child into his Church to have him receive all the blessings that he has promised to those who are faithful to him. First, we will present this child to God through our prayer, saying together with humble hearts:

Lord God, eternal and all-powerful Father, since it has pleased you by your infinite mercy to promise us that you will be our God and the God of our children, we pray that you would confirm this grace on this child, born of a father and mother that you have called into your Church. And as this child is offered and consecrated by us, please receive this child into your holy care, declaring yourself as his God and Savior, and remitting his original sin, of which all the descendants of Adam are guilty. Then sanctify him by your Spirit, so that when he reaches the age of discernment, he may recognize and adore you as his only God, glorifying you his whole life long, always turning to you for the forgiveness of his sins. And in order that he may receive these mercies, we ask that you include him in the communion of our Lord Jesus, to participate in all his blessings as one of the members of his body. Hear us, Father of mercy, so that the baptism that we are administering to him according to your ordinance produce its fruit and effect, as we are told in your Gospel.

Our Father, who art in Heaven. Hallowed be Thy Name. Thy Kingdom come. Thy will be done on earth as in Heaven. Give us this day our daily bread. And forgive us our debts, as we forgive our debtors. And lead us not into temptation, but deliver us from evil. Amen.

Since the intent is to receive this child in the company of the Christian church, you promise, when the child will have reached the age of discretion, to teach him the doctrine accepted by the people of God, as it is concisely expressed in our common confession of faith:

I believe in God the Father almighty, Creator of Heaven and earth. And in Jesus Christ his only Son, our Lord, who was conceived by the Holy Spirit, born of the virgin Mary, suffered under Pontius Pilate, was crucified, died, and was buried. He descended into hell. On the third day he rose from the dead. He ascended into Heaven and is seated at the right hand of God the Father almighty. From thence he will come to judge the living and the dead. I believe in the Holy Spirit, in the holy universal church, in the communion of saints, in the forgiveness of sins, in the resurrection of the body, and in life everlasting. Amen.

Note the importance of the parents' status as the gateway for baptism.

The "you" here refers to the father and godparents who presented the baby for baptism — mothers traditionally did not attend, as they were still recovering from the birth.

The Lord's Prayer and the Apostles' Creed recited by everyone were a sign of the unity of belief in the congregation, and a sign of the father's and godparents' ability to transmit at least these basic teachings to the child being baptized.

You promise, therefore, to carefully instruct him in all aspects of this doctrine, and generally in everything contained in the holy Scriptures of the old and new Testament, so that he might receive this as the sure Word of God, coming from Heaven. Furthermore, you will teach him to live according to the rule given to us by our Lord in his law, which is summarized in these two points: That we love God with all our mind, heart, and strength, and our neighbor as ourselves. Similarly, and based on the teachings of God conveyed through his Prophets and Apostles, that he turn away from himself and his own desires, and dedicate and consecrate himself to glorify the name of God and of Jesus Christ, and edify those around him.

Once the promise is made, the child is given his name, and the minister then baptizes him:

In the Name of the Father, and of the Son, and of the Holy Spirit.

All of this is said aloud in the language of the people, since the faithful who are present are to be witnesses of what is done, and therefore have to comprehend what is said, and also that all may be edified, recognizing and recalling to mind what is the fruit and purpose of their baptism.

Another critique of Roman Catholic liturgies, which were in Latin — the Reformers were quick to highlight the significance of worshipping in the language of the people, so that everyone could understand what was going on.

We know that in other places, many other ceremonies are carried out, which, we admit, are very old, but . . . they were invented to please people or at least for very insubstantial reasons; in any event, since they were crafted without the Word of God, and furthermore, given that so many superstitions have resulted from these, we have had no qualms in abolishing them, so that there will no longer be any impediment to prevent the people from going directly to Jesus Christ. First of all, that which God has not commanded us to do is left to our free choice. Furthermore, anything that does not serve for purposes of edification should not be adopted in the church, and if it has been introduced, it should be removed. More importantly, that which is a source of scandal and is like a tool of idolatry and wrong beliefs should never be tolerated. Indeed it is clear that the chrism, candles, and other such ceremonials are not ordered by God, but have been added in by human beings. In the end, things have gone so far that these practices have taken over and have been more revered than the actual institution by Jesus Christ. At least we have a form of baptism according to Jesus Christ's instructions, one which the Apostles kept and followed, that the early church practiced, and no one can condemn us for anything apart from our desire to not be wiser than God himself.

"Chrism" is anointing with holy oil, a key part of Catholic baptismal liturgies.

Again, Calvin and his colleagues emphasized their direct links to worship practices of the early church, legitimizing what otherwise was condemned by the Roman Catholic Church as dangerous novelties.

_____

Source: Form for the Celebration of Baptism (1542), translated by Karin Maag from the French, *La Forme des Prieres et Chantz Ecclesiastiques avec la maniere d'administrer les Sacremens, et consacrer le Mariage: selon la coustume de l'Eglise ancienne,* published in the nineteenth-century collected edition of Calvin's works: *Joannis Calvini Opera Quae Supersunt Omnia,* ed. W. Baum, E. Cunitz, and E. Reuss (Braunschweig: Schwetschke and Son, 1867), Vol. VI, cols. 185-92. The editors of the *Opera* established their version by comparing the original 1542 edition of *La Forme des Prieres* ([Geneva: Jean Girard], 1542) with later editions published in 1545, 1547, 1559, 1562, 1563, and 1566.

The Manner of Celebrating Holy Matrimony (1545)

The Genevan marriage liturgy was adapted largely from the wedding liturgy prepared by Guillaume Farel. The ritual was straightforward, emphasizing the promises of the bride and groom to each other in front of witnesses and in the presence of God, and scriptural teachings on the respective roles and responsibilities of the spouses in marriage.

The public and solemn ceremony to ratify marriages was put in place by Christians to hold genuine and legitimate marriage in higher reverence and honor, and to prevent any fraud or trickery enacted by either party. Instead, everything should be done in good faith and loyalty, and the church is to pray for the salvation of the spouses. Therefore, the responsibility of the pastors of the church is to declare publicly from the pulpit the names of those who want to be joined in marriage, to approve and confirm the said marriage in the presence of the faithful, and to show them through Scripture the worth and excellence of the married state.

Notice the careful reference to the presence of the faithful, i.e., the congregation. Marriages were supposed to take place during regularly-scheduled church services, and were not private ceremonies for the couple and their families.

He must then tell them of the duties of spouses, namely, how the husband should behave towards his wife, and how the wife should similarly behave towards the husband, so that they may be one, according to God's commands in Genesis 2, Matthew 19, 1 Corinthians, Colossians 3, 1 Timothy 3, Titus 2, and 1 Peter 3. It would be neither disrespectful nor pointless for the minister to gather [from these texts] the exhortations and words of comfort relevant and appropriate to this matter. And in order that all things be done decently, devoutly, and in good order, the entire wedding party must enter the church without any drums or other musical instruments. After the sermon or exhortation is done, the minister of the Word of God or the deacon will turn to those who have come to the church to be joined in marriage in the following manner:

This section is a preamble intended for the use of the pastor, so that every wedding ceremony be undertaken in the same way. Compare this rubric with the practice of Pastor Perrot and to the Ecclesiastical Ordinances' section on marriages.

It must be noted that before the Sunday on which the marriage is to be celebrated, it must be published in the church for three Sundays: in order that anyone who knows an impediment may declare it in good time; or if someone else has an interest, they have time to oppose it.

Our help is in the name of God, who made Heaven and earth. Amen.

God our Father, after creating the Heaven and the earth, and everything which is in them, created and formed man after his image and likeness, who had dominion and lordship over the beasts of the earth, the fish of the sea, the birds of Heaven. He said after having created man: It is not good that the man should be alone: let us make for him a helper similar to himself. And our Lord made a great slumber fall upon Adam. And as Adam slept, God took one of his ribs from him, and formed Eve, giving us to understand that man and wife are one body, one flesh and one blood. For which cause the man leaves father and mother, and is joined to his wife, whom he should also love, as Jesus loves his Church, that is to say, the true faithful and Christians, for whom he died. And also the wife should serve and obey her husband, in all holiness and honesty. For she is subject, and in the governance of her husband as long as she lives with him. And this holy marriage, honorable, instituted by God, is of such virtue that the husband has no power over his own body, but the wife: also the wife has no power over her body, but the husband. For this reason the ones joined by God cannot be separated, unless for a time by mutual agreement, to devote to fasting or prayer, guarding well that they are not tempted by Satan through incontinence. And for that reason, they should return together again. Because for avoiding fornication, each man needs to have his wife, and each woman her husband: so that all those who cannot be continent, and who do not have the gift of continence, are obliged, by the commandment of God, to marry: so that the holy temple of God — that is to say, our bodies — may not be violated and corrupted, because since our bodies are members of Jesus Christ, it would be a great outrage to make them members of the harlot. Wherefore everyone must preserve themselves in all holiness, for whoever violates the temple of God, God will destroy him.

See Numbers 5:31 and John 8:3-5.

You, then, N and N, having knowledge that God has thus ordained it, do you wish to live in this holy estate of marriage which God has so greatly honored? Have you such a purpose as you testify here before his Holy Assembly, requesting that it approves?

They reply: Yes.

The Minister:

I take you all, who are present here in witness, requesting you to have recollection: moreover, if anyone who knows some impediment or if one of the parties has promised marriage to another, let them in Christian charity declare it and make it public.

Here is confirmation that the wedding ceremony was held during regular worship times, since the congregation was present.

If no person contests it, the Minister says this:

Since no one has contested, and no one has pointed out an impediment, our Lord God confirms your holy intention which he has given you. And that same one who created and made the heaven and the earth wishes to give increase to your [beginnings] and to [fill] them with happiness. And your [beginning] is in the name of God, who made Heaven and earth. Amen.

Speaking to the groom, the Minister says this:

Do You, N, confess here before God and his holy congregation that you have taken and do take N here present to be your wife and spouse, whom you promise to protect, in loving her and holding together faithfully, at the same time having the duty of a true and faithful husband to his wife: living in holiness with her, keeping faith and loyalty in all things, according to the Holy Word of God and his Holy Gospel?

Answer: Yes.

Then speaking to the bride, he says:

Do you, N, confess here before God, and his Holy Assembly, that you have taken and do take N for your lawful husband, whom you promise to obey, serving him and being subject to him, living in holiness with him, keeping faith and loyalty in all things, as one whose duty is as a faithful and loyal spouse to her husband, according to the Word of God and the Holy Gospel?

Reply: Yes.

Then the Minister says:

The Father of all mercy, who by his grace has called you to this holy estate of marriage, for the love of Jesus Christ his Son, that by his holy presence has sanctified marriage, making it the first sign before the Apostles, give you his Holy Spirit, to serve him and honor him in this noble estate. Amen.

The reference here is to the wedding at Cana; see John 2.

Hear the Gospel how our Lord wishes to have marriage regarded, and how it is firm and indissoluble, as it is written in St. Matthew in the 19th chapter: (Gospel reading). Believe these holy words, that our Lord Jesus pronounced, as the Evangelist recites them; and be certain that our Lord God has joined you in this holy estate of marriage. Wherefore live together holily, in good love, peace, and unity, keeping true charity, faith, and loyalty one to the other, according to the Word of God.

Let us all now pray with one heart to our Father:

Almighty God, all good and all knowing, who has foreseen from the beginning that it is not good for man to be alone, and for this reason you created for him a help similar to himself, and has ordained that the two should be one: We pray you, and humbly request, since it has pleased you to call these here to the holy estate of marriage, that by your grace and goodness you would give them and send your Holy Spirit; in order that, through a true and firm faith, and being willing to accept your goodness, they may live in holiness, surmounting all naughty affections. Living in purity and building up one another in all honesty and chastity, may they receive your benediction, as you gave to your faithful servants Abraham, Isaac, and Jacob. Having a holy lineage, may they praise you and serve you, and be nurtured to your praise and glory, and serve their neighbor (*l'utilite du prochain*) in the advancement and exaltation of your Holy Gospel. Grant us, Merciful Father, through our Lord Jesus Christ your most dear Son, Amen.

Our Lord fill you with all graces, and in all good things, giving you a long and holy life together.

Go in peace. God be with you always. Amen.

Source: The Manner of Celebrating Holy Matrimony (John Calvin, Geneva, 1542), in *Worship in Medieval and Early Modern Europe,* ed. Karin Maag and John Witvliet (Notre Dame: University of Notre Dame Press, 2004), pp. 252-54. The English translation is by Bryan Spinks, using the French text in J*oannis Calvini Opera Selecta,* ed.

P. Barth and D. Scheuner (Munich: Kaiser, 1952), Vol. II, pp. 50-56. The same French text appears in the nineteenth-century collected edition of Calvin's works: *Joannis Calvini Opera Quae Supersunt Omnia,* ed. W. Baum, E. Cunitz, and E. Reuss (Braunschweig: Schwetschke and Son, 1867), Vol. VI, cols. 203-8. In both cases, the editors of Calvin's collected works used the French text in the 1545 edition of *La Forme des Prières et Chantz Ecclesiastiques* (Strasbourg: [no printer], 1545). Karin Maag translated from the French the first two paragraphs that appear right after the header, which are missing from Bryan Spinks's translation.

Prayers from the 1542 Genevan Catechism

Calvin's 1542 catechism included a series of prayers at the end that were to shape daily private worship. It is unlikely that these prayers were to be learned by heart and recited by rote since Calvin and his fellow Reformers were uncomfortable with reciting non-biblical or non-credal texts. Instead, these prayers were meant to serve as training models, encouraging regular prayer and teaching young people in particular how to pray on a daily basis. The prayers are interspersed with extracts from the Psalms, which could certainly be memorized.

Assess the probable impact of these prayers on someone who would commit to praying this way regularly through their day. What are the strengths of these prayers? What might be missing from them?

Prayer to be recited in the morning, when getting up:

My God, my Father, and my Savior, since you have been pleased to give me the grace to bring me through the night to the present day, may you also now grant me the gift of spending this day entirely in your service, so that I may not think, or say, or do anything except to please you and obey your good will, so that in this way all my works be done to the glory of your name and to the edification of my neighbors. And just as you are pleased to make your sun shine on the earth to give us bodily light, so illuminate my understanding and my heart through the light of your Spirit, to guide me along the straight paths of your justice. Thus, whatever my undertaking, may my main goal and intention always be to walk in the fear of you, to serve and honor you, expecting that all good and prosperity comes to me from your blessing alone, so that I do not attempt anything that is not pleasing to you. Furthermore, while I work hard for the sake of my body and for the present life, may I always cast my gaze further, namely, toward the heavenly life that you have promised to your children. Yet may it please you to be the protector of both my body and my soul, strengthening me against all the devil's temptations, and delivering me from all the earthly dangers that may threaten me. And because a good beginning is worthless without perseverance, please guide me onto your holy paths, not only for today but for my whole life, daily continuing and increasing your grace in me, until you bring me to full unity with your Son, Jesus Christ our Lord, who is the true Sun of our souls, shining endlessly and perpetually day and night. And in order that I may obtain these graces from you, please forget my previous faults, forgiving me for them according to your endless mercy, as you have promised to all those who wholeheartedly ask this of you.

Notice how personal and individually-focused this prayer is; it does not include any prayers for others, beyond a reference to serving one's neighbors.

From Psalm 143:

Already in the morning let me hear of your mercy, for I have trusted in you.

Help me to know the way in which I should walk, for I have lifted my heart to you.

Deliver me from my enemies, O Lord, for I have cried out to you.

Teach me to do your will, for you are my God, and your Spirit leads me on the right path.

Prayer to be said before starting lessons at school:

From Psalm 119:

How shall a child direct his way? By directing himself according to your Word, O Lord.

Open my eyes, and I will see the wonders of your law.

Grant me understanding, and I will keep your law, and preserve it with my whole heart.

This prayer was particularly well-suited to the main audience for the catechism, namely young people. The use of Psalm 119, with its strong focus on learning wisdom from God, fits very well with this particular prayer.

O Lord, fount of all wisdom and knowledge, since you have been pleased to provide the way for me to be taught in my youth, to know how to chart the course of my life in a holy and upright way, may you also shed light in my understanding, which on its own is blind, so that my mind may understand the doctrine I am taught. Strengthen my memory, so that I may retain this teaching, and prepare my heart to receive it willingly and with appropriate eagerness, so as to avoid ruining through my ingratitude this opportunity you have given me. To do so, please pour your Holy Spirit upon me, the Spirit of all intelligence, truth, judgment, prudence, and doctrine, that makes me able to benefit from what I learn, so that the pains taken to teach me will not be wasted. No matter what subject I study, make it so that I direct this learning to the true goal, namely, to know you in the person of our Lord JESUS Christ, to have full confidence of salvation and life in your grace, and to serve you in a pure and upright way according to your will, such that everything that I learn may be as an instrument to help me towards this goal. And given that you promise to give wisdom to the lowly and the humble, and to bring down the proud in their vain confidence in their own understanding, and to show yourself to the upright of heart, and in contrast to shut the eyes of the wicked and perverse, may you teach us true humility, through which I may grow biddable and obedient, first to you and second to my superiors, whom you have charged with overseeing and teaching me. Furthermore, may you shape my heart to seek you without guile, leaving aside any carnal or evil affection. And may I in this way prepare myself now to serve you in whatever condition and vocation you will choose for me when I am old enough.

The upper-case letters appear in the original French text.

This prayer gives insight into Calvin's understanding of the purpose of education.

From Psalm 25:

The Lord reveals his secrets to those who fear him, and makes his covenant known to them.

Prayer to be said before eating:

From Psalm 104:

All things wait for you, O Lord, and you give them food in their season.

When you give it to them, they gather it up, and when you open your hand, they are replete with good things.

Lord, in whom is the fullness of all good things, please grant your blessing to us, your poor servants, and bless the gifts which we receive from your bounty, so that we may make use of them in a temperate and pure fashion, according to your good will, that we may hence acknowledge you as Father and author of all mercy and always seek first the spiritual bread of your Word, which feeds our souls eternally, through Jesus Christ, your Son, our Lord, Amen.

Deuteronomy 8:

Man does not live by bread alone, but by the word that comes from the mouth of God.

Calvin and his fellow pastors were always keen to make sure that God's gifts of food and drink were appreciated but not abused by over-indulgence. Geneva had specific laws to prevent excessive feasting, for instance.

Notice that this prayer is much shorter than the others, not surprisingly if it was said while hungry people were waiting to eat.

Thanksgiving after the meal:

From Psalm 107:

Let all the nations praise the Lord, let all the people praise him.

For his mercy is spread over us, and his truth is from everlasting to everlasting.

Lord God, we thank you for all the blessings we continuously receive at your hand, in that you are pleased to sustain us in our bodily life, providing for all our needs, and especially that you have been willing to regenerate us in the hope of a better life, which you revealed to us in your Holy Gospel. We pray that you may prevent our affection from being rooted in these corruptible things, but that we instead may always raise our gaze higher, awaiting our Lord Jesus Christ, until he returns for our redemption. Amen.

A prayer of thanks after eating is much less common today — why might Calvin have felt it important to include this prayer?

Prayer to be recited before sleeping:

Here and elsewhere in his writings, Calvin uses "man" (*l'homme*) to refer to all people, both men and women.

Notice that here too, like in the prayer before eating, Calvin emphasizes moderation and temperance: too much food or too much sleep is to be resisted.

Lord God, since it has pleased you to create the night for man's rest, just as you ordained the day for work, grant me the grace to have my body rest this night so that my soul is always awake to you, and that my heart is raised up in your love. Given my weakness, may I find such relief in laying down my earthly concerns that I may always remember you. May the record of your goodness and your grace remain always imprinted on my memory, and in this way may my conscience take its spiritual rest, just as my body takes its physical rest. Furthermore, may I not overindulge in sleep to unduly satisfy the desire of my flesh, but only sleep enough to satisfy my fragile nature in order to be fit for your service. Please also preserve my purity of body and soul and keep me from all dangers, so that even my sleeping is done to the glory of your name. And because the day that is past has not gone by without me offending you in various ways, given that I am a poor sinner, just as everything is now concealed by the darkness you send over the earth, may you also bury all my faults by your mercy, so that I will not be cast away from your face because of these sins. Hear my prayer, my God, my Father, my Savior, through Jesus Christ our Lord, Amen.

Source: Prayers from the 1542 Genevan Catechism from the *Joannis Calvini Opera Quae Supersunt Omnia,* ed. W. Baum, E. Cunitz, and E. Reuss (Braunschweig: Schwetschke and Son, 1867), Vol. VI, cols. 135-43. Translated by Karin Maag. The editors of the *Opera* used both the earliest available French and Latin editions of the Genevan Catechism: *Le catéchisme de L'Eglise de Geneve: c'est à dire, le Formulaire d'instruire les enfans en la Chrestienté* ([Geneva: Jean Girard], 1545); and *Catechismus ecclesiae Genevensis, hoc est, formula erudiendi pueros in doctrina Christi* (Strasbourg: Wendelin Rihel, 1545). Although this catechism was first published in 1542, no copies of the original edition have survived.

The Title Page of La Forme des Prieres et Chantz Ecclesiastiques

LA FORME
DES PRIERES ET
CHANTZ ECCLESIASTI‑
ques, auec la maniere d'administrer les Sacre‑
mens, & consacrer le Mariage : selon la cou‑
stume de l'Eglise ancienne.

Psalme 159.
Chantez au Seigneur chanson nouuelle, &
que sa louënge soit ouye en la Congregation
des debonnaires.

Psalme 150.
Que tout ce qui respire, louë le Seigneur.

M. D. XLII.

This work was the first prayer/service book used in the Genevan church after the Reformation. Calvin based much of his worship practice and liturgy on the lessons he learned and put into practice during his time as pastor of the French refugee church in Strasbourg between 1538 and 1541. Notice how comprehensive its advertised contents were: the title translates as "The form of prayers and church singing, together with the way to administer the sacraments and consecrate marriages, following the practice of the ancient church." Note the specific connection made between Genevan liturgical practice and the worship of the early church (l'église ancienne).

Source: *La Forme des Prieres et Chantz Ecclesiastiques* (Geneva: Jean Girard, 1542). Image supplied by the Meeter Center Rare Book Collection, Hekman Library, Calvin College.

Genevan Psalm VIII from La Forme des Prieres *(1542)*

One of the key components of La Forme des Prieres *was Psalms set to music so that the congregations in Geneva could sing together in unison, using the words of Scripture. As Calvin noted in his preface to the Genevan Psalter, "We shall find no better songs nor more appropriate to the purpose than the Psalms of David, which the Holy Spirit made and spoke through him." Calvin's awareness of metrical Psalm-singing, in which the Psalms were first versified and then set to music, began in Strasbourg during his period as pastor of a congregation of French refugees. While Calvin did some of the earlier versifications, his work was later superseded by that of more talented poets, including Theodore Beza and Clément Marot.*

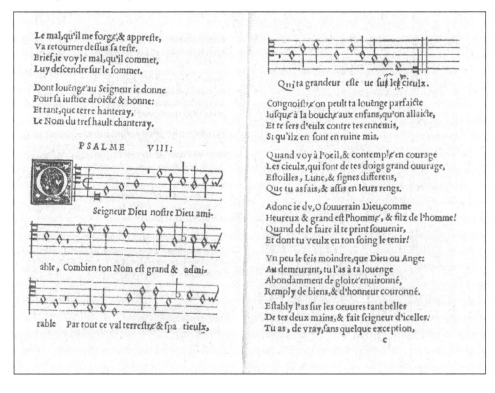

Source: *La Forme des Prieres et Chantz Ecclesiastiques* (Geneva: Jean Girard, 1542), fol. 11 verso and fol. 12 recto. Image supplied by the Meeter Center Rare Book Collection, Hekman Library, Calvin College.

The Song of Simeon and the Lord's Prayer from La Forme des Prieres *(1542)*

Because the process of versifying the Psalms and setting them to music was a slow process, early editions of La Forme des Prieres *did not provide a complete set of Psalms. Only fifty were ready by 1546, and only eighty-nine by 1551. Not all the biblical texts set to music in* La Forme des Prieres *were Psalms. The work also included several other key biblical texts set to music, in this instance the Song of Simeon (the prophet who spoke about Jesus and blessed him during his purification in the Temple in Jerusalem) and the Lord's Prayer.*

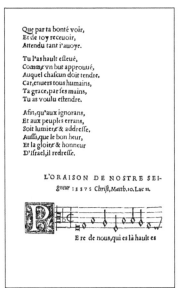

Here are two versifications of texts that are not Psalms: the Song of Simeon, and the Lord's Prayer. Why set these texts to music?

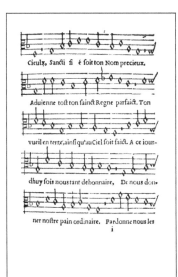

Source: *La Forme des Prieres et Chantz Ecclesiastiques* (Geneva: Jean Girard, 1542), fol. h8 r. and v. and fol. i1 r. and v. Images supplied by the Meeter Center Rare Book Collection, Hekman Library, Calvin College.

The First Page of the Psalter at the Back of the 1567 Genevan Bible

By 1567 the entire set of 150 Psalms had been versified and set to music. As noted on this first page, the French poet Clément Marot and the Reformer Theodore Beza were given credit for the French versifications of the Psalms. Binding the Psalter, the Genevan catechism, prayers, and orders of service together with the Bible allowed Genevans to purchase a multipurpose worship resource that could be used equally well at church and at home during family devotions.

Source: *La Bible, qui est toute la saincte Escriture, contenant le vieil & le nouveau Testament, autrement, la vieille & la nouvelle alliance* (Geneva: François Estienne, 1567), fol. Aaiii recto. Image supplied by the Meeter Center Rare Book Collection, Hekman Library, Calvin College.

Prayers and Creeds from the 1567 Bible Psalter

As in the 1542 Psalter, the 1567 Psalter included a range of other biblical texts set to music, including in this instance the Lord's Prayer (L'Oraison de Nostre Seigneur Jesus Christ) and Moses' song from Deuteronomy 32 (Cantique de Moyse). Musical settings of other key non-biblical texts could also be included, in this instance the prayer to be said after meals (Priere apres le repas) and the Apostles' Creed (Les Articles de la Foy). While the Song of Simeon and the Ten Commandments remained standard musical additions to the Psalter, other texts' appearance was more episodic, and depended to a certain extent on the need to fill up the available pages and on the preferences of the publishers.

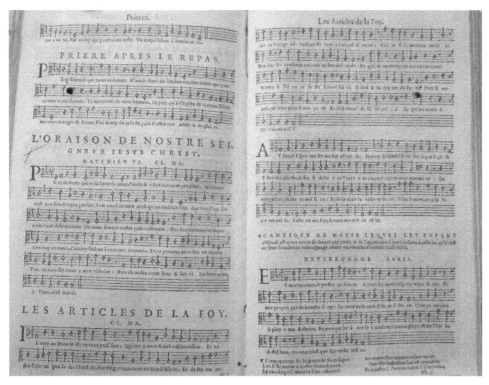

Source: *La Bible, qui est toute la saincte Escriture, contenant le vieil & le nouveau Testament, autrement, la vieille & la nouvelle alliance* (Geneva: François Estienne, 1567), fols. Hhi verso-Hhii recto. Image supplied by the Meeter Center Rare Book Collection, Hekman Library, Calvin College.

A Chart from the Psalter in the 1567 Genevan Bible

This chart that appeared already in the 1562 Genevan Psalter divided up the 150 Psalms over the course of 25 weeks, allowing the entire Psalter to be sung twice a year. The chart provides important information about the use of the Psalms in the Genevan liturgy, showing, for instance, that Genevan worship began with the singing of a Psalm "apres le second coup de la cloche" or "after the bells have rung for the second time." The chart also split the longer Psalms over several services. At the end of the chart, on the second page, the instructions noted that the Ten Commandments were sung at each of the quarterly celebrations of the Lord's Supper.

Source: "Table pour trouver les Pseaumes," in *La Bible, qui est toute la saincte Escriture, contenant le vieil & le nouveau Testament, autrement, la vieille & la nouvelle alliance* (Geneva: François Estienne, 1567), fols. Hhiii recto-verso. Images supplied by the Meeter Center Rare Book Collection, Hekman Library, Calvin College. English translation of the chart (see facing page) by Karin Maag.

CHART TO LOCATE THE
PSALMS ACCORDING TO THE ORDER
in which they are sung in the Church of Geneva,
both on Sunday mornings and evenings,
and on Wednesdays.

Sunday morning after the second bell				*Sunday morning at the sermon time*			
1 Do not, O Lord			6	1 My God, I hope in you			7
2 Lord, the King will rejoice			21	2 Why then	11	Give help	12
3 All you princes 29. I have put 31, *to* Among				3 Lord, be my refuge &			16
4 Then I will *rest of* 35. Do not 37, *to* But				4 Lord, listen to my plea			17
5 I am so *from* 38, *to* Come then				5 To you, O Lord, I lift my heart			25
6 With noble themes, my heart			45	6 Vindicate me, O Lord			26
7 O my God, grant my petition			55	7 The Lord is my light			27
8 Thou hast rejected us, O God			60	8 O God who is 18 The evil one			36
9 May God bless us 67 May God 68, *to* Then				9 Because you have rescued me, Lord			30
10 Alas, Lord 69, *to* Approach				10 Awake 33, *to* The Lord			
11 I will praise Thee again *rest of* 71				11 I will never cease 34, *to* God holds			
12 O Lord 75 Give ear 78, *to* But				12 I said that I would closely			39
13 Yet he *rest of* 78 O Shepherd 80, *to* In former times				13 I waited, waited for the Lord			40
14 O God, do not 83 I will sing 89, *to* It is				14 How truly God 73, *to* Then each			
15 Sing to God a new song			96	15 O Lord, you have been our refuge			90
16 Thou hast made the moon *rest of* 104				16 Lord, hear my 102, *to* this shall be written			
17 Praise God for 106, *to* But they forgot				17 Praise the Lord, my soul			103
18 Give to the Lord 107, *to* Those who				18 Give to God 118, *to* The Lord's right hand			
19 May his line be doomed *rest of* 109				19 I love the Lord			116
20 119 *Aleph* 1, Blessed *Beth* 2, As				20 My God, my King			145
21 *Zain* 7, Remember *Heth* 8, O God				21 Lord, I will sing 101 O God, all 54			
22 *Mem* 13, O may your Law *Nun* 14, Your Word				22 May the Lord hear 20 When at last 126			
23 *Qoph* 19, I prayed *Resh* 20, See				23 Unless the Lord 127 Blessed is 128			
24 How good it is 133 Come now, servants 134				24 Out of the depths 130 I must 138			
25 O God, you know 139 O God, grant 140				25 Unto the hills 121 As soon as 122			

[. . . chart continues through Sunday evening and Wednesday services . . .]

The Commandments of God (Lift up your hearts, open your ears, Exodus 10) are sung after the sermon on days when the holy Supper of our Lord Jesus Christ is celebrated. The Lord's Supper is celebrated four times a year, namely at Easter, Pentecost, on the first Sunday of September and on the Sunday closest to the nativity of our Lord Jesus.   At the thanksgiving the Song of Simeon (Now, Lord, Luke 2) is sung.

Sermons

Calvin preached regularly both on weekdays and on Sundays as part of the roster of preachers that took turns giving sermons in Geneva's churches. More of Calvin's sermons have survived, compared with those of his colleagues, because even his contemporaries recognized how important his sermons were. Beginning in 1549, a man named **Denis Raguenier** *was paid by the deacons of the Bourse française (the charitable fund that supported French religious refugees in Geneva) to take down Calvin's sermons as he preached them; Calvin preached without a text or notes in front of him. Raguenier took down the sermons in an early form of shorthand and then transcribed them into a clean copy. Calvin reviewed the text briefly before it was typeset and printed. The printed copies were sold in Geneva and in France, and the money from the sales went to support the care of the poor in Geneva. Calvin preached in French, but the French texts were also subsequently translated into other languages, so that Reformed believers who did not know French could still benefit from Calvin's teachings. After Raguenier's death in 1560 or 1561, other scribes took over. Not all the sermons were published — many remained in manuscript form. Calvin preached on books of the Bible sequentially, that is, he began at chapter 1, verses 1-8, and then for the next sermon he covered chapter 1, verses 9-20, and so on, until he reached the end of that particular book. He began his series of sermons on 2 Samuel on 23 May 1562. The sermon below is one of them.*

Calvin's Sermon on the True Worship of God (1562)

Again David assembled all the chosen men of Israel, thirty thousand. Thus David arose and went, and all the people who were with him of the men of Judah, to bring up the ark of God, of which the name is called: the name of the Lord of hosts who dwells between the Cherubim upon it . . . (2 Sam. 6:1-7).

We are told here that when David realized that his kingdom was at peace, he turned his attention to restoring the integrity of the worship of God. In the time of Saul, as we gather from the First Book of Chronicles, there had been a great falling away so that the ark of God was practically forgotten and despised (1 Chron. 13:3). When he [David] saw that he could not prosper unless the Lord was worshiped in purity, he recognized that God had made and established him as king for that very purpose. David assembled 30,000 men, as we read here (2 Sam. 6:1). Apparently, we have a discrepancy here from the other passage, where we read that he assembled all Israel from Egypt to the other end of the land, which reached to the Euphrates (1 Chron. 13:5). If he had literally assembled all Israel, the number would have been infinite. But the Scripture is simply using everyday language. When one gathers people together from all over a country, one can say that the whole country is assembled. But there it is speaking of his deliberations with his captains and officers (1 Chron. 13:1). Here it simply says that he gathered everyone together.

The way that he assembled them is specified in the other passage, where he inquired of them whether it would not be good to bring back the ark of God from where it was. When the matter was concluded, we read that he published it throughout the whole country and assembled the people. In other words, no city or town failed to send several people — perhaps five or ten to represent the population. These were the chosen ones, the cream of the crop. So in that sense, the whole country was assembled into a great company which acted in the name of all. That is how we harmonize what on the surface seems contradictory.

We must keep in mind what we saw above — that the ark of God has been in a borrowed place in the house of Abinadab (1 Sam. 7:1) since its return by the Philistines, who had captured it. In explaining that unbelievers could not have had the ark except by permission of God, we have mentioned the passage from the Psalms, where God subjected his name to similar contempt in order to punish the iniquities of the people. Kiriath-jearim received the ark and took it to Gibeon, where it was lodged in the house of Abinadab.

Now the ark was in a place to which it had not yet been assigned. Moreover, we can gather that it was seriously profaned. We are clearly told that people were not seeking God in the time of Saul (1 Chron. 13:3). Of course, there were always some faithful people (1 Sam. 14:19); indeed, Saul took the priest with him when he went to battle (1 Sam. 14:36). Although there was an outward appearance of religion, it was very coldly and grudgingly performed. We must realize that it takes far more than making a formal profession and merely declaring that we are God's people and want to serve him. When we hear what was pronounced by the Spirit of God, it should encourage us to seek him voluntarily, and not in such a cold manner.

If someone had asked all the people in the time of Saul, "Do you not want to seek God?" each one would have replied, "Yes, this is my intention." But so what? God disdained their talk, and declared that they were despising and rejecting him, and in fact denying him. Why? Because they had no zeal and no pure and true affection for him. Let us, therefore, be careful not to seek God halfway. On the contrary, let us earnestly seek his face, driving ourselves

Calvin does not shy away from dealing with discrepancies in the biblical text. He expects his congregation to remember other Scripture passages and be able to compare them.

Here he is referring to a previous set of sermons on 1 Samuel, again, expecting a great deal of recall among those in attendance at his sermons.

Notice the important shift from a discussion of the meaning of the Scripture passage to modern-day application to his hearers' lives and practice of worship. The use of the pronoun "we" is very important and worth commenting on. Why might Calvin use "we" rather than "you", addressing his audience directly?

Calvin's approach in this section is a good antidote to the notion that the Calvinist doctrine of predestination must necessarily lead to people becoming very passive about their life of faith.

Calvin looks forward to later sermons as another way to heighten the interest of his congregation and link his sermons together.

forward as we realize that he is the mainspring of our whole life, upon whom we must concentrate all our thoughts and study in order to be pleasing to him.

It is true that David was not given further information concerning where God wanted to be worshiped (1 Chron. 21:18; 2 Chron. 3:1). We will see later that when Mount Zion was finally chosen, these words of the Psalms were fulfilled: "I rejoiced with those who said to me: Let us go and worship God in his holy mountain, Jerusalem will be his dwelling, and Zion will be the place of his habitation; then God shall have a lasting abode" (Ps. 122:1; 99:9; 76:2; 1 Kings 8:13). It was not for mortal men to assign him a place. Moses had said, "When the Lord your God has shown you where his name is to be called upon, and where you are to come and worship and sacrifice" (Deut. 12:11). So we see, then, that God reserved to himself the authority to declare where they should come solemnly to worship him.

David presumed to remove the ark from the house of Abinadab to another place, without being specifically commanded to do so, because he expected God to do what he had announced through Moses. He wanted the ark to be lodged in the center of the country — away from the remote location where it had been left by the people when the Philistines were forced to return it, after God's hand grievously afflicted them. Because the ark was in a corner, it could scarcely be honored as it deserved [to be], and the people who opposed it had an excuse for not coming to the solemn feasts, as the law commanded. That, in turn, caused religion to grow cold, in addition to the fact that men were far from devoted to it. That is why David brought back the ark: so that it would be in a place where people could come more easily, and so that everyone could more readily do their duty. For men seek nothing but excuses to draw further away from God, as we see too frequently. When things are not easy, we think that we can "wash our hands of the matter." We pretend that we would like to do it, but lack the opportunity. That is why David wanted to remove every obstacle, so that those already too careless could not say that the ark of God was in an out-of-the-way place too far to reach.

We must gather from this that insofar as we see the same kind of laziness in ourselves, along with a lack of inclination to worship God and an absence of convenient means of worship, then we will never profit from worship as we should. Why is it that the church chooses the hours which are the most appropriate, a definite place to assemble, and a bell to ring, with all these matters carefully arranged? It is because we humans have practically no desire to give ourselves to God unless we are first drawn to do so. Therefore, on the one hand let us note how feeble we are when we ought to be stiffening ourselves to honor God, and then let us use every available means to move ourselves to break through this coldness and laziness to which we are so strongly inclined. That, in sum, is what we must remember from this passage.

Now it says that "the ark carried his name: the eternal God dwells between the cherubim" (2 Sam. 6:2). Some explain it: where on the ark the name of God was revealed. In fact, the passage in Chronicles cannot be taken otherwise (1 Chron. 13:6). But because this word is

Would you classify this paragraph as analysis or interpretation? Is Calvin really explaining the text or adding his own interpretation to make a point he feels strongly about, concerning modern-day believers?

What is your reaction to Calvin's psychological reading of human beings' reaction to worship — do you think his assessment is correct? Why or why not?

repeated here — "The name (of the eternal), the name of God" — undoubtedly the Holy Spirit wanted to state this honorable title so as to emphasize that this ark was a definite sign and a seal of the presence of God. Indeed, Scripture speaks in this way all the way through. Psalm 24 says, "Lift up your heads, great gates, so that the Lord of Hosts may enter in" (Ps. 24:7). David addressed the same words to the temple, as if he were saying, "Here is God, who wants to make his entry." Therefore, his majesty must be known even to the doors, that they may be lifted up in order to receive such grandeur. It is certain that this was nothing but an ark, but it was named, as I have said, "the Living God." And why? Because the promise was given, and Scripture often says, "You shall come before the face of God" (1 Chron. 16:11; Ps. 100:1); and then: "Lord, according as you have commanded your people, I have ever sought thy face, and will yet seek it" (Ps. 27:8). And what was this face of God? It was this ark in which the Law was placed (1 Kings 8:9; Heb. 9:4).

Notice the profusion of scriptural references.

In order to understand better what this means, let us note in the first place that the majesty and glory of God are incomprehensible. Not only do we not see God with our eyes, since he is of a spiritual essence, but when we apply all our senses to know him, we will certainly be dazzled a hundred times over, before we can even approach him. For we are too crude and weak. We can only crawl upon the earth, while "the heaven of heavens cannot contain him" (1 Kings 8:27), as the other passage says. So when we want to approach God, it is certain that we will not be able to and that he is totally inaccessible to us. Therefore, he must come down to us when we cannot reach up to him. And how does he come down? It is not that he changes his place as far as his essence is concerned, but he must make himself known in a familiar manner. So when he conforms himself to our smallness, he does it only insofar as he abases himself. Not that there is change in him, but his coming down refers to our capacity.

Calvin is explaining his concept that God accommodates himself to human perception and understanding. Why might this idea help Calvin's interpretation of the text? Read the next two paragraphs of Calvin's sermon to see how he applies the idea to the passage.

Therefore, consider how God, who from all times has had pity on the crude capacities of men, has for that very reason come down to them, since they could not reach up to him. How has he come down? He has done so in the fashion of men, as if to say, "Here am I, and when I come through these means, it is the same as if I were manifest to you and you were seeing me with the naked eye" — that is what the ark meant. It was a means by which God made himself known to the people so they would be without excuse and could not say, "We do not know which way to begin when we ought to pray to God and honor him. We do not know how he will be our Protector, and how we will feel his help." On the contrary, the ark was a standing witness that God wanted to dwell in the midst of the people.

Calvin here implicitly criticizes Roman Catholic worship practices that featured images of saints and of Christ on the cross.

Notice that there was absolutely no idol or representation of God in it, because that would have served to hold the people in superstition; rather, the Law was enclosed in this box. This shows us that God declares himself only in his Word. So when we want to have a living image of him, we must not forge idols, of stone or wood or any other material, but we must know him in his Word. If we fall away from his Word, we wander astray; we will be like vagabonds — indeed, like straying beasts. When God says that he wants to show his face, it is eminently reasonable for us to believe that, because he placed his Law in the ark — the two tables which he had written with his own power, without human help (Exod. 31:18; Deut. 10:4-5). This is what we must remember.

Again, it is not enough to state that God must not be represented by statues and paintings, but his declaration ought to make the people reach above the heavens. Indeed, we see how the Jews were reproved in their superstitions for thinking that they could keep God contained (1 Kings 8:27; Acts 17:24). Solomon, in dedicating the temple, clearly told them that they could not enclose God in any particular habitation by saying, "The heavens cannot contain God," and "He cannot dwell in a place made by the hand of man." Whenever the Jews glorified themselves by saying, "The temple of the Lord, the temple of the Lord" (Jer. 7:4), they wanted to keep God almost as their prisoner. That is why Isaiah cries with a loud voice, "And what place do you think to build for me? For the earth is only my footstool, and my seat is above the heavens, and do you think to make me a house there?" (Isa. 66:1). "Do you come to seek me in a superstitious manner so that you can say that I am with you?" This shows how the Jews abused this familiarity which God had granted them.

Thus, we must note that when God declares himself to us, we must not cling to any earthly thing, but must elevate our senses above the world, and lift ourselves up by faith to his eternal glory. In sum, God comes down to us so that then we might go up to him. That is why the sacraments are compared to the steps of a ladder. For as I have said, if we wanted to go up there, alas, we do not have wings; we are so small that we cannot make it. God, therefore, must come down to seek us. But when he has come down, it is not to make us dull-witted; it is not to make us imagine that he is like us. Rather, it is so that we might go up little by little, by degrees, as we climb up a ladder one rung at a time. The sacraments are like this, and the ark was like a sacrament — at least in principle. The people had to be moved to seek God in a very tangible manner.

When Scripture says that God was between the cherubim, that did not make the ark into an idol. For the cherubim had their faces hidden, and their wings covered the ark (Exod. 25:20) to show that God was invisible in his essence, and that even the angels adored him in all humility, and that there was a shadow so obscure over the ark that making God a mouth or nose or anything else terrestrial was totally out of the question. So much, then, for the ark.

Now let us apply this to ourselves, for we are no more competent than the Jews. Yet we need God to make himself small, so that we can have access to him; otherwise we would be completely shut out. However, he does not make himself so small because he wants his glory to be lessened, but rather he does this out of goodness to lift us up to admire his glory and to adore him with the reverence that he deserves.

When we have access to the preached Word, God speaks in a common and ordinary fashion to us. It is an illustration of his condescension. Hence, the preaching of the Gospel is like

---

Calvin repeatedly emphasizes the need to remember specific concepts: it was not enough for congregations to attend church and listen to the sermons, but they were also to engage their minds by actively recalling key concepts.

See Calvin's use of the ladder imagery in his commentary on Psalm 9 (p. 115).

Calvin again makes a strong connection between something his congregation would be familiar with (the sacraments) and something he is trying to explain to them (the importance of the ark as a sign of God's presence and a way to God).

Why was Calvin so determined to differentiate the Jews' veneration of the ark of the covenant from idolatry?

God descending to earth in order to seek us. We must not abuse this simplicity of the Word of God by disdaining it. Rather, we must receive it all the more, recognizing that he indeed deigns to transfigure himself, so to speak, that we might approach him. He is not content with giving us his Word, but he adds baptism to confirm it. When we are baptized — though only a little water is used — it stands for crucifying our old man, for renewing our souls, and for being united with the angels. Baptism is performed to ensure that we inherit the eternal kingdom, to make us enjoy adoption, by which we are companions and brothers of the angels — but can a little water do that? The point, of course, is that since God has come down to us (in this symbol), we must go up to him (in faith).

It is the same way with the Lord's Supper, which the Papists greatly abuse and corrupt by wanting God to be present in it, and wanting him to come down in an earthly fashion to suit their appetite. But we are shown here that he descends to us, not to stupefy or bind our senses in these low and feeble things. The Papists are far too dull-witted, for under the excuse that our Lord Jesus Christ has left a testimony and a pledge of his body and blood under the bread and wine, so that men might know that truly he is the nourishment of their life, what have they done? They have turned it into an idol, as though he entered into a piece of bread and wanted to be adored there in a gross fashion, with the result that men become so bewitched with such poison that they have no longer enough discretion to discern anything. Even this is not enough for them, for under the excuse of this presence, they say he had to hide in a sacramental cup and be held captive in it as a prisoner. Furthermore, they handle the sacrament like apes and make a farce of it.

Well, when we see how very much inclined the world is to superstition, we must all the more remember the rule which I have given: namely, that when God has come down, it is not that we should remain down here, but rather that we should be lifted on high to adore him spiritually, and that we should thereby rise above the world by our faith.

Nevertheless, in order that we might know that God does not want to frustrate us, and that the signs which he gives us are not frivolous and empty baggage, like toys for little children, it says that God truly dwells between the cherubim. This does not mean that his essence is enclosed in the ark, but that he wishes to display his virtue there for the salvation of his people. Similarly, today in the waters of baptism, it is the same as if the blood of our Lord Jesus Christ poured down from Heaven to water our souls and cleanse them from their uncleanness. When we have the bread and wine in the Lord's Supper, it is the same as if Jesus Christ were coming down from Heaven and making himself our food, so that we could be filled with him. We must not, therefore, take these signs as visible things and figures which are to feed our spiritual senses, but are to realize that God joins his virtue and truth to them, so that the thing and the effect are joined to the figure. We must not put asunder what God has joined together. That, in sum, is what we must keep in mind from the statement that the ark of God has the name: the name of the God of hosts, dwelling between the cherubim.

Calvin had a high view of preaching. What might be the consequences, both positive and negative, of such a high view of preaching?

Calvin's critique of the Catholic mass and its theology was very strong. He was following the path of other Reformed leaders before him who articulated similar criticisms.

What are the possible implications of Calvin's insistence that the faithful must "be lifted on high" and "rise above the world"?

This passage deserves serious reflection. How likely was it, in your opinion, that a congregation would be able to follow Calvin's logic?

Note how regularly and carefully Calvin returns to his text for the day.

In fact, that is also why David invokes him in this way: "Lord God of Israel, who dwells between the cherubim, hear my prayer, look upon me in pity; continue no longer to afflict me as you have done" (Ps. 80:1). Now if David had not had the ark as a sign, he might have become lost in seeking God. But he knew by the Law that God wanted the ark to be a pledge of his presence. He was certain of this and assured himself that he would be heard, and that he could perceive God or communicate familiarly with God, as though he inhabited the country of Judah as his own residence.

Of course, today we have no such ark, but we do have the fulfillment of all that it implied in our Lord Jesus Christ. Even the covering of the ark was truly a type of Jesus Christ (Exod. 25:17ff.). However much one may deduce about Christ from this "covering," it certainly means "propitiation," in that sins are blotted out. Therefore, Jesus Christ is called our propitiator today. He is called our propitiation so that we may no longer be taken up with these ancient symbols in themselves, but rather that God may draw us to himself by using these humble signs as a help in our present weakness (see Heb. 4:16; 9:5; Rom. 3:25).

Let us, therefore, learn that every single time that we want to invoke God, if his majesty is terrible to us, or if we want to say that he is too far from us and that we cannot have access to him, even though we recognize our infirmity — still let us recall that the prophet says that he is Emmanuel, which means: "God with us" (Isa. 7:14). Let us also remember that our Lord Jesus Christ, who dwells in eternal glory, has left his mark upon us by baptism; that we have the knowledge of him by his Word, which assures us that he will employ his power in our lives; and that we will be filled with his own substance in the Lord's Supper. In brief, he dwells in us by faith, as St. Paul says (Eph. 3:17). This is how we must follow David, making use of the humble means which are available to us — whenever we are prevented by our lack of trust from coming to God.

Further, it says that the "ark of God was placed in a new cart" (2 Sam. 6:3). David cannot be excused for doing this, because this duty was assigned to the Kohathites, who were a portion of the tribe of Levi (Num. 4:15). They should have carried the ark; since God had ordained it this way, it should have been done in obedience to him. Why did they tamper with his requirements? This shows us what happens when people are not used to participating in the worship of God and are total novices in it. Here was David, who had the high priest with him and the Levites following him, who could have taught him. He had the gift of prophecy as a master and doctor in the church (1 Sam. 16:13). Nevertheless, he did not know how to carry out what was expressly stated in the Law concerning this matter. Instead, he took a new cart. What was the cause of this failure except that the people had increasingly adulterated themselves, were not accustomed to the worship of God, and were ignorant of the simple elements of it?

We have certainly seen this sort of thing, and we see it again today in the corruptions and villainies of the Papacy, which are so bad that one scarcely knows which way to start restoring

Notice the sermon's Christological turn. How does Calvin link the role of Christ to his exegesis of this Old Testament passage?

Calvin's pastoral heart and his awareness that believers may feel God is too distant to care or to be attentive, comes through strongly in this paragraph.

Notice Calvin's interest in even the smallest details of the passage: nothing is left unexplained or uninterpreted.

the true order of the Church of God. Instead, we see very little willingness among the Papists to do this. There are many who will make a profession of the Gospel, but when you want to lead them to a pure rule of practice, when you do not want to tolerate a halfway religion but rather a pure and whole religion, they reply, "We do not want any of that!"

Why? You cannot reclaim them and make them submit to the obedience of God, simply because they have been stupefied by their pollutions and nourished by their villainy. Let us be aware, then, that we are — with good reason — greatly exhorted to take thought of ourselves day and night (Matt. 26:41; Col. 4:2) and to be vigilant (1 Pet. 5:8) to know how God wants to be worshiped and served. That is why we are to apply all our powers to serve him and are to bring back to memory things which we may have too quickly forgotten. This, in sum, is what we must remember when it says that David took a new cart to carry the ark of God. The ark should have been placed, instead, on the shoulders of the Kohathites, who would have done their duty cheerfully if David had required it of them. His failure to do so showed contempt, both on his part and on the part of the people, for since they were so asleep in their religion, they were truly novices in it, which is why they did not follow the rule of the Law.

Certainly, they could have given some reason for taking a new cart — but these reasons came from imitating the Philistines and from their own ideas. But when it is a question of the service of God, it must be separated from everything which belongs to this terrestrial life. Our filthy and profane affairs must not be mingled with what is sacred. We must, when we eat and drink, says St. Paul, do all in the name of God (1 Cor. 10:31). All must be blessed and sanctified by him. But nonetheless, we must clearly be separated (from merely human ideas) in the worship of God. Thus, for example, we cannot mingle our prayers and petitions with our worries, and so when we have to pray, we have to lay aside everything which is otherwise good. If we try to pray to God in the manner of unbelievers, our prayer is a pollution and sacrilege. A woman, for instance, is doing well when she does her housework, makes up her bed, cleans the house, boils the pot, and governs her children; all of this is very appropriate. But on the other hand, if, like some of the Papists, she half-heartedly mumbles through her devotions while she is doing these things, muttering the Lord's Prayer and seven psalms while she is working her way through the house with her mind on other matters, in effect God and the devil are thrown together. Is it not a sheer mockery of God, who wants "to be served and worshiped in spirit and truth" (John 4:24)?

Hence, we must separate ourselves from everything which concerns our earthly welfare when we have to pray to God. Moreover, when we want to serve him in purity, if we instead think of our domestic affairs, our needs, our household, and our possessions, then we cause villainous and detestable confusion. We certainly profane the name of God by doing this.

Of course, David had a certain amount of good intention when he chose a new cart, which had not carried anything else, to carry the ark. But that by no means totally excuses him, for "obedience is better than sacrifice," as we have seen in the First Book of Samuel (1 Sam.

Again, would you classify these two paragraphs as analysis or interpretation? Is Calvin stretching the link between the biblical text and the modern-day application he is trying to make?

Here is a good instance of Calvin using examples that would be very familiar to his hearers, including the women in attendance.

It is worth pointing out that the people most likely to persist in Catholic worship practices even after the Reformation in Geneva were women, who had been nurtured in the Catholic faith and found great comfort and familiarity in its rituals. Calvin's example was undoubtedly deliberately chosen.

What can you deduce about Calvin's views of women, of household management, and of the role of religious devotion in daily life?

15:22). Since this regulation was given by the Law, it should have been observed, but this was not done, because the people had neglected the Law for a long time.

The text adds that Abinadab walked in front of the ark, and "his sons one after the other led it" (2 Sam. 6:3). Now it could well be (as we shall see more fully) that there was some ambition involved, and that this man very much wanted to show that he had lodged the ark of God and that his house had been like the inner sanctuary. But still, he was showing reverence toward God when he and his sons conducted the ark. Indeed, we see that he did not resist the removal of the ark, as many do who are resentful against God when they lose such a privilege. Here was Abinadab, who had been like the host of God. This was a greater dignity than anything else. But they came to remove the ark, so that his house was stripped of this honor, which excelled all that is excellent in this world, for there is no royal scepter which can be compared with the temple of God. That is the degree to which the ark had ennobled his house. If Abinadab had been annoyed when David came to remove the ark, he could simply have left the scene, to show that he was compelled by force and that he could not have resisted the king with the 30,000 men who kept him company. So it was a sign of humility and modesty when he led the ark and voluntarily ceded this privilege, which he had enjoyed for a long time. He gave visible proof that he was not sad that the ark should be put in a place where all the people could easily come to worship God, so that everyone should be encouraged to go there, and all the regions of Israel might assemble there, as was commanded in the Law (Deut. 12:2f.).

Here is a good example of Calvin's astute observation of human character and motivations, bringing the biblical text to life.

On the other hand, it says that "David and Israel sang a hymn to God, that is, with instruments" and music (2 Sam. 6:5). David assembled such a multitude that all might worship God with one accord. He well knew that God had not made himself known to him alone, but had established the whole family of Abraham. Thus, David wanted everyone to imitate him and showed the way for there to be mutual accord, that small and great might demonstrate that they wanted to serve God. Here we see the true use of hymns: we are to encourage one another to celebrate and magnify the name of God in our hymns (Eph. 5:19-20). It would be enough for each one to pray to God in his heart and for each one to give him thanks. This is the true worship of God: "Call upon me in the day of your trouble" (Ps. 50:15), says the Lord, "and then praise me when you know that I have answered." We can surely do that from the heart, but our mouth must state ever more clearly the very concerns which cause us to pray to God. Even though everyone can still privately invoke God by themselves, we have this privilege of assembling in public in order to testify to our faith, and then to encourage others by our example. When we pray to God here in the church, and sing the psalms, it is not to show ourselves off, as hypocrites do, but to declare that we seek nothing but that God may be glorified among us. Our assembling in his name also should certainly serve as a thorn to prick us because of our laziness. That is how we are to encourage one another (Heb. 3:13), and that is why people were not to sing hymns of praise to God for only a temporary period of time, but until the end of the world. Since we are surrounded with flesh and blood, we need means such as these (to lift our spirit up to God), and thus the obligation to sing hymns of praise is common both to us and to the ancients.

There is a difference, however, concerning the instruments of music. It would be nothing but mimicry if we followed David today in singing with cymbals, flutes, tambourines, and psalteries. In fact, the Papists were seriously deceived in their desire to worship God with their pompous inclusion of organs, trumpets, oboes, and similar instruments. That has only served to amuse the people in their vanity and to turn them away from the true institution which God has ordained. We must, at the same time, be aware of all the privileges which we have in common with the fathers who have lived under the Law and, on the other hand, be aware of the things wherein they are separated from us. All those things which we have in common with them are lasting and must be maintained until the end of the world. But we are not to keep observing these things which were only for the time of the Law, unless we want to make a confused mixture which confounds heaven with earth. In a word, the musical instruments were in the same class as sacrifices, candelabra, lamps, and similar things. There is nothing that the Papists have not turned to some use. Because there was the chandelier with the lamps (in the Old Testament), thus there had to be candles (in the church); because there was perfume then, there had to be incense now. There were ritual washings then, so there had to be holy water now. The Papists, in brief, have shown themselves in every possible way to be apes without any discretion!

As I have said, we must notice that what God has instituted for the time of symbols (before the coming of our Lord Jesus Christ) must be put aside and not enforced today. It is true that God ought to be heartily praised, both by musical instruments and by mouth. But it is another matter when we conduct the worship of God in church. If we want to sing praises in the name of God, we would do much better to have psalms instead of common dissolute songs. We sing in order to give him thanks — not in order to produce a solemn ceremony as a meritorious work that we do for God. Those who take this approach are reverting to a sort of Jewishism, as if they wanted to mingle the Law and the Gospel, and thus bury our Lord Jesus Christ. When we are told that David sang with a musical instrument, let us carefully remember that we are not to make a rule of it. Rather, we are to recognize today that we must sing the praises of God in simplicity, since the shadows of the Law are past, and since in our Lord Jesus Christ we have the truth and embodiment of all these things which were given to the ancient fathers in the time of their ignorance or smallness of faith. They did not have such revelation as we have today in the Gospel.

In sum, we see how God was adored both in truth and in type. He was adored in truth because, in giving him praises, people magnified his name and recognized that all came from him. Nevertheless, there were types joined with the reality insofar as they were necessary at that time. Today, we certainly have some ceremony, but it is not like old times. We have it

Calvin's justification of corporate worship highlights several key points — which ones seem most significant to you?

Is Calvin's argument in this section convincing?

What seem to be the main reasons Calvin was uncomfortable with the idea of instruments accompanying singing in church?

in sobriety. The pure worship of God today is called heavenly, in that it is not enclosed amid these shadows, and with a half-effect. This is the meaning of the account of their moving the ark.

This comment provides clear evidence of the sequencing of sermons in a series.

The text then adds that "Uzzah touched it and God smote him" (2 Sam. 6:6-7) because of his hastiness. But that cannot be explained today; it is reserved for tomorrow.

Let us be content with knowing that David's intention was to awake the people, who had for a long time been asleep toward God, to seek him. He wanted to put the ark in a place appropriate and available for all the people, so as to stir them up to do all that the Law commanded. David did this not out of superstition nor against the ordinance and command of God, but to influence the people, because the true religion had for a long time been put under foot and forgotten. In spite of that, he endeavored to honor and treat the name of God in all reverence. Let us also be aware that when the name of the ark is spoken, the very name of the eternal God is given so that we might learn to embrace the promises of God in his sacraments. His name is given so that whenever we truly seek him with a faith that has no superstition mixed with it to hold us back, we may not doubt that we have him with us and, indeed, inside us — so that we may go to him in true affection, looking for his eternal glory.

This concluding section is Calvin's closing prayer, which he proclaimed at the end of each of his sermons, though the wording following "Now let us prostrate ourselves before the majesty of our good God" varied from sermon to sermon.

Now let us prostrate ourselves before the majesty of our good God in recognition of our faults, praying that he may make us so to feel them as to draw us to him more and more; and to incline us to his service in such a way that we do not imitate the hypocrites, who have only forms and external ceremonies. But rather [let us act] out of a heartfelt affection. May we be so enthusiastic to sing his praises that it becomes our main pursuit. May we so profit each other that, with one accord, we proclaim that truly all our good consists and lies in him, and may that encourage us more and more to come to seek him, that we may find rest. May he not only bestow this grace upon us, but upon all people and nations of the earth. . . .

Source: John Calvin, "The True Worship of God," Sermon on 2 Samuel 6:1-7, preached on 3 July 1562, from *Sermons on 2 Samuel,* chapters 1-13, trans. Douglas Kelly (Edinburgh: The Banner of Truth Trust, 1992), pp. 229-43. Kelly based his translation on the French text published in the *Supplementa Calviniana,* Volume I, ed. Hans Rückert (Neukirchen: Neukirchener Verlag, 1961). This edition was based on the manuscript transcription of Calvin's sermons on 2 Samuel included in ms. fr. 16, held by the Bibliothèque publique et universitaire at the University of Geneva, Switzerland.

Theology of Worship Documents

Calvin's Teaching on Baptism (1561)

Very little is known about the circumstances surrounding Calvin's writing of this text beyond its date (1561), though Calvin and his fellow pastors were regularly consulted by other churches and pastors who were dealing with difficult worship-related issues and wanted the Genevan pastors' advice. Geneva's role as a reference point for other churches continued well into the late sixteenth century. Although Calvin was involved in several polemical exchanges with German Lutherans over the Reformed understanding of the Lord's Supper, his writings on baptism tended to be more pastoral and more practical, as in this case. Calvin does not indicate who his correspondents were, but from the information he provides, we can infer that they were a body of Reformed Protestants living in exile in a reasonably supportive community.

Your letter pleased us greatly, dearest brothers, because a place has been granted you in the city at last, and freedom of assembly has been given. God will increase this remarkable benefit with other, even greater ones. New and constant conflicts await you, and the fury of the devil will burst forth for a short time, perhaps, but you must press on vigorously.

We have not answered your earlier letter until now because there was no one to carry our reply safely. This is our opinion on the question put to us: No layperson can legitimately administer baptism, and you must oppose this evil severely; it is a clear profanation of baptism. This perverse custom originated in superstition when the need for salvation was attached to a symbol, and this twofold evil should therefore be nurtured all the less.

Augustine speaks uncertainly about this, saying that if a layperson performs a baptism when necessity compels it, this either is not a sin or is a venial sin. And yet the inviolable command of Christ ought to be of more weight: "Go, teach, baptize" [Matt. 28:19].

This knotty problem cannot be resolved without sacrilege. There is, in addition, the apostle's opinion: "And no man takes this honor unto himself except the one who is called of God" [Heb. 5:4]. We think, therefore, that a baptism performed by a layman is spurious; this

There was no regular postal service in the sixteenth century. Instead, people entrusted their letters to travelers, including merchants, students, or others, and hoped the letter would make it safely to its destination.

Calvin seems to cite Augustine with a measure of respect, even when he clearly disagrees with the early church father. Why?

107

temerity would not be tolerated in a properly established church. Because this has happened in your midst at an early stage, however, before the church's order was restored and when circumstances were still confused, the error should be forgiven, and the baptism (of whatever sort it is) should be tolerated.

This baptism, performed improperly and only once, should not serve as an example. God condones many things in a fragmented church that it would be wrong to allow in a well-ordered church. In former times, when religion was corrupt, circumcision was undoubtedly involved in many faults and corruptions, but we have read that it was not revoked when the people were recalled to a pure worship. It is not necessary, therefore, or even useful to investigate all the circumstances anxiously; this would produce countless worries. What God forgave under the Papacy we should also lay to rest. . . .

We feel differently about baptism by women. Women went beyond the law of nature and forced themselves upon the office of baptism with monstrous audacity. We do not doubt that such shameful behavior should be strongly repudiated. Meanwhile, there is no danger that weak consciences are going to suffer damage, unless someone worries for no reason, out of excessive inquisitiveness. No one knows that he was baptized by a woman, and in the second place, an ancient decree of the Carthaginian Council prohibited women from the office of baptizing, so that the novelty of it (which would have been a fearful thing to men) will not shock anyone.

Farewell, best and purest brothers. May the Lord guide you with spiritual wisdom, sustain you with his virtue, and enrich you with all gifts. We pray for good health for the elders and for the whole church.

Geneva. November 13, 1561

Source: *Calvin's Ecclesiastical Advice,* trans. Mary Beaty and Benjamin Farley (Louisville: Westminster John Knox Press, 1991), pp. 97-98. This translation is based on the Latin text published in the nineteenth-century collected edition of Calvin's works: *Joannis Calvini Opera Quae Supersunt Omnia,* ed. W. Baum, E. Cunitz, and E. Reuss (Braunschweig: Schwetschke and Son, 1872), Vol. X, cols. 214-15. The Latin text in the *Opera* is taken from the first edition of John Calvin's *Epistolae et Responsa* (Geneva: Pierre de Saint-André, 1575), p. 334.

Calvin's Teaching on Public Prayer (1560)

This extract is taken from Calvin's most famous work, the Institutes of the Christian Religion, *which he first published in Latin in 1536 and reworked extensively throughout his lifetime, publishing revised editions in Latin and in French up until a few years before his death. He intended it as a guide to Reformed theology, and it was translated into nearly every major European language before 1600.*

This point is crucial: Calvin was acknowledging the validity of a baptism performed by a lay-person, albeit under exceptional circumstances.

Calvin's approach here is very pastoral. When people converted from Roman Catholicism to the Reformed faith in the sixteenth century they were not rebaptized: their original Catholic Trinitarian baptism was viewed as valid by the Reformed church.

Why might Calvin have been so adamantly opposed to baptisms done by women?

29. Although mainly focused on private prayers, ceaseless prayer also includes public prayers. While it is good to gather together, public prayers cannot be continuous and must be carried out according to the practices set out by the common consent of the church. However, there are certain set times which do not matter to God but are necessary for human practice, so as to accommodate everyone's schedule and so that, as Saint Paul says [1 Cor. 14:40], everything should be done in the church in an orderly and harmonious fashion.

This should not prevent individual churches from encouraging more frequent prayer, especially when impelled by a specific need. We will say more at the end about perseverance, which is closely linked to unceasing prayer. Yet none of this provides any support for superstitious lengthening and repetition of prayers, which is prohibited by our Lord [Matt. 6:7]. For he does not prohibit persistence in prayer, nor returning to it frequently, ardently, and often. But he teaches us not to believe that we can constrain God to give in to our pleas by bothering him with empty words, as if he could be moved by our chatter like humans are. For we know that hypocrites, not realizing that they are dealing with God, pray with great pomposity, as if at a triumph. They are like the Pharisee who thanked God that he was not like others, and who patted himself on the back in public as if he wanted to gain a reputation for holiness by proclaiming his allegiance to God.

Such lengthy prayers are popular today in the Papacy, and stem from the same source: some waste their time by murmuring endless Ave Marias and saying their rosary a hundred times, while others, like the canons and hypocrites, sell their fakery to the people by chanting in church day and night and muttering their breviary. Because such vain verbosity is akin to treating God like a small child, we should not be surprised if Jesus Christ shuts the door against such practices and does not allow them into his church, where the only prayers to be heard are genuine and authentic.

There is a second similar abuse that Jesus Christ also condemns, namely, that of attention-seeking hypocrites who look for many witnesses by planting themselves in the middle of the marketplace rather than miss out on the opportunity to flaunt themselves in their prayers so as to receive worldly praise. As we have already said, since the goal of prayer is to lift our spirits to God, to desire his glory and proclaim his praise, and to ask him for help in our need, we can infer that the essence of prayer lies in the heart and the spirit. In fact, prayer is only this inner desire transforming itself and addressing itself to God, who knows the secrets of the heart. Yet when he wanted to give us a good set of rules for prayer, our Lord Jesus Christ told us to go into our room, close the door, and pray there in secret to our heavenly Father, so that he who sees and knows all secrets will grant our petitions [Matt. 6:6]. For after having pulled us away from the example of the hypocrites who through their attention-seeking prayers aim to be praised and favored by the people, Christ adds and teaches us therefore what we should do, namely, to go into our room and pray with the door closed. As I understand it, through these words he teaches us to seek out a haven of this kind that helps

Articulate in your own words the distinction Calvin makes in this section between different kinds of prayer.

A breviary is a prayer book containing scriptural texts and orders of service, usually used by Catholic clergy.

How does this defini-
tion fit with your
understanding of
prayer?

us mindfully enter into our hearts. He promises us that God will be fully present to our inner longings, for our bodies are to be his true temples. In saying so he was not denying that it is both appropriate and necessary to pray in other places, but he only wanted to make it clear that prayer is a hidden thing that is based mainly in the heart and the spirit. Prayer calls for peace of mind, removed from all desires of the flesh and earthly troubles and concerns. For this reason our Lord Jesus himself when he wanted to pray drew apart from human clamor. Indeed, he drew apart to incite us to follow his example and not to disdain such methods which can encourage us to turn our hearts more ardently to pray effectively, for our will on its own is much too weak and evaporates.

However, just as he did not fail to pray in the midst of the crowds if the opportunity presented itself, so we too should not balk at raising our hands to Heaven in all places, whenever appropriate [1 Tim. 2:8] . We should even be sure of the following: he who refuses to pray in the gathering of the faithful does not know what it means to pray in private, or in solitude, or at home. Similarly, he who takes no interest in private and individual prayer, even if he attends public worship, will only offer empty and frivolous prayers there, given that he relies more on human opinion than on the secret judgment of God. However, to avoid any disparagement of the church's common prayers, God underscored their importance, especially by calling his temple a house of prayer [Isa. 56:7]. In doing so, he showed that prayer is the foundation of his service. In giving orders to build up the temple, he raised a banner calling on the faithful to gather together in praise of him. There is also this notable promise: Lord, praise waits for you in Zion, and to you vows shall be paid [Ps. 65:1]. Through these words the prophet means that the prayers of the church are never useless or fruitless, especially as God always gives his people reasons to praise him and sing for joy. And while the shadows of the Law have fled, yet because God also wants to maintain the unity of faith among us through such a ceremony, there is no doubt that this promise also belongs to us. Indeed, Jesus Christ ratified it in his own words, and Saint Paul teaches that it will always be in force.

Read the Gene-
van Ecclesiastical
Ordinances and
the Ordinances for
the Supervision of
Churches in the
Country (p. 148,
p. 182) to see how
Calvin's ideas
about the status of
church buildings
were worked out in
practice.

30. Indeed, since God commands all his people to pray together, it is necessary to have temples dedicated to this purpose. Those who refuse to gather with the people of God in prayer cannot make excuses for themselves by claiming that they go into their rooms to obey God's command. For he who promises to grant everything that two or three people gathered together in his name ask for [Matt. 18:20] provides sufficient evidence that he does not reject public prayers, so long as no ambition or vainglory creeps in. In contrast, true and pure affection in the depths of the heart is called for. If this is how temples should legitimately be used (and that is certainly true), we must be careful not to believe (as has been the case for many years) that the buildings themselves are God's real dwelling place, and that God listens to us more attentively there. We are not to ascribe to the buildings any hidden holiness which would make our prayers more acceptable to God.

For if we are the genuine temples of God, we have to pray to him from within ourselves if we want to call on him in his true temple. Let us leave this crude and earthly perspective to Jews or Gentiles, since we have been commanded to worship the Lord in spirit and in truth, without regard to place [John 4:23]. It is true that the temple was formerly dedicated by God's command as the place to offer prayer and sacrifices, but that was during the time when truth was veiled. Now that this truth is declared to us openly, we have no right to get attached to any physical building. Furthermore, the temple was not commended to the Jews on the condition that they confine God's presence to its walls, but to train them to contemplate the image and likeness of the true Temple. Indeed, those who believed that God lived in temples made by human hands were sharply criticized by Saint Stephen, just as their ancestors were by Isaiah [Acts 7:48; Isa. 66:1].

31. In the same way, it is obvious that speaking and chanting, if used in prayer, are worthless and rejected by God unless they are grounded in love from the depths of the heart. Instead, such prayers irritate him and cause his anger to swell against us if the prayers arise and emerge only from our mouths. To do so is to mock his most holy Name and disparage his majesty, as he declares through his prophet. Even though the prophet was speaking in general about all hypocrisy, he includes this error with the rest. These people, he says, draw near to me with their mouths and praise me with their lips, but their hearts are far from me. They fear me because of human laws and doctrines. Yet I will generate a great wonder and a stunning miracle for these people. For the wisdom of all their sages will perish, and the understanding of their leaders and elders will be destroyed [Isa. 29:13; Matt. 15:8].

We are not saying, however, that speech or singing is bad. In fact, we value these practices, so long as they are grounded in the fervor of the heart and strengthen it. For in doing so, singing and speaking help the human resolve (which is otherwise fragile and easily distracted if it is not consistently reinforced) and keep it focused on meditation on God. Furthermore, since all of our body parts, each in its own realm, are to glorify God, it is appropriate that even the tongue that is specially created by God to proclaim and magnify his Name be put to use for this purpose, either in speech or in song. And the tongue is mainly needed in public prayers offered when Christians gather. There we are to show how we honor God with one spirit and one faith, and thus we praise him with one common voice and as if from one mouth. This praise takes place in public so that each person can hear clearly his brother's confession of faith and be edified and encouraged to do the same.

32. As for the way to sing in church, I will say briefly that not only is it a very long-standing practice, but even the Apostles made use of it, as can be inferred from these words from Saint Paul: I will sing with my mouth and I will sing with my mind [1 Cor. 14:15]. Also to the Colossians: Teach and exhort each other with hymns, Psalms, and spiritual songs, singing to

the Lord in your hearts with grace [Col. 3:16]. For in the first passage he shows that we must sing with our hearts and our mouths, and in the second passage he praises spiritual songs through which the faithful are mutually edified. However, as we can see from Saint Augustine, this practice was not always universally observed [*Confessions*, Book 9, chap. 7]. For he says that singing began in Milan at the time of Saint Ambrose, when Justine, the mother of Emperor Valentinian, was persecuting Christians, and that the practice of singing spread from there to the western churches. A little earlier, he said that this practice had come from the East, where it had always been carried out. Augustine also shows in his second book of retractions that the practice was common in Africa in his day. And certainly if singing is done with the seriousness of purpose that is appropriate in the presence of God and his angels, then it enriches the praise of God, giving it more grace and dignity.

Singing is also a good way to rouse the heart and inspire it with greater fervor to pray, but we should always be careful not to have our ears more attentive to the harmony of the singing than to have our minds focused on the spiritual meaning of the words. Augustine admits in another passage [*Confessions*, Book 10, chap. 33] that he was afraid of exactly this, saying that he wished everyone followed Athanasius's way of singing, which was closer to reading than to singing. But elsewhere he added that when he recalled the benefit and edification he received from hearing people singing in church, he favored the opposite, and approved of singing. Therefore, when adopting a similarly moderate approach, there is no doubt that it is a very holy and useful practice. In contrast, songs and melodies that are composed only to delight the ears, like all the chirping and droning of the Papists, and what they call part-singing or polyphony, or music in four parts, are totally unsuited to the majesty of the church and clearly greatly displease God.

33. Therefore it is also clear that public prayers should not be offered in Greek among the Romans, nor in Latin among the French or the English (according to recent universal practice), but rather in the common tongue of the area, one that can be understood by the whole gathering. Indeed, these prayers are to be done for the edification of the whole church, which cannot receive any benefit from incomprehensible noise. Even those who disregard compassion or concern should take to heart in some small measure the authority of Saint Paul, whose words on the subject are rather clear. If you give thanks with unintelligible sounds, how will the untaught man say Amen to your praise, since he does not understand what you are saying? Indeed, you are giving thanks, but your neighbor is not edified [1 Cor. 14:16]. Who can then not be greatly astounded at the Papists' zealous daring then and now, who go against the apostle's commands and sing and bellow in a strange and unknown tongue, which in most cases they themselves do not understand at all, and which they do not want others to understand? Saint Paul shows us that we must follow another road. What then will I do? he asks. I will pray with the voice, and I will pray intelligibly. I will sing with the voice, and I will sing intelligibly. In this passage, he uses the word *Spirit,* which I translate as Voice, meaning

---

Augustine of Hippo (354-430) was an early church father and renowned theologian. Calvin cited Augustine's writings regularly and with approval in his works.

Why might Calvin have found it so important to include specific historical examples?

Compare this section to Calvin's foreword to the Genevan Psalter (p. 143). What seem to be Calvin's key points?

the gift of tongues, which many take advantage of for their own glory, making a distinction between that gift and intelligible speech.

However, we must always realize that the tongue is useless without the heart: whether in private or public prayer, such an approach can only be displeasing to God. Furthermore, the fervor and deep ardor of the will should be so great as to soar over anything that can be expressed with our tongues. Finally, in private prayer words are not even necessary unless the mind on its own is too unfocused, or unless the mind, driven by burning emotion, pushes the tongue into action and impels speech. For though at times the best prayers are silent, in many cases the inner fervor is so strong that both tongue and other members are propelled into action, without any desire to show off. Thus Samuel's mother, Hannah, murmured in an undertone as she prayed [1 Sam. 1:15]. And the faithful experience similar things on a daily basis, when their prayers contain unplanned sighs and broken cries. As for the postures and external stances for prayer that are customarily done (such as kneeling and removing one's hat), these are practices through which we try to prepare ourselves for a more reverent approach to God.

Source: Karin Maag translated Book III, Chapter 20, sections 29-33 from the French 1560 edition of the *Institutes:* Jean Calvin, *Institution de la religion Chrestienne. Nouvellement mise en quatre Livres: & distinguée par Chapitres, en ordre & methode bien propre: Augmentee aussi de tel accroissement, qu'on la peut presque estimer un livre nouveau* (Geneva: Jean Crespin, 1560), fols. Kvi verso — Lii recto. Paragraph divisions have been introduced to improve the readability of the text.

Calvin's Commentary on Psalm 9 and Psalm 50 (1557)

Calvin's commentaries on the Psalms were first published in Latin in 1557, and in French in the following year, with a revised French edition published in 1561. Calvin had taught on the Psalms in his public lectures on the Old Testament beginning in 1552, and the Psalms had also been the focus of the weekly "congrégations" or pastoral Bible-study sessions beginning in 1555. Calvin's main audience for his lectures was future pastors, who spent a period of time (from a number of months up to a few years) in Geneva learning how to interpret Scripture and then how to teach it to their congregations in their sermons. Just as in his sermons, Calvin worked through the Psalms in order, commenting on them verse by verse in sections. Here only the sections dealing with worship have been included.

Psalm 9

1. *I will praise the Lord.* He [David] uses this starting point to gain favor with God, so that God will rescue him from the ills that press in on him. For since God's grace toward the faithful is always constant, all the good he has done for us in the past must give us assurance and hope

that he will be gracious and merciful to us in the future. It is true that David's words include an acknowledgment of God's past favor, but in recalling these things to mind, David encourages himself more and more to hope for help and aid in the future, and in so doing, he opens the door to prayer. When he says "with all my heart," he means with a pure and whole heart, rather than in a duplicitous way. And therefore he not only makes a distinction between himself and those heavy hypocrites who praise God only with their lips, leaving their hearts stone cold, but he also acknowledges that everything praiseworthy he has done so far stems entirely from the pure grace of God. For even though secular men are ashamed not to give God the praise he deserves after having won a significant victory, we see that after having briefly admitted that God saved them, they begin to boast openly and sing of their own mighty deeds, as if they owed nothing to God. In short, they are only pretending, every time they highlight God when recounting their valiant deeds, because after having made an oblation to God, they in fact pay homage to their own counsels, dexterity, courage, weapons, and people. . . . Therefore David rightly states that he is not like the children of this world, whose hypocrisy and fraudulent behavior is uncovered by the vastly unequal shares they dole out to God and to themselves, giving themselves the greater share of the praise that they pretend to want to ascribe to him. For when a mortal man dares to take for himself even the smallest part of the praise owed to God, that action definitely contradicts the idea of praising God with all one's heart. It is bad enough to have to bear with the sacrilegious pride of those who try as much as they can to conceal God's glory by praising themselves. . . .

2. *I will rejoice and exult in you*. Here is how the faithful are to praise God purely and without pretense, namely, when they do not rely on themselves and are not intoxicated by an overconfident dependence on the flesh, but rejoice in God alone. This simply means finding joy in his pure grace, since in it complete happiness is found. For we must remember the sharp contrast between people delighting in themselves, and [those] seeking their happiness in God. And so that David can express more clearly the idea that he turns away from anything that could hold him back or provide him with empty amusement, he adds "and exult," meaning that he finds God to be the complete source of joy, so much so that there is not a drop of it to be found elsewhere. Furthermore, we must recall what we previously said, namely, that David recalls to mind the earlier testimonies of God's grace, so as to open his heart more readily to God and make his petitions to him. For the one who acknowledges at the start of his prayer that the source of his joy stems from God is grounded in a firm confidence.

How would you summarize Calvin's thoughts on the appropriate starting point for prayer?

3. *When my enemies*. He testifies here about his reasons for singing praises to God, namely, because he acknowledges that he has gained so many victories not due to his strength, or that of his soldiers, but by the unmerited favor of God. . . .

10. *God never abandons those who seek him.* This is done in two ways: either by invocation and prayers, or by seeking and working at living a good and holy life. It is true that the one is always connected to the other, but because the issue here is God's protection, which is the source of the faithful's salvation, I interpret "to seek God" as meaning turning to him.

11. *Sing to the Lord.* Not satisfied with having given thanks in private, David for his part urges the faithful to praise God together with him, not only because we should encourage each other in this practice of piety, but because God's acts of deliverance were worth public and solemn praise. This is stated even more clearly in the second part, where he orders that the saving acts be "told among the peoples." In other words, unless the story is told throughout the world, God's acts of deliverance will not get the praise they deserve. Furthermore, even though it was like talking to deaf people, God [*sic*, for David] wanted to show through this figure of speech that the territory of Judea was too small to contain the infinite scope of God's praise. David calls God the one who "lives in Zion," to distinguish him from all the false gods of the Gentiles. Here is an implied comparison between the God who made a covenant with Abraham and Israel, and all the gods who were commonly worshiped around the world according to human whims. Indeed, it is not enough to honor and venerate some vague divine force, but instead to know how to recognize the one and only true God, whom one should serve appropriately and according to his commands. However, because God had specifically chosen that place, so that the faithful would call on his name there, it is right that David assigned that place as God's own dwelling, not that one can legitimately encompass God in one place, given that the highest heavens cannot hold him, but he had promised to settle there forever, as we shall see elsewhere. For David had not assigned this dwelling place to God at random, but he had learned through a revelation that God was pleased to have it this way, as Moses had often predicted. This also goes to show what I said earlier, namely, that this Psalm was not written at the time of Goliath's defeat, for it seems that the Ark was only moved to Zion according to God's commandment toward the end of David's reign. Those who suggest that David was speaking prophetically about something yet to take place seem to constrain and force the text. Furthermore, we see that the holy Fathers, when they gathered in Zion to offer sacrifices to God, did not decide on this location for themselves. Instead, being established in their faith in the Word of God, they were approved by God in their obedience. Therefore there is no point to use their example to justify the services of God generated by the minds of superstitious men. Moreover, in those days it was not enough for the faithful to rely on the Word of God, for with the help of outward ceremonies, they raised their hearts higher, and served God spiritually. It is very true that God had given genuine signs of his presence in this visible Sanctuary, but the goal was not to bind people's senses to earthly elements. Instead, he wanted these external signs to serve as ladders to draw the faithful to Heaven. For right from the start God had the same goal for the Sacraments and

Notice how Calvin weaves in critiques of others' interpretations of the passage. What can you infer about Calvin's approach to Scripture and scriptural exegesis?

This image of the ladder is one of Calvin's favorite ways of explaining how God uses the elements of this world to draw believers to a deeper and more spiritual understanding of their faith.

all other outward practices of the faith, namely, to accommodate the weakness and minimal capacity of his people. Therefore yet today their true purpose is to help us seek God spiritually in his heavenly glory, and not to keep us in this world or distract us with the vanities of the flesh, a matter which is better handled in a later section. The Lord was called "He who dwells in Zion" when he wanted to give his people a full and unwavering reason for confidence, rest, and joy. But now that the Law has gone out of Zion and that from this source the covenant of grace is flowing over us, let us be sure that he fully presides in the midst of the faithful who worship him purely and worthily according to his Word.

14. *That I may retell.* While David simply means that he will make God's praises known in every solemn assembly and in all places where lots of people will gather (for in those days assemblies took place at the city gates), it seems however that he was referring to the gates of death, of which he has just spoken. It is as if he said that because he had been rescued from the grave, he was going to work to make God's grace known in broad daylight. But given that it is not enough for the praise of God to be on our tongues, unless they come from the heart, he adds inner joy, as if he had said that he had no desire to live in this world for any other reason than to rejoice in his deliverance thanks to the grace of God. . . .

Notice how Calvin intersperses historical information to explain the text more thoroughly.

Psalm 50

[4.] . . . God calls them his faithful ones, not because they all truly deserve to be called holy, but to make them consider more carefully the goal of their calling. Thus God is using irony to underscore in passing that these phony and corrupt Jews were not fulfilling their calling. A more subtle way of putting it, which still fits the intention of the prophet and his subject matter, is to say the following: Separate out for me the small number of those who serve me in purity and simplicity of heart from the milling crowd of those who dishonor my name too easily. Then this multitude cannot hide any longer beneath the false cloak of these outward ceremonies. However, it is not absurd for us to say that while the church was corrupt, the small number of the faithful and pure-hearted that remained within it was still worthy of such honor that for their sake, this blended gathering of good and evil people was called the holy people of God. The next phrase is interpreted differently by various commentators. Some think that the phrase "over the sacrifices" in this context means above or beyond the sacrifices, as if God was praising here his true servants, who recognize that his covenant calls for something greater (not outward ceremonies), and who do not get lost in earthly shadows. Others think that the spiritual service of God is completely in contrast to sacrifices, as if the text read: As for or instead of sacrifices, the people appropriately reaffirm their covenant with me, for they dedicate and consecrate a pure obedience of the heart to me. But in my opinion,

What important point is Calvin making here, and how does his approach refine and reframe our view of Calvin's attitude towards non-Reformed Christians?

the prophet is recommending here the true and natural practice of the service decreed in the Law. Indeed, it was no small matter to know rightly why God required sacrifices in the Law. Yet the prophet here states clearly that the sacrifices are only signs and seals or helps to confirm and ratify God's covenant. He even refers to the common custom of holding sacrifices to ratify agreements, alliances, and contracts and ensure that they were more carefully and solemnly observed. Thus God commanded sacrifices to increase his people's sense of obligation toward him and to ensure an authentic and well-founded covenant. This passage is worth noting, indicating that those whom God considers true members of the church are people who are merciful, who treat their brothers fairly and with equity, and who ratify through the pure obedience of their faith the covenant of adoption offered by God. Therefore all those who advocate a different form of worship and who turn away from the pure Law can proclaim as loudly and as often as they like that they are the church of God. However, the Holy Spirit for its part banishes them and rejects them from the Church of God, because the sacrifices and all the rituals should only have one goal, namely, to be a seal and sign of the pure truth of God in us. Hence all the ceremonies that are not grounded in the Word of God are false and illegitimate, and all the service that is not regulated and based on the Word of God is nothing but a misuse and corruption of the pure service God requires.

> Based on this passage, articulate in your own words what Calvin's criteria would be for assessing whether a particular form of worship, ritual, or ceremony would constitute true worship of God.

8. *I will not rebuke you.* Here is the key point: God does not care about sacrifices, and he does not value them in and of themselves. Now it is not the case that the Jews sacrificed in vain and fruitlessly, because it would be ridiculous to say that God had commanded something that had no purpose. But because God simply receives and approves such services as praiseworthy and because he accepts the practices of piety when these are directed to their proper goal, God rightly rejects outward services in which the sign and its true meaning are incompatible. The prophets speak this way fairly regularly, as we have previously said several times, and especially in Psalm 40. Since therefore the rituals are not intrinsically important, God says that he does not require them, as if he wanted his servants to be less anxious about these, since they only assist in spiritual worship. In Jeremiah 7:22, he says he did not order sacrifices, and the prophet Micah asked (Mic. 6:7), "Does God require of you to sacrifice flocks of sheep, and does he take pleasure in thousands of rams?" Instead, he asks you to do justice, and love equity, etc. Similarly in Hosea (Hos. 6:6) he says, I want mercy, not sacrifice. In short, the prophets all present this truth, especially in several places in Isaiah: 1:12, 58:1, and 66:3. For we often see that where God complains that sacrifices have been corrupted by evil men, he not only rejects the sacrifices and declares that they are fruitless, but he adds that his anger is kindled by this corruption. We have to bear in mind the following distinction: when men observe God's ordinance and use ceremonies to nourish and fortify their faith, these rituals assist and strengthen the genuine worship of God. However, when hypocrites simply follow rituals without engaging their hearts and believe that these rituals serve to appease God, then

God not only dismisses the ceremonies as useless trash, but in fact rejects them and fiercely condemns them as filth and vile doings that pervert his worship.

[Verses 14 and 15]

14. *Make a sacrifice of praise to God.* This second part sheds light on the doctrine we saw earlier, for if God had only said that sacrifices were useless, we could well have wondered why God ordered people to offer such acts of worship to him. Now the contrast with true sacrifices offered to God removes this difficulty. God does not reject sacrifices, so long as they are put to proper use. The aim of serving God is a principle that is naturally and profoundly imprinted in human hearts. But since human nature is totally incapable of serving God purely and spiritually, people have made up and imagined something to cover themselves. While men see that they gain nothing by serving God according to their own whims, they still remain stuck in their superstitions, because they fear or are even terrified of rejecting all religion and service of God. Therefore, until the way to serve God rightly and appropriately is known, ceremonies are always popular. Furthermore, the words *Praise* and *Prayer* are synecdoches because the prophet only touches on a part of the true service of God when he orders that God be acknowledged as the source of all good, and that he be given the praise he deserves. We are to give God his due, to turn to his goodness, to place all our cares in his lap, and to seek deliverance only through him, and finally, to give thanks to him for delivering us. Indeed faith, self-denial, new life, patience in tribulations — all of these are the true sacrifices that God favors. It is hardly surprising that the prophet summed up the whole in a few words, given that prayer stems from faith. Faith is always linked to patience and to the mortification of the flesh, and a true acknowledgment of God's blessings originates only in the warmth of a true and pure heart. To show that prayer and praise are a spiritual service, he contrasts them to all ceremonies and outward claims to serve God. It is wrong to say that he reverses the order when he begins with praise. It is true that this approach can seem ridiculous, given that prayer is the starting point for thanksgiving. However, since the foundation of prayer is rooted in giving God the honor he deserves, and since the first principles of faith are to look to God as the only source of all good things, the prophet [in these verses] had good reason to put praise first. Furthermore, given that God bestows his gifts on us even before our birth and before we have any need to call on his name, we owe him the testimony of our thanks. In short, those who use their powers of good judgment and reasoning will know to start with the sacrifice of praise. And yet there is no need to work at this issue, since the prophet has taken into account the limited understanding of the people by giving a simple description of the spiritual service of God, which includes praise, prayers, and thanksgiving. The added injunction to make one's vows is a reference to the practices under the law, as in Psalm 116:12, "What shall I render to the Lord for all his benefits to me? I will take the cup of salvation,

A synecdoche is a figure of speech, where (in this instance) the part (praise and prayer) stands in for the whole (worship).

and call on the name of the Lord." Overall, he calls on the children of God to acknowledge the divine gifts, which they usually testified to via solemn sacrifices in ancient times. But given that this passage is wonderfully worth considering, we should reflect on this teaching at greater length. First, we should note that what it says about serving God spiritually applies equally to the Old Testament Jews and to us. For when Christ wanted to show that there was no service more acceptable to God, he used as a basis the idea that God is a Spirit (John 4:24). And God did not suddenly start to be a Spirit after the ceremonies of the Law were abolished. Therefore, it is clear that God wanted to be served by the patriarchs in the same way as now. God put the ceremonies in place for the sake of the time period. When he abolished the ceremonies, he did so for our sake. In fact, the service is identical in its essence: it only differs in its outward form, since God wanted to accommodate himself to the level of his unlearned and weak people. He held his hand out to them through these ceremonies and other starting points, but he is more straightforward with us, who have emerged into adulthood following the coming of Christ — and yet God remains always the same. The **Manicheans'** claim that God changes because of the varied forms of government of the church is as foolish an objection as someone who would hold that God was changeable because the weather is not constant throughout the year: spring follows winter, and summer follows spring, and fall follows summer in an unceasing circuit. Thus all outward rituals are barren and minimally significant on their own. They only serve to edify the people's faith if they call upon God with pure hearts. . . .

15. In verse fifteen, we are first told to pray, with the connected promise that the prayers of those who turn to God will not be offered in vain, and then we are called to offer thanks. The reference to the day of affliction does not mean that our obligation to pray to God should be limited to such times, but rather the faithful should pray daily, and even at every moment of each day. Thus, even if we are at peace and safe from harm, and everything is going well and no evil threatens us, we should persevere in prayer, especially since we know that we will be done for if God takes even a small measure of his grace away from us. But because our faith is tested more during times of adversity, the phrase "day of affliction" is there for a purpose, as if the prophet were saying that we should seek God in all our times of need, especially because he is our sole harbor of salvation. Furthermore, given that men usually quake with fear in the presence of God, either because his infinite glory terrifies them, or because the knowledge of their own worth casts them down, God's promise follows on immediately to encourage or even prod us to pray with sure and certain trust. However, when God promises to grant our desires and supplications, he also requires us to show our gratitude to him. Indeed, when we see here that prayer is the first key step in the service of God, we must diligently do full homage to God if we want to show that we are God-fearing. Therefore, the current and continuing corruption in the Papacy is all the more vile and detestable in that they decided to intermingle angels, the

Calvin uses a range of scriptural references in his analysis. What can you infer both about Calvin's biblical knowledge and about his audience's familiarity with Scripture?

Evaluate Calvin's reasoning here. Does his interpretation make sense? What preconceptions about different faith practices lie at the root of his analysis?

The Manicheans were followers of the teachings of a Persian named Mani, who lived in the 3rd century AD. Manicheans had a strongly dualist worldview and felt that the physical world in all its aspects (meat eating, procreation, etc.) impeded the human soul's ascent to the divine light.

deceased saints, and God. They allege that they are seeking advocates who can intercede for them before God. But first of all, since Christ's role as mediator is not being acknowledged, it is clear that their patrons and advocates are put in his place. And second, their form of prayer shows clearly that they make no distinction between God and a saint, whether great or small. They indiscriminately petition Saint Claude as much as God, and they mutter their **paternosters** in front of Saint Catherine's image in the same way as if they were presenting their requests to God. Now according to the Papists, they do not think that they harm God's honor by praying to the dead, for they do not think that these prayers conflict with God's service. They babble so much about veneration (*latrie*) that they leave nothing for prayer. But if we evaluate the words of the prophet accurately, it will be easy to see that all of the honor and reverence owed to God dissipates if he alone is not the focus of prayer, as he should be. If the Papists are asked if sacrifices to the dead are allowable, they will deny it vigorously, and rightly so. Even today they agree that it is wrong to offer a sacrifice to Saint Peter or Saint Paul, especially since common sense rejects such a great sacrilege. And when God prefers prayers directed to him over and against any sacrifice, is he not showing clearly that praying to the dead is a heinous offense? Therefore it follows that even though the Papists kneel before God a thousand times, they still steal away most of his glory when they turn to the saints. As for the explicit mention of suffering [in the Psalm], it provides a large measure of comfort to weak consciences that are not yet firmly secure. For as soon as God takes away from us the testimony of his grace and his love for us, we fall into doubt, wondering whether he is taking care of our salvation or not, and we are even tempted to distrust him. But in fact, God is urging us through these very afflictions and adversities from his hand to seek him and pray to him, as if prodded by a spur. . . .

16. *But to the evil one.* He [the Psalmist] now rebukes more openly those who pretended to serve God and who had no other religion than carrying out their ceremonies, as if they could dazzle God's eyes. Indeed, we know that for their part the people of this world love to conceal themselves under these false disguises. Here God asserts that those who try to hide the impurity of their heart and their wicked lives under the cloak of the rituals they follow do not gain any favor with him. This pronouncement that should have been accepted by all has been badly received by the Jews. It is true that everyone agrees that God's service is tainted unless it is heartfelt. Even the pagan poets were forced to admit this truth, and we know that evildoers were not allowed to attend sacrifices or enter temples. Yet what was engraved on everyone's heart was choked by hypocrisy and abolished to such an extent that the worst of the worst dared to present themselves before God, as if by their antics God could be indebted to them. Therefore, the prophets had good reason to reiterate this doctrine so regularly, namely, that the more that evil people work to pretend to honor God, the more they incur his wrath because of their fraud and deceit. Again we see how God's Spirit proclaims loud and clear that to pretend to serve God for show without true faith and repentance is a sacrilege and a dreadful

In this context paternosters refer to repeated rote prayers, such as the Lord's Prayer (*Pater Noster* in Latin), usually recited in Latin.

misuse of God's name. However, it seems to be impossible to get the Papists to leave aside their diabolical error, namely, that these empty gestures find God's favor if they are done for a worthwhile cause and with good intentions. They do admit that only those in a state of grace deserve to be honored, but they maintain that simple acts of worship serve to prepare us to receive God's grace even if the heart is not completely virtuous. Thus if a monk were to rise from his bed of fornication and present to God his stinking and polluted mouth and sing Psalms with a cold and indifferent heart, or if a fornicator, or a perjurer, or a swindler were to buy off his evil deeds by paying for Masses to be sung, going on pilgrimage, or carrying out similar foolishness, they would not accept that to do so is a waste of time. In contrast, God states that those who perform these outward acts of faith without a pure heart not only waste their time but are also guilty of sacrilege, given that they wickedly misuse his name. . . .

23. *Offering praise.* For the third time the prophet says that God is most pleased by our sacrifice of praise, through which we testify to our thanksgiving for the gifts we have received from him. This repetition is not superfluous for two reasons. First, we are much too quick to forget God's benefits, and hardly take the time to appreciate one out of every thousand, and even then only superficially and in passing. Second, we do not value praising God as much as we should. Even though it is the main obligation and practice of piety that God wants us to practice for our whole life, we look down on it as a common and frivolous thing. Yet the Psalmist states that the true service of God lies in the sacrifice of praise, for the phrase "will glorify God" means that he is truly and properly served in this fashion, and that God receives the glory due to him when men praise and give thanks for his blessings with pure hearts and humble thanksgiving. In contrast, the other rituals carried out so diligently by the hypocrites are rejected by God and do not form part of his service. However, we must also bear in mind what I said earlier, namely, that the word "praise" includes both faith and prayer. For only personal experience can lead us to open our mouths in praise of God. And we cannot get a sense of God's goodness except through faith. Thus we must conclude that based on the result or the effect, the word "praise" means all spiritual worship. This is why later on the prophet tells those who want their worship to be approved by God to "walk on the right paths." Some think that "to walk on the path" means simply to confess one's sins, while others explain it as removing stumbling blocks from the path and preparing the path that everyone should follow. Both of these interpretations seem forced to me. For my part, I am convinced that he is contrasting the right path to the path of errors that is full of wrong turns, followed by those who pretend to seek God. Thus the Psalmist means that there is no way to reach God except by walking in purity of heart, honesty, and simplicity.

Based on this passage, would any human worship be acceptable to God, since sinful humans cannot claim purity of heart?

Source: Karin Maag translated these sections from Calvin's commentary on Psalm 9 and Psalm 50 from the 1561 French second edition: *Commentaires de M. Jean Calvin sur le livre des Pseaumes* ([Geneva]: Conrad Badius, 1561). Psalm 9: fols. ciiii verso – cv recto; cvi verso; cvii verso; Psalm 50: xviii verso; yi recto – yiii verso; yiv recto. The first French edition was published in 1558, and was a translation of the first Latin edition of 1557.

Calvin's Commentary on John 4 (1553)

Calvin's commentary on John's Gospel was first published in 1553, in two editions in that same year, one in Latin and the other in French. Calvin dedicated the work to the Genevan city council. In this section, commenting on John 4, in which Jesus met the Samaritan woman, Calvin sought to make clear distinctions between Jewish (and Catholic) worship practices and those of the Reformed faith, which Calvin felt were most closely based on the teachings of God's Word.

John 4:22-26

22. *Ye worship*. This is a sentence worth remembering. By it we are taught that we are not to essay anything in religion rashly or unthinkingly. For unless there is knowledge present, it is not God that we worship but a specter or ghost. . . .

. . . What it all comes to is that God is only worshiped properly in the certainty of faith, which is necessarily born of the Word of God; and hence it follows that all who forsake the Word fall into idolatry. For Christ plainly declares that an idol or an empty image is put in God's place when men are ignorant of the true God; and he accuses of ignorance all to whom God has not revealed himself. As soon as we are deprived of the light of his Word, darkness and blindness reign in us.

And we must notice that when the Jews in their faithlessness annulled the covenant of eternal life made with the Fathers, they were deprived of the treasure which they had possessed until then; for they had not yet been rejected from God's Church. But now that they deny the Son, they have nothing in common with the Father. The same is true of all who have left the pure faith of the Gospel for their own and other men's inventions. However much in their obstinacy those who worship God from their own notions or men's traditions flatter and praise themselves, this one Word thundering from Heaven overthrows every divine and holy thing they think they possess: "Ye worship that which ye know not." And so, if our religion is to be approved by God, it must needs rest on knowledge conceived of his Word.

23. *But the hour cometh*. Now follows the latter clause on the repealing of the worship of the Law. When he says that the hour cometh or will come, he teaches that the order handed down by Moses is not for everlasting; when he says that the hour is now come, he puts an end to the ceremonies and so declares that "the time of reformation" has been fulfilled. Meanwhile he approves of the temple and the priesthood and all the ceremonies pertaining to them, so far as their past use is concerned (Heb. 9:10). Moreover, to show that God does not wish to be worshiped either in Jerusalem or in Mount Gerizim, he takes up a higher principle — that the true worship of him lies in the Spirit. Whence it follows that he may be worshiped properly in all places.

Calvin is willing to wrestle with seeming inconsistencies between his own perspective and what the text is saying. He acknowledges that in this passage Jesus was supporting the ritual and religious practices of the Jews of his day, even though that admission weakens Calvin's argument that the Jewish ceremonies were put to an end by Christ.

But here we must ask, first, why and in what sense the worship of God may be called spiritual? To understand this we must note the antithesis between the Spirit and external figures, as between the shadow and the substance. The worship of God is said to consist in the Spirit because it is only the inward faith of the heart that produces prayer and purity of conscience and denial of ourselves, that we may be given up to obedience of God as holy sacrifices.

This gives rise to another question: Did not the Fathers worship him spiritually under the Law? I reply, Since God is always true to himself, he did not, from the beginning of the world, approve any other worship than the spiritual, which is consistent with his nature. This is abundantly attested by Moses himself. He declares in many places that the only aim of the Law is that the people shall cleave to God in faith and with a pure conscience. The Prophets express it still more clearly when they harshly attack the people's hypocrisy in that they thought they had satisfied God when they had performed the sacrifices and the outward display. There is no need here to cite the many testimonies which come everywhere, but the most remarkable passages are Psalm 50; Isaiah 1, 58, 66; Micah 6; and Amos 5. But although the worship of God under the Law was spiritual, it was wrapped up in so many outward ceremonies that it had a flavor of carnality and earthliness. This is why in Galatians 4:9 Paul calls the ceremonies "flesh" and "the beggarly elements of the world." Similarly, the author of the Epistle to the Hebrews says that the old Sanctuary with all that belonged to it was earthly (Heb. 9:1). Hence we may well say that the worship of the Law was spiritual in its substance but something carnal and earthly in its form. For that whole economy whose reality is now openly manifested was shadowy.

We now see what the Jews had in common with us and in what way they were different. In all ages God wanted to be worshiped by faith, prayer, thanksgiving, purity of heart, and innocence of life. And never did he delight in any other sacrifices, though in the Law there were various additions so that the Spirit and truth were concealed under coverings. But now that the veil of the temple has been rent, there is nothing obscure or hidden. There are indeed among us today certain outward exercises of godliness which our childishness needs. But they are moderate and sober enough not to obscure the naked truth of Christ. In short, what was sketchily outlined to the Fathers is now openly displayed to us.

But under the Papacy this distinction is not only confused but altogether overturned. For there the shadows are no less dense than they used to be under Judaism. It cannot be denied that here Christ is making a plain distinction between us and the Jews. By whatever subterfuges the Papists may try to get out of it, it is certain that we differ from the Fathers only in the outward form, because in their spiritual worship of God they were bound to ceremonies which were abolished by the coming of Christ. Therefore all who burden the Church with an excessive host of ceremonies despoil her of the presence of Christ, so far as lies in them. I think nothing of the weak excuse that many ordinary folk in our day need those aids as

Notice again how Calvin cross-references scriptural passages to support his exegesis. In what ways could these references contribute to active learning on the part of his hearers and readers?

What might Calvin have in mind? What "outward exercises of godliness" might he have been thinking about?

Articulate in your own words the main points of Calvin's argument — why were the ceremonial worship practices of ancient Israel acceptable in some way, when the present-day Catholic ceremonial worship practices were not?

much as the Jews did of old. For we must always pay attention to the way the Lord wished his Church to be governed, for he alone knows best what is advantageous for us. But it is sure that nothing is more contrary to the divine ordinance than the gross and doubly carnal show which prevails in the Papacy. The shadows of the Law certainly hid the Spirit, but these masks of the Papacy disfigure him altogether. Therefore we must on no account connive at such horrible and unworthy corruptions. However cleverly men or those too timid to correct abuses may argue that these things are indifferent and should be regarded as neither good nor bad, it is simply unbearable that the rule laid down by Christ should be violated.

The true worshipers. Christ seems in passing to reprove the obstinacy which later broke forth in many. For we know how obstinate and contentious the Jews were in defending the ceremonies they were used to when the Gospel was revealed. The statement has, however, a wider significance. He knows that the world will never be free from superstitions, and therefore he separates the godly and true worshipers from the perverted and hypocritical. Armed with this testimony, let us not hesitate to condemn the Papists in all their inventions and despise their reproaches. For why should we fear when we hear that God is pleased with this bare and simple worship, which is disdained by the Papists because it is not swollen with a mass of ceremonies? And what good does the empty show of the flesh do them, which Christ says quenches the Spirit? What it is to worship God in Spirit and truth appears plainly from what has already been said. It is to remove the coverings of the ancient ceremonies and retain simply what is spiritual in the worship of God. For the truth of the worship of God rests in the Spirit, and ceremonies are, so to say, adventitious. And here again it must be observed that truth is not contrasted to falsehood but to the outward addition of the figures; so that it is, as they say, the pure and simple substance of spiritual worship.

24. *God is Spirit.* Here is confirmation from the very nature of God. Since men are flesh, it is not surprising that they delight in what corresponds to their natures. This is why they invent many things in the worship of God which are full of insubstantial display. They should first consider that they are dealing with God, who no more agrees with the flesh than fire does with water. When we are concerned with the worship of God, it ought to suffice in restraining the wantonness of our mind if we just think that God is so unlike us that those things which please us most are to him disgusting and boring. What if hypocrites are so blinded by their pride that they are not afraid to subject God to their will, or rather lust? Let us know that modesty does not hold the lowest place in the true worship of God and regard with suspicion whatever is pleasing to the flesh.

Source: John Calvin, *Calvin's Commentaries: The Gospel according to St John 1-10,* trans. T. H. L. Parker, ed. David W. Torrance and Thomas F. Torrance (Grand Rapids: Eerdmans, 1961), pp. 98-103. This translation is a revision of the 1847 English translation done by William Pringle. Pringle based his work on the "original Latin," presumably the 1553 first edition, albeit likely a later edition. Nineteenth-century scholars were notoriously bad at giving specific information about their sources.

Calvin's Commentary on 1 Corinthians 11 (1546)

Calvin's commentary on 1 Corinthians was first published in Latin in 1546, with the first French edition (translated by an unknown translator) appearing in the following year. Calvin's analysis of the eleventh chapter of 1 Corinthians gave him an unparalleled opportunity to lay out both his understanding of the sacrament of the Lord's Supper and his challenges to other interpretations of the sacrament.

1 Corinthians 11:23-30

Up to this point Paul has been showing what was wrong; now he begins to teach them [the Corinthians] the best way to rectify matters. For the institution of Christ is a fixed standard, so that the slightest deviation from it means that you fall into error. Since the Corinthians had departed from this standard, he calls them back to it. This passage ought to be carefully studied, for it shows that the only remedy for removing and correcting corruptions is to get back to the unadulterated institution of God. That is what our Lord himself did when he was speaking about marriage (Matt. 19:3). The scribes made reference to custom and also to the concession which Moses allowed, but he himself only brought forward his Father's institution, because it is an inviolable principle. When we do this today, the Papists make loud protest that we are tampering with and spoiling everything. We make it quite clear that it is not just that they have departed from the primary institution of our Lord in one way only, but that they have corrupted it in a thousand ways. Nothing is more obvious than that their Mass is poles apart from the Holy Supper of Our Lord. I go a step further. We point out that it is swarming with wicked abominations. It therefore stands in need of correction. Our demand is this, and it is clear that Paul had to make it too, that the institution of our Lord be the common standard for us, and that both sides be in agreement about that. They [the Papists] make violent protest against that. Now you know the nature of the controversy about the Lord's Supper in our own day.

23. *I have received from the Lord.* By these words Paul means that the only authority that carries any weight in the church is that of the Lord. For he might have put it this way: "I have not delivered to you something I have made up. When I came to you, I had not invented a new supper, the product of my own imagination; but I regard Christ as its originator, and from him I have received what I have personally delivered to you. Return therefore to this fundamental source." Therefore, when we have turned our backs on the rules which men make, the authority of Christ alone will remain, unshaken.

On the night in which he was betrayed. The reference to the time reminds us that the

Returning to the source was a hallmark of early modern Christian humanism — in this instance, the original source was the words of Scripture.

purpose of the mystery is that we may be confirmed in the blessing that the death of Christ gives. For the Lord could have entrusted the covenant to the disciples on some earlier occasion, but he was waiting for the time of his sacrifice, so that the Apostles would not have long to wait before seeing what he had foreshadowed in the bread and wine actually fulfilled in his body.

If anyone infers from this that we therefore ought to celebrate the Supper at night, and after eating an ordinary meal, I answer that when we look at our Lord's actions, we must consider what he intended us to do. It is certain that he had no intention of delivering instruction to them about nocturnal rites, something like those of Ceres, and also that he did not mean to invite his people to his spiritual feast after they had eaten a hearty meal. Such actions of Christ as we are not asked to imitate should not be regarded as belonging to his institution. That is why there is no difficulty about refuting the cunning arguments of the Papists, by which they evade what I have already said about retaining and preserving what Christ actually instituted, and only that.

"Therefore," they say, "we will only receive the Lord's Supper at night, and after we have dined, not after fasting." Such talk, I say, is a waste of breath; because it is an easy matter to determine what the Lord did for the express purpose that we should follow his example; one should rather say, what he did in order to direct us to do it also.

24. *When he had given thanks.* Paul says in 1 Timothy 4:5 that every gift we receive from God's hand is sanctified to us through the Word of God and prayer. Nowhere, therefore, do we read of our Lord eating with his disciples, without the fact that he gave thanks being recorded. There is no doubt that he has taught us, by his own example, to do the same thing. Yet this thanksgiving goes deeper than that, for Christ is giving thanks to his Father for his mercy toward the human race, and his priceless gift of redemption; and he encourages us by his example, so that, as often as we approach the Holy Table, we may lift up our hearts in acknowledgment of the boundless love of God toward us, and be inflamed with true gratitude to him.

Take, eat, this is my body. Since it was Paul's intention here to teach us about the right way to observe the sacrament, and since he does it briefly, we should, on our part, study what he has to say with careful attention, not passing over anything lightly, in view of the fact that everything that he says very much needs to be known, and deserves the closest consideration.

In the first place let us note that here Christ divides the bread among the disciples so that they may all eat it together; and in this way all may share and share alike. Therefore when a common table is not prepared for all who believe, when they are not invited to the common breaking of bread, when, in short, the faithful do not share with each other, there are no grounds for describing the proceedings as the Lord's Supper. But why do they call people

How strong is Calvin's argument here? Does the Catholic critique of the Reformed church's selective following of Christ's Passover meal carry weight?

Notice the centrality of thanksgiving in the sacrament — does that hold true in the liturgies and practices of Reformed churches today?

together for the Mass? Perhaps the answer is that they may be sent away again unsatisfied, after seeing a pointless show. It has, therefore, nothing in common with the Supper.

From this verse we also gather that the promise of Christ no more applies to the Mass than to the feast of the college of priests of Mars. For when Christ promises that he will give us his body, he similarly commands us to take the bread and eat it. If we do not obey this commandment of his, all our boasting about having his promise is to no avail. Let me put this in another way, in language that is more customary: the promise is bound up with the commandment, as if the latter were a condition; the promise therefore only becomes effective if the condition is fulfilled. To take an example: it is written (Ps. 50:15), "Call upon me: I will hear you." What we have to do is to obey God's commandment so that he may carry out what he has promised us; otherwise we deprive ourselves of its fulfilment. But what about the Papists? They ignore the question of sharing, and consecrate the bread for a totally different purpose, at the same time making it their boast that they have the body of the Lord. Since they cause an ungodly divorce in separating the things which Christ has joined together, it is plain that their boasting is a hollow thing. Therefore, as often as they quote the words "This is my body," we must retort with the other words which precede them, "take" and "eat." For the meaning of the words is: "By sharing in the breaking of bread, according to the order and rite which I have commanded, you will also be sharing in my body." Thus when a person eats it on his own, the promise is non-effective in that case. Besides, these words teach us what the Lord wants us to do. "Take," he says. Therefore, those who sacrifice to God take their lead from some other teacher than Christ, for he does not give us instructions in these words to carry out a sacrifice.

But what do the Papists actually say about the Mass? At first they were presumptuous enough to allege that it was right and proper for it to be called a sacrifice. They now admit that it is a commemorative sacrifice indeed, but in this way, that by their daily offering the blessing of redemption is brought to the living and the dead. Whatever it may be, they certainly present something that looks like a sacrifice (*immolationis spectaculum*). In the first place it is a high-handed thing to do, seeing that there is no command of Christ to justify it. But they commit a still more serious sin in doing this, because, while Christ intended that the purpose of the Supper should be that we take and eat, they have corrupted it to serve exactly the opposite purpose.

This is my body. I shall not go over once again the unhappy battles which have been disturbing the church in our time over the meaning of these words. I only wish it were possible to bury all remembrance of them in everlasting oblivion! I shall give my own views about the words, not only sincerely and honestly, but also without any reservation, as I usually do.

Christ calls the bread his body. I reject, without further argument, the absurd notion that our Lord did not show the bread to the Apostles, but his own body, which was plain before

Why might Calvin have wanted to forget about all the controversies in the church over the interpretation of these words?

their eyes; for immediately afterwards there come the words, "This cup is the new covenant in my blood." Let there be no further questioning of the fact that here Christ is referring to the bread.

But now we turn to the question, What does he mean when he refers to the bread? In order to arrive at the meaning we must bear in mind that he is speaking figuratively; and he would be an exceedingly bold man who would deny that. Why, then, is the term *body* applied to the bread? I think everybody would agree that it is for the same reason that John calls the Holy Spirit a dove (John 1:32). So far we are in agreement. Further, in the case of the Spirit the reason was that he had appeared in the form of a dove; therefore the name, Spirit, is transferred to the visible sign. Is there any reason why we should not say that metonymy is used here in a similar way, and the name *body* given to the bread, because it is a sign or symbol of the body? If any disagree with me, they will perhaps pardon me; but it seems to me that it is only causing trouble to persist in arguing about that. I am therefore quite clear in my own mind that this is a sacramental way of speaking (*sacramentalem loquendi modum*), when the Lord applies to the sign the name of the reality signified (*rei signatae*).

> A metonymy is a figure of speech in which a word associated with another is used in place of it.

We must now go a step further, and ask why metonymy is used. My answer to that is that the name of the reality signified is not given to the sign simply because it stands for it (*sit figura*); but rather because it is a symbol by which the reality is held out to us (*exhibetur*). For I do not accept the comparisons which some people make with secular or worldly things, for they are in a different category from the sacraments of our Lord. The statue of Hercules is called "Hercules"; but it is nothing else but a bare, empty representation (*figura*). But the dove is described as the Spirit, because it is a definite pledge (*tessera*) of the presence of the invisible Spirit. Therefore the bread is the body of Christ, because it bears indubitable witness to the fact that the very body, which it stands for, is held out to us; or because, in offering us that symbol, the Lord is also giving us his body at the same time; for Christ is not one to deceive us, and make fools of us with empty representations. Accordingly, it is as clear as day to me that here the reality is joined to the sign; in other words, we really do become sharers in the body of Christ, so far as spiritual power is concerned, just as much as we eat the bread.

We must now look into the mode of participation. The Papists press their doctrine of transubstantiation upon us. They hold that, when the consecration has taken place, the substance of the bread no longer remains, but only the accidents. Over against this fabrication we set not only the plain words of Scripture, but also the very nature of the sacraments. For what will the signification (*significatio*) of the Supper be, if there is no analogy between the visible sign and the spiritual reality (*si nulla sit inter signum visibile et rem spiritualem analogia*)? They think that the sign has the false and misleading appearance (*speciem*) of bread. What, then, about the reality signified? It can only be a mere piece of make-believe. Therefore, if there ought to be a corresponding relationship (*convenientiam*) between the sign and the reality (*veritate*) behind it, then the bread must be real (*verum*) bread, not imaginary, in

> "Accidents" here means the outward appearance of bread.

order to represent the real (*verum*) body of Christ. Besides, this verse shows that it is not just that the body of Christ is given to us, but that it is given to us as food. Now, it is not the color at all, but the substance of the bread that nourishes us. To put it in a nutshell, if the reality itself is to be a genuine reality, the sign must also be a genuine sign.

Therefore, having rejected the nonsense of the Papists, let us see the way in which the body of Christ is given to us. Some people's explanation is that it is given to us when we are made sharers in all the benefits, which Christ procured for us in his own body; by that I mean when, by faith, we embrace Christ, crucified for us and raised from the dead, and, in that way, come to share effectively in all his benefits. Those who think like this have every right to their point of view. But I myself maintain that it is only after we obtain Christ himself that we come to share in the benefits of Christ. And I further maintain that he is obtained, not just when we believe that he was sacrificed for us, but when he dwells in us, when he is one with us, when we are members of his flesh, when, in short, we become united in one life and substance (if I may say so) with him. Besides, I am paying attention to the implication of the words, for Christ does not offer us only the benefit of his death and resurrection, but the self-same body in which he suffered and rose again. My conclusion is that the body of Christ is really (*reali-ter*), to use the usual word, i.e., truly (*vere*), given to us in the Supper, so that it may be health-giving food for our souls. I am adopting the usual terms, but I mean that our souls are fed by the substance of his body, so that we are truly (*vere*) made one with him; or, what amounts to the same thing, that a life-giving power from the flesh of Christ (*vim ex. Christi carne vivifi-cam*) is poured into us through the medium of the Spirit, even though it is at a great distance from us, and is not mixed with us (*nec misceatur nobiscum*).

Only one problem remains: How is it possible for his body, which is in Heaven, to be given to us here on earth? Some people think that the body of Christ is boundless, and is not confined to any one place, but fills both Heaven and earth, like the essence of God. That notion is so absurd that it does not need to be refuted. The Schoolmen discuss the question of his body of glory with more acuteness, but all their teaching simply amounts to this, that Christ is to be found in the bread, as if he were shut up (*inclusus*) in it. The outcome is that men look with amazement upon the bread, and give adoration to it as if it were Christ. Should anyone ask them whether it is the bread they worship, or its appearance (*speciem*), they are certain to answer him with a firm "Neither," but all the same, when they are going to give Christ their adoration, they turn in the direction of the bread. By that I mean that it is not merely a matter of turning their eyes and their whole body, but also their thoughts. Now, what else is this but pure idolatry? But the sharing in the Lord's body, which, I maintain, is offered to us in the Supper, demands neither a local presence, nor the descent of Christ, nor an infinite extension of his body, nor anything of that sort; for, in view of the fact that the Supper is a heavenly act, there is nothing absurd about saying that Christ remains in Heaven and is yet received by us. For the way in which he imparts himself to us is by the secret power of the

Calvin is referring here to medieval theologians.

This emphasis on rising up to heaven draws on an early church phrase, *sursum corda* ("lift up your hearts"), often used in Lord's Supper liturgies. It echoes the language of Col. 3:1-2.

Holy Spirit, a power which is able not only to bring together, but also to join together, things which are separated by distance, and by a great distance at that.

But to be capable of this impartation, we must rise up to Heaven. In this connection our physical senses are of no avail to us, and so it is faith that must come to our help. When I speak of "faith," I do not mean any kind of opinion, which depends upon what men make up, since there are many people constantly boasting about their "faith," and who are extremely wide of the mark on the point at issue here. What then? You see bread, and nothing else, but you hear that it is a sign of the body of Christ. Be quite sure that the Lord will really carry out what you understand the words to mean: that his body, which you do not see at all, is spiritual food for you. It seems unbelievable that we are fed by the flesh of Christ, which is so far away from us. Let us remember that it is a secret and wonderful work done by the Holy Spirit, and it would be sinful of you to measure it by the little standard of your own understanding. In the meantime, however, get rid of stupid notions, which keep your eyes glued on the bread. Let Christ keep his flesh, which is real flesh (*veram carnis naturam*), and do not hold the mistaken view that his body stretches all over Heaven and earth. Do not tear him into pieces by your fanciful ideas, and do not worship him in this place or that according to your carnal apprehension (*pro carnali tuo sensu*). Let him remain in his heavenly glory; and aspire to reach Heaven yourself, that, from it, he may impart himself to you.

These few thoughts will satisfy the minds of right-minded, humble people. My advice to the inquisitive is to look elsewhere for the satisfaction of their craving for information.

Which is broken for you. Some think that this refers to the distribution of the bread, because it was necessary that Christ's body be preserved intact, to conform to the prediction in Exodus 12:46: "not a bone of him shall be broken." For myself, while acknowledging that Paul has made allusion to the breaking of the bread, yet I take "broken" to be used here in the sense of sacrificed; certainly this is not the proper use of the word, but it is not out of place. For even if "not a bone of him" was damaged, yet, since his body was exposed first of all to so much torture and suffering, and then to the punishment of death in its cruelest form, it cannot be said that it was uninjured. That is what Paul means by its being broken. This, however, is the second part of the promise, and it must be not passed over lightly. For the Lord does not offer his body to us, just his body with nothing else said about it, but his body as having been sacrificed for us. The first part, then, tells us that his body is held out to us; this second part brings out what we come to enjoy through it, viz., a share in redemption, and the application to us of the benefit of his sacrifice. That is why the Supper is a mirror which represents Christ crucified to us, so that a man cannot receive the Supper and enjoy its benefits unless he embraces Christ crucified.

This do in remembrance of me. The Supper is therefore a memorial (μνημόσυνον) provided to assist our weakness; for if we were otherwise sufficiently mindful of the death of Christ, this help would be superfluous. This applies to all the sacraments, for they help us in our weakness. But we shall soon learn what sort of memorial of himself Christ wanted us to keep in the Supper.

Some draw the inference from this phrase that, in these circumstances, Christ is not present in the Supper, because there can only be a memorial (*memoria*) of something that is absent. That can be easily answered: according to this way of thinking of the Supper as remembrance (*recordatio*), Christ is indeed absent from it. For Christ is not visibly present, and is not seen by our eyes as are the symbols, which, by representing him, stir us up to remember him. Finally, in order to be present with us, he does not change his place, but from Heaven he sends down the efficacy of his flesh to be present in us.

25. *The cup, after they had taken their supper*. The apostle seems to suggest that there was a certain interval of time between the giving out of the bread and the cup; and the Evangelists do not make it quite clear if the whole was a continuous action. Indeed, that does not matter very much, because it may well have been that the Lord gave some discourse, which would have come in between his giving out of the bread and the cup. But, since he was doing and saying nothing that was unrelated to the mystery, there is no need for us to say that its administration was disorganized or broken up. I did not want to adopt Erasmus's rendering, "when supper was over," because ambiguity should be avoided in a matter of such great importance.

This cup is the new covenant. What is predicated of the cup applies also to the bread; and so he is using these words to express what he had already said more briefly, that the bread is his body. For we have it for this reason, that it may be a covenant in his body, i.e., a *covenant* which has been once for all ratified by the sacrifice of his body, and is now confirmed by eating, namely, when believers eat that sacrifice. And so, where Paul and Luke speak of the *covenant in my blood*, Matthew and Mark speak of *the blood of the covenant*, which amounts to the same thing. For the blood was poured out to reconcile us to God, and now we drink it spiritually in order to have a share in that reconciliation. Therefore, in the Supper we have both the covenant (*foedus*) and a reinforcing pledge of the covenant.

If the Lord spares me, I shall speak about the word "covenant" or "testament" (*testamentum*) in the commentary on the Epistle to the Hebrews. But it is well known that sacraments are described as "testaments," because they provide us with "testimonies" of God's goodwill, in order to make our minds all the surer of it. For the Lord deals with us in a similar way to men, who make their covenants with each other with solemn rites. This way of speaking is by no means unsuitable, because, by reason of the connection between word and sign, the covenant of the Lord really is bound up with the sacraments, and the term *covenant* (*foedus*) bears a relation to us, or embraces us. This will be of great value for understanding the nature of the sacraments, for, if they are covenants, then they contain promises, which may awaken men's consciences to an assurance of salvation. It follows

Erasmus of Rotterdam (1466-1536), the great Christian humanist, was known for his Greek edition of the New Testament, in which he went back to the original sources rather than to the standard Latin Vulgate Bible. Notice how Calvin engaged with his contemporaries as he sought to present and explain the biblical text.

from this that they are not only outward signs of the faith we profess, for men to see, but also aids to our own inner life of faith.

This do, as oft as ye drink. Christ has therefore instituted a twofold sign in the Supper. Those things which God hath joined together, let not man put asunder. Therefore to distribute the bread without the cup is to mutilate the institution of Christ. For we are listening to the words of Christ. As he commands us to eat the bread, so he commands us to drink of the cup. Complying with one half of the commandment and disregarding the other is nothing else but making a mockery of what he has laid down. But debarring the people from the cup which Christ gives to everybody, as happens under the tyranny of the Pope, is without a doubt a diabolical presumption. Their [the Papists'] quibble that Christ was speaking to the Apostles, and not to the ordinary people, is exceedingly childish, and is easily refuted from this very passage; for here Paul is addressing himself to men and women without distinction, and to the whole church in fact, and says that he has delivered this to them in accordance with the Lord's commandment. By what spirit will those who have dared to annul this institution allege they were directed? And yet this gross corruption is also doggedly defended in our own day. Little wonder that they are brazen enough to use speeches and writings in an attempt to justify something which they are defending by fire and sword in such a cruel way!

26. *For as often as ye eat.* Paul now adds a description of the way in which the memorial ought to be kept, viz., with thanksgiving. It is not that the memorial depends completely upon the confession of our lips, for the main point is that the power of the death of Christ should be sealed upon our consciences. But this knowledge ought to move us to praise him openly, so as to let men know, when we are in their company, what we are aware of within ourselves in the presence of God. The Supper is, therefore, if I may say so, a kind of memorial (*quoddam memoriale*) which must always be maintained in the church until the final coming of Christ; and which was instituted for this purpose, that Christ may remind us of the benefit of his death, and that we, on our part, may acknowledge it before men. That is why it is called the *Eucharist.* Therefore, in order that you may celebrate the Supper properly, you must bear in mind that you will have to make profession of your faith.

This shows us quite clearly how impudently they make a mockery of God, who boast that in the Mass they have something answering to the nature of the Supper. For what is the Mass? They admit (for I am not speaking about the Papists, but about the would-be followers of Nicodemus) that it is packed full of detestable superstitions, to which they pretend to be giving their approval by their outward posture. What sort of way is this to proclaim the death of Christ? Are they not rather abandoning it?

Until he come. Since we always stand in need of an aid such as this, as long as we are living in this world, Paul points out that we have been entrusted with this act of remembrance (*re-cordationem*) until Christ appears for judgment. For, in view of the fact that he is not present

One of the hallmarks of Protestant celebrations of Communion was that the people received both the bread and the wine, whereas during a Catholic Mass at the time, people only received the bread or host.

Calvin is referring to people who were Protestant or Protestant sympathizers, but who lived in Catholic areas (in France, for instance) and kept their Protestant beliefs hidden, outwardly conforming to Catholic worship practices, in order to avoid detection and persecution. Why might Calvin have labeled them "followers of Nicodemus"?

with us in a visible form, we need to have some symbol of his spiritual presence with which to occupy our minds.

27. *Wherefore whosoever shall eat the bread . . . unworthily.* If the Lord expects gratitude from us when we receive this mystery; if he wants us to acknowledge his grace with our hearts and make it known with our lips, then the man who has offered him insult rather than honor will not escape without punishment; for the Lord will not tolerate the despising of his commandment.

Now, in order to grasp the meaning of this verse, we must know what "eating unworthily" means. Some people make it apply only to the Corinthians, and to the corruption which had got such a hold in their midst. But my own view is that Paul, as he usually does, moves from that particular suggestion to general teaching, or from one example to a whole class. The Corinthians had one particular fault. Paul takes advantage of this to speak of every kind of fault to be found in the administration or receiving of the Supper. He says: "God will not allow this mystery to be desecrated without punishing it severely."

Therefore, to "eat unworthily" is to ruin the pure and proper use by our own abuse. That is why there are various degrees of unworthiness, so to speak; and some people sin more seriously, while others do so only slightly. Any fornicator, perjurer, drunkard, or cheat, without a shred of penitence, may force his way in. Since reckless contempt such as that bears the mark of a cruel insult to Christ, there is no doubt that anyone like that receives the Supper to his own destruction. Another will come who is not in the grip of any obvious or perceptible fault, but all the same is not as prepared in his heart as he ought to be. Since this complacency or carelessness is a sign of irreverence, it also deserves the punishment of God. Thus, since there are various degrees of eating unworthily, the Lord inflicts lighter punishments on some, severer on others.

Now this verse has given rise to the question, which some people later went on to debate far too hotly, whether people who eat unworthily are in fact eating the body of Christ at all. For some people were so carried away by the controversy as to say that it is received by good and bad alike; and in our own day many loud-mouthed persons are doggedly maintaining that in the very first Supper Peter received no more than Judas. I am indeed reluctant to enter upon a rather fierce debate with anyone about this matter, which, in my opinion, is a peripheral one. But as others take it upon themselves to adopt the attitude of a schoolmaster, and, without any justification, to declaim what suits themselves, and to shout down anyone offering the slightest suggestion of the opposite point of view, we will therefore be pardoned if we quietly give reasons to support what we consider to be the truth.

It is an axiom to me, and I will not allow myself to be shifted from it, that Christ cannot be separated from his Spirit. That convinces me that when we receive his body, it is neither

This concern over possible unworthy participation in the Lord's Supper shaped church discipline in Geneva — see the Consistory records for cases of people barred temporarily from the Lord's Supper because of a range of moral and confessional failings.

It is fair to take with a hefty pinch of salt Calvin's seeming reluctance to get involved in the controversy.

his dead, passive body, nor his body divorced from the grace and power of his Spirit. I will not spend much time in proving what I have just said.

Now if a man has not a vestige of a living faith or of repentance, and nothing of the Spirit of Christ, how can he receive Christ himself? More than that, since he is completely under the control of Satan and sin, how will he be fit to receive Christ? Therefore, on the one hand, I grant that there are persons who truly receive Christ in the Supper and are yet, at the same time, unworthy. Many of the weak, for example, are in that category. On the other hand, I do not take the view that those who bring simply a faith in the historical events of the Gospel (*fidem historicam*), without a lively awareness of repentance and faith, receive only the sign. For I cannot bear to tear Christ apart, and I am horrified at the absurd notion that to unbelievers he gives himself to be eaten in a lifeless form, as it were. And Augustine is thinking along these lines when he says that the wicked receive Christ in the Supper insofar as it is a sacrament (*sacramento tenus*). He puts that more clearly in another passage, when he teaches that, while the rest of the Apostles ate the bread, i.e., the Lord (*panem Dominum*), Judas, however, ate only the bread of the Lord (*panem Domini*).

But the objection is made here that the efficacy of the sacraments does not depend upon the worthiness of men, and that the promises of God are not in the least impaired or destroyed by the badness of men. I agree with that, and for that very reason I say further, and in explicit terms, that the body of Christ is offered to bad men just as much as to good, and that is all that is required so far as the effect of the sacrament and the faithfulness of God are concerned. For in the Supper God does not cheat the wicked by a mere representation of the body of his Son, but really does hold it out to them; and the bread is not an empty sign for them, but a pledge (*tessera*) of his faithfulness. Their rejecting it does not damage or alter the nature of the sacrament in any way whatever.

We must still deal with an objection arising from what Paul says in this passage. "Paul says the unworthy are guilty, because they do not discern the Lord's body, therefore they do receive his body in it." I say that that conclusion is wrong. For, apart from their rejecting it, it is right to call them guilty, because they desecrate and dishonor what is offered to them by the way they use it, as if they were throwing it on the ground and trampling it underfoot. Do you call that an insignificant sacrilege? So I see no difficulty in what Paul says, so long as you pay attention to what God is offering and holding out to the wicked, and not to what they receive.

28. *But let a man prove himself.* The following exhortation is drawn from the threat that has just been given. If those who eat unworthily are guilty of the body and blood of the Lord, then let no one approach the table without being well and truly prepared. Let everyone, therefore, take care not to fall into this sacrilege through neglect or indifference.

But the question is now asked: When Paul summons us to an examination, what ought the nature of it to be? The Papists think that it consists in auricular confession. They order all those who are about to receive the Supper to examine their lives carefully and anxiously, so that they may unburden all their sins in the ear of a priest. That is their method of preparation! But I myself maintain that the holy examination of which Paul is speaking is far removed from torture. Those people think that they are clear after they have tortured themselves with their thoughts for a few hours, and have let the priest into the secret of their shamefulness. It is another kind of examination that Paul requires here, one corresponding to the proper use of the Holy Supper.

This is the quickest or easiest method of preparation for you. If you want to derive proper benefit from this gift of Christ, you must bring faith and repentance. Therefore, so that you may come well prepared, the examination is based on those two things. Under repentance I include love, for there is no doubt that the man who has learnt to deny himself in order to devote himself to Christ and his service will also give himself wholeheartedly to the promotion of the unity which Christ has commended to us. Indeed, it is not perfect faith or repentance that is asked for. This is said because some people, by being far too insistent upon a perfection which cannot be found anywhere, are putting a barrier between every single man and woman and the Supper forever. But if you are serious in your intention to aspire to the righteousness of God, and if, humbled by the knowledge of your own wretchedness, you fall back on the grace of Christ, and rest upon it, be assured that you are a guest worthy of approaching this table. By saying that you are worthy, I mean that the Lord does not keep you out, even if in other respects you are not all you ought to be. For faith, even if imperfect, makes the unworthy worthy.

Articulate in your own words Calvin's pastoral advice to those coming to the sacrament. How should they prepare?

29. *He who eats unworthily, eats judgment to himself.* Paul had already clearly pointed out the seriousness of the offense, in saying that those who "eat unworthily shall be guilty of the body and blood of the Lord." Now he is giving them cause for alarm by the threat of punishment. For many people are not disturbed by the sin itself, but only if they are visited by the judgment of God. So that is what Paul is doing when he declares that this food, which is otherwise beneficial, will be turned into poison and cause the destruction of those who eat unworthily.

Paul adds the reason for this, viz., because they "do not discern the Lord's body," as something that is holy and not common. What he means is that they handle the sacred body of Christ with unclean hands, and, worse, they treat it as if it were worthless, giving not a thought to its great value. They will therefore pay the penalty for desecrating it so much. But let my readers bear in mind what I said a little ago, that the body of Christ is offered to them, even if their unworthiness prevents them from sharing in it. . . .

[30.] . . . If, in Paul's time, an abuse of the Supper which was not of the most serious kind could stir up the wrath of God against the Corinthians, so that he punished them so severely, what are we to think about the situation in our own day? Throughout the range of Popery we see not only horrible desecrations of the Supper, but also a profane and detestable thing set up in its place.

Calvin is referring here to private or memorial Masses, at which the only person in attendance might be the priest celebrating the Mass.

(1) In the first place, it is prostituted to sordid gain and moneymaking. (2) It is a mutilated thing, because the cup has been taken away. (3) Its form has been quite changed, since it has become the custom for each one to have his feast on his own, so that sharing with each other is done away with. (4) No explanation of the mystery is given in it, but all that is to be heard is a murmuring, which is more like the incantations of magicians, or the horrible sacrifices of the heathen, than our Lord's institution. (5) There are countless ceremonies, abounding not only in senseless things, but also in superstition, and, on that account, obvious corruptions. (6) There is the devilish invention of sacrifice, which amounts to a wicked blasphemy against the death of Christ. (7) It is well designed for causing wretched men to become drunk with a carnal confidence, when they set it before God as an expiation, and think that by this charm they are driving away everything that could hurt them, and that without faith and without penitence. Yes, and more than that, when they are so sure that they are armed against the devil and death, and that, as far as God is concerned, they are securely protected against him, they make so bold as to sin with much greater freedom, and they grow in stubbornness. (8) In it an idol is worshiped in the place of Christ. In short, it is swarming with all sorts of abominations.

Masses were celebrated in Latin, with the priest facing the altar (with his back to the congregation).

Calvin is referring to the veneration of the consecrated host.

Now, we administer the Supper in its purity, after it has been restored to us as though it had come back from exile. But even among us how much irreverence there is! How much hypocrisy there is in the case of many people! What a shocking mix-up there is, when no distinction is made, and scoundrels and people who are openly dissolute push their way in, people whom no decent or respectable person would have anything to do with in ordinary social relations! And still we wonder what is the reason for so many wars, so many plagues, so many failures of the harvest, so many disasters and calamities, as if the cause was not in fact as plain as a pikestaff. And we certainly cannot look for an end to misfortunes until we have removed their cause by correcting our faults.

Source: Text from *Calvin's Commentaries: The First Epistle of Paul the Apostle to the Corinthians*, trans. John W. Fraser, ed. David W. Torrance and Thomas F. Torrance (Grand Rapids: Eerdmans, 1960), pp. 232-55. The translation is based on the Latin edition of 1546 published in *Joannis Calvini Opera Quae Supersunt Omnia*, ed. W. Baum, E. Cunitz, and E. Reuss (Braunschweig: Schwetschke and Son, 1892), Vol. XLIX, and was checked against the French 1562 edition.

Calvin's Commentary on Hebrews 13 (1549)

Calvin's commentary on Hebrews was first published in 1549, appearing in both a Latin and a French edition in the same year. In his commentary on Hebrews 13, Calvin focused on explaining the differences between the sacrifices required of the Jews under the Law of Moses and the sac-rifices Christians were to make following the time of Christ. While Calvin commented on all the verses in Hebrews 13, only the sections dealing with worship have been included here.

Hebrews 13:10-16

10. *We have an altar.* This is a fine analogy (*anagoge*) from the old rite of the Law to the present state of the church. There was a solemn kind of sacrifice that is mentioned in Leviticus 16, of which no part was given back to the priests and Levites. He [the writer of Hebrews] says, using a neat allusion, that this has now been fulfilled in Christ, since he was sacrificed on the condition that those who serve the tabernacle should not feed on him. By the ministers of the tabernacle he understands all those who performed the ceremonies. He therefore means that we must renounce the tabernacle in order to have a share in Christ. Just as the word "altar" includes a sacrifice and a victim, so the tabernacle includes all the outward types which were joined to it. The sense is that it is no wonder that the rites of the Law have ceased today, for what was prefigured in the sacrifice, which the Levites carried outside the camps to burn it there, was that just as the ministers of the tabernacle tasted nothing of it, so if we serve the tabernacle, that is, if we retain its ceremonies, we shall not participate in the sacrifice which Christ once for all offered, nor in the atonement which he performed once for all in his own blood. He brought his own blood into the heavenly sanctuary in order to atone for the sins of the world.

13. *Let us therefore go forth unto him.* In case this allegory and its spiritual comparison becomes lifeless, he joins to it the earnest duty which is required of all Christians. Paul is also in the habit of using this mode of teaching to show to believers what God wishes them to be engaged in in his anxiety to lead them away from vain ceremonies. It is as if he were saying, "This is what God demands of you, and not that by which you tire yourself in vain." That is what the apostle is now doing. In calling us to leave the tabernacle and follow Christ, he is advising us that something is demanded of us very different from the service of God in the shade beneath the wonderful glory of the temple, because it is to be performed through exiles, flights, reproaches, and all kinds of trials. He contrasts this warfare, in which we are to labor to the point of blood, with the shadowy practices in which alone the masters of the ceremonies engaged. . . .

15. *Let us offer up a sacrifice of praise.* He returns to that particular doctrine which he had touched on of the abrogation of the old ceremonies. He anticipates an objection that could be raised. Since the sacrifices were attached to the tabernacle as appendages, it follows that

when it was abolished, they too must cease. Yet the apostle had taught that since Christ suffered outside the gate, we were also called thither, and therefore that the tabernacle was deserted by those who wished to follow him. Hence arose the question whether any sacrifices remained for Christians, for this would be absurd, since they were ordained to serve the worship of God. The apostle meets this timeously, and says that another form of sacrifice is left for us which is no less pleasing to God, namely, the offering to him of the calves of our lips, as the prophet Hosea says (14:2). The sacrifice of praise is not only equally pleasing to God but more so than all the outward things that were used under the Law, as clearly appears from Psalm 50. There God rejects all these things as of no account, and orders the sacrifice of praise to be offered to him. We see therefore that it is the finest worship of God, and the one which is to be preferred to all other exercises, that we should celebrate the goodness of God by the giving of thanks. This, I say, is the rite of sacrifice which God commends to us today. At the same time, there is no doubt that the whole act of calling on the name of God is included in this single part, for we cannot give thanks to him unless we are purged by him, and no one obtains anything unless he prays. In short, he means that without brute beasts we have something to offer God and that in this way he is rightly and perfectly worshiped by us.

As it is the apostle's plan to tell us what is the proper way of worshiping God under the New Testament, he reminds us in passing that we cannot honestly call on God and glorify his name except through Christ as our Mediator. It is he alone who hallows our lips, which are otherwise defiled, to sing the praises of God, who opens the way for our prayers, who in short performs the office of priest by standing before God in our name....

16. *But to do good.* He is here pointing out another way of offering due and proper sacrifices, in the fact that all the duties of love are equivalent of so many sacrifices. In this he shows that those who think that something is lacking if they do not offer beasts to God according to the Law are stupidly and perversely avaricious, since God supplies us with frequent and manifold materials for sacrifice. Although he can derive no benefit from us, yet he looks on our calling on his name as a sacrifice, and indeed as the principal one which suffices for all the others. Moreover, whatever benefits we show to men he regards as done to himself, and gives them the name of sacrifice, so that it is clear that the elements of the Law are now not only superfluous but harmful, since they draw us away from the true way of sacrificing.

In short, the meaning is that if we want to sacrifice to God, we must call upon his name, make known his goodness by giving thanks, and do good to our brethren. These are the true sacrifices with which true Christians should be engaged, and there is neither time nor place for any other.

"Timeously" means "in a timely manner."

Calvin connects different parts of Scripture together in his analysis. See his commentary on Psalm 50 above (pp. 116-22).

Calvin connects worship (prayer, thanksgiving) and action (doing good to one's neighbor).

Source: John Calvin, *Calvin's Commentaries: The Epistle of Paul the Apostle to the Hebrews and The First and Second Epistles of St. Peter,* trans. William B. Johnston, ed. David W. Torrance and Thomas F. Torrance (Grand Rapids: Eerdmans, 1963), pp. 209-12. This translation is based on the 1834 Latin edition of Calvin's New Testament commentaries, which itself was based on the edition of Calvin's works prepared in Amsterdam by J. J. Schipper between 1667 and 1671.

Calvin's Response to Arguments in Favor of the Worship of Images (1562?)

Very little is known about the circumstances surrounding Calvin's writing of these responses to a series of questions about religious images. Calvin was not alone in his opposition to the presence of images in churches, as his perspective was shared by Reformed leaders across Europe. Yet because religious images had been so integral a part of pre-Reformation church life, their often-violent removal during episodes of iconoclasm generated a great deal of popular opposition to the actions of the Reformed community.

A Refutation of Arguments Proposed in Favor of the Worship of Images

Madame, since you are willing for me to respond to your report, I shall proceed by summarizing the arguments that are advanced by those who disagree with us.

They argue that the resolution to this question should be based on the exposition of the Second Commandment, which is correct, for it is the sole and unique ground of our dispute. Hence we must determine whether our exposition is in conformity with the truth or whether we ought to accept images.

They also admonish us not to take the commandments' prohibitions so literally, because St. Paul says, "The letter kills but the spirit gives life." I reply that their citation of this passage is improper. For in the apostle's passage "the letter" refers to the entire law, and the manner in which the Jews practiced this commandment shows that it was meant to be taken literally, as written.

Moreover, God had a reason for keeping the commandments brief, but he wanted his people to learn them. Nor did he want to obscure their truth, which is otherwise so clear.

Furthermore, they have cited this commandment against us, "Thou shalt not kill," in order to show that the commandments must be understood with exceptions in mind, seeing that it is lawful for magistrates to kill, as, for example, Phinehas did. I reply that whenever any exceptions have to be made in the commandments, they are made in deference to legislators, not to men in general. They cite against us the Manichean abuse in which the Manicheans claimed that it was unlawful to eat animals.

In order to prove their argument, however, they would have to produce a passage that expressly commands the making of images and their adoration. Besides, there are numerous

Notice the focus on Scripture and its interpretation as the pre-eminent source of authority. Also, keep track of how many different sources of authority Calvin cites, many of which he agrees with. If he wants to base himself solely on Scripture, why bring in these other authorities?

See Numbers 25:1-9 for the story of Phinehas.

passages that approve of the executions which princes carried out in the name of justice in order to keep the public peace.

As for the Sabbath, I know that some want to see it as a ceremonial commandment. But I accept it as a safeguard for pure morals.

As for their reference to cherubim, I would reply with Tertullian in his treatise *On Idolatry*, in which he addresses certain Christian workers who saw nothing wrong with making images for pagans, saying, "Why then did Moses in the desert make the likeness of a serpent from brass?" [Num. 21:8-9]. My answer is that figures which were designed for some hidden purpose, not to set the law aside, but to be types, are in a separate category. That is to say, we must set aside those things which have been ordained for secret purposes. And if that seems to argue against our point, then let us hear what Tertullian writes next: "Otherwise, if we understand them to be against the law, are we not ascribing inconstancy to God?"

How would you rate Calvin's argument here? Is his case persuasive or not? Explain.

It has been said that one can interpret a commandment by considering what precedes and follows it. First of all it is said, "You shall not make for yourself any foreign gods," and finally, "You shall not worship them."

We must insist that the commandment is broken when our opponents worship and honor images, which they do when they attribute to them what ought to be offered to God alone.

Now sacrifices, consecrations of temples and the like, and incense are due God. But when you offer these to the images of the saints, you are offering them to "foreign gods."

When I reflect on it, I find nothing that the Gentiles offered their idols that is not being offered to images. It has been argued that the ancients thought that their images were animated. I would respond that a few of the uncultivated among them held such a view, but the majority did not.

For example, we find in St. Augustine's passage on Psalm 113 a reference to the same excuses which people propose today. This clearly shows that no images existed in the church then and that people contented themselves with vessels only. Lactantius in his book on false religion says, "Why do you not address yourselves instead to him who is in heaven?" Arnobius says the same. "Sacrifice we owe only to God," says Augustine in *Against Faustus the Manichean*, book 20 [chapter 22]. As for incense, it represents only one aspect of sacrifice and was something unheard of during the time of Tertullian, who says, "We do not offer frankincense." The same is said of "crowning," which are conferred today according to the book *The Soldier's Crown*.

Why does Calvin make so many references to statements from the early church fathers? What is he trying to show?

As for prostrations, I have held that there is a "religious" reverence that is owed to God and a "civil" reverence that is owed to men. In fact, St. Augustine in his discussion of *dulia* says that there are two forms of worship: one that is owed to God and another that is civil and is owed to princes. Now why would a "civil" bow require the same toward images? It is without order or reason.

The term *dulia* means "veneration."

I further maintain that there are things chanted in the church that are repugnant to God, such as [this one addressed] to the image of the Virgin: "Although not in everything, thou art everything." There is another verse that claims: "Rule according to your Mother's law." Are these not, I ask, genuine forms of impiety and idolatry?

Pagans attributed future events to idols, but the same are attributed to St. Anthony of Padua, to Our Lady of Good News, and to others.

It has been said that the law of nature does not prohibit images. But St. Paul says that those who worship them have exchanged "the glory of the incorruptible God" for "corruptible things" [Rom. 1:23]. As for what occurred at Bethel, no image was erected, rather only a testimony that Jacob had seen the vision of God [Gen. 28:18-22].

As for the "adoration" [of images], our opponents argue that they are offering only an "interior adoration," not an "exterior" one. But I argue, to the contrary, with Origen in his Eighth Homily on Exodus 20: "Restrain from both." He says the same in book 1 on Romans 1. Hence, I conclude that in accordance with the Word's true meaning, we ought to interpret "to adore" in its proper sense and prohibit all honoring of images, whether "interior" or "exterior."

It has been said that anyone ignorant enough to worship images cannot help but say, "Images, I worship you!" Our opponents reply that they have given the image the name of that which is signified in the name they call it. Nevertheless, they continue to address the image. And that is why the people, being distracted by certain images, attach the saint to the image.

As for the cross, idolatry pertains to it when it has been consecrated — as it is the church's custom to do with wooden objects — when it is called "the cross of our hope." However, I acknowledge that the sign of the cross is very old in the church, and that the wooden cross falls somewhere between the sign and images. For this reason, the earliest usage of the cross was sound, but as time has elapsed it has become worse.

Nothing but the sign of the cross was practiced until the time of Constantine, who lived between the third and fourth centuries, and at the time it received no adoration. But when [his mother] Helena found the cross [supposedly in Jerusalem] and sent it to Constantine, he set it up in the Forum. As for the nails, they say she threw one into the sea; from a second she made a bridle for Constantine's horse; and the third was set in Constantine's diadem — for which she was praised. We can only respond to this, however, in accordance with what the Word of God shows concerning that raised serpent which was shattered by Hezekiah when he saw that it led the people into idolatry [2 Kings 18:4].

As for Theodoret's *On Sacrifices*, I would hold that the sacrifices which God has ordained predate those of the Gentiles, but the devil has sought to substitute these lawful sacrifices of God with signs and imitations of his works.

The tenth chapter of Acts and the [nineteenth] of the Apocalypse prove that neither St. Peter nor the angel ever found worship [of themselves] good. Some argue that Cornelius was a pagan. But, on the contrary, he is called "religious," and St. Peter went to him to lead him to the true Messiah. Cornelius was accepted by St. Peter not because he prostrated himself before Peter, for Peter had to rebuke him for that, but because what Cornelius said surpassed what was required.

Moreover, God's servants in Scripture never received the praise that was accorded princes. St. Augustine in *Against Faustus the Manichean*, book 20, chapter 21, says the same. Similarly, the angel [in Revelation] says, "I am your fellow servant. Worship God" [Rev. 19:10]. Hence, I conclude that if the prototype refuses to be worshiped, then even less ought we to worship images and other types.

As for martyrs who have been interred under altars, St. Augustine says in the passage cited above, "We honor the martyrs by imitating them and having a share in their company." In chapter 16 of his book *On True Religion*, where he is addressing Christians instead of Gentiles, he says that the saints are honored for the sake of "imitation," not "worship." And of the angels he says, "We honor them by loving them, not by worshiping them." In his *On the Morals of the Catholic Church* Augustine says that in his time there were worshipers of images and pictures — both of whom he soundly condemns.

As for St. Basil, who teaches various things about a monastic life, I cannot think of anything he says that would contradict this.

Our opponents cite St. Paul and St. James on faith and works. But I will respond to this later in another context.

The Second Council of Nicaea met in 787; the Council of Frankfurt met in 794.

Why would the absence of these delegates make a difference in Calvin's mind?

Why was this accusation so damaging?

There exists today the same kind of ignorant idolatry as existed in ancient times. The **Council of Nicaea** cannot be accepted without leading faith into error. This council was called without the churches of Gaul and Germany being present. At the **Council of Frankfurt** the pope's ambassadors were present. We ourselves remove images. For Charlemagne, who prohibited their adoration, did not remove them, which resulted in our succumbing to idolatry. However, we do not reject all the councils, as we accept the first four.

As for our confession, which they maintain was derived by our ministers alone, everyone [present] contributed his advice and concurred to adopt the testimony of the Holy Scriptures. Other churches that have also separated from Rome and that are now dispersed maintain the same doctrine.

As for the Council [of Nicaea (787)] that reinstated images, I am unable to place any confidence in a council that denies its ecclesiastics the power [to vote their consciences], or one in which we are not guaranteed security, notwithstanding the ordinance of the **Council of Constance**, although it was made an appendix of the **Council of Trent.** Nor can I accept a council unless it proceeds in accordance with the authority of Scripture and operates free of prescriptions.

The ecumenical Council of Constance met from 1414 to 1418. The Catholic Council of Trent met (with interruptions) from 1545 to 1563.

We do not despise the church, nor have we separated ourselves from it. And if they should ask, "Where has the church been since the introduction of images?" I can reply, "Where was it during the time of Eli?" I think that our church has been in the hands of poor husbandmen indeed!

_____

Source: John Calvin, "A Refutation of Arguments Proposed in Favor of the Worship of Images," in Calvin's *Ecclesiastical Advice,* trans. Mary Beaty and Benjamin Farley (Louisville: Westminster John Knox Press, 1991), pp. 71-75. This translation is based on the French text published in the nineteenth-century collected edition of Calvin's works: *Joannis Calvini Opera Quae Supersunt Omnia,* ed. W. Baum, E. Cunitz, and E. Reuss (Braunschweig: Schwetschke and Son, 1872), Vol. X, cols 193-97. The French text in the *Opera* comes from an undated manuscript headed "Pour envoyer à M. de Beze" ["To be sent to M. de Beze"]. Théodore de Bèze was one of Geneva's leading pastors and Calvin's right-hand man. The *Opera* editors tentatively suggest 1562 as the year in which Calvin wrote this response to a series of questions.

Calvin's Foreword to the Psalter (1545)

The Genevan Psalter is one of the best-known and most enduring outcomes of the Genevan Reformation. Calvin first encountered Psalm-singing in Strasbourg and brought the practice back with him to Geneva. Although Calvin himself did versify some of the Psalms, poetry was not his strong point, and his versions were superseded by others prepared by more talented poets, especially Theodore Beza and the French Renaissance poet Clément Marot. The first Genevan Psalters did not include all 150 Psalms, and many of the texts used the same melody. Only by the 1560s was the Psalter completed in its final form. The practice of singing rhymed or metrical Psalms to Genevan melodies spread from Geneva to other Reformed areas, including France, Scotland, the Netherlands, parts of the Holy Roman Empire, and Hungary.

Epistle to the Reader

As it is a thing required by Christianity, and one of the most necessary, that each of the faithful observe and maintain the communion of the church in his neighborhood, attending the assemblies which are held on Sunday as well as on other days to honor and serve God, so it is also expedient and reasonable that everyone know and understand what is said and done in the temple in order to receive benefit and edification from it. For our Lord did not institute the order which we are bound to observe when we gather together in his name merely to amuse the world by a spectacle, but rather desired that from it profit would come to all his people, as Saint Paul testifies, commanding that everything which is done in the church be directed to the common edification of all (Rom. 15:2; 1 Cor. 14:26; Eph. 4:29), something which the servant would not have commanded had it not been the intention of the Master.

Now this cannot be done unless we are taught to understand everything which has been ordained for our use. For to say that we can have devotion, either at prayer or at ceremony, without understanding anything about them, is a gross delusion, no matter how much it is

Calvin put participation in communal worship front and center as one of the key requirements of life as a Reformed believer.

Notice the continued importance Calvin places on understanding as a key component of genuine worship and devotion.

commonly said. A good affection toward God is a thing neither lifeless nor bestial, but is a quickening movement proceeding from the Holy Spirit when the heart is truly touched and the understanding enlightened. And in fact, if one could be edified by things which one sees without understanding what they mean, Saint Paul would not so vehemently forbid speaking in an unknown tongue (1 Cor. 14:16), and would not use the argument that there is no edification unless there is doctrine. Nevertheless, if we wish truly to honor the holy ordinances of our Lord which we use in the church, the most important thing is to know what they contain, what they mean, and to what purpose they tend, in order that their observance may be useful and salutary, and in consequence rightly regulated.

Now there are in sum three things which our Lord has commanded us to observe in our spiritual assemblies, namely, the preaching of his Word, the public and solemn prayers, and the administration of his sacraments (cf. Acts 2:42). I refrain from speaking of preaching at this time, inasmuch as it is not in question. Touching the two other parts which remain, we have the express commandment of the Holy Spirit that prayers be made in the common language and understood by the people. And the apostle says that the people cannot respond "Amen" to the prayers which have been made in an unknown tongue (1 Cor. 14:15-17). Now since prayer is made in the name of all and on behalf of all, everyone should be a participant. Wherefore this has been a very great affront to those who have introduced the Latin language into the churches where it is not commonly understood. And there is neither subtlety nor sophistry which can excuse them from this custom, which is perverse and displeasing to God. For one must not presume that he will consider agreeable what is done directly contrary to his will, and, as it were, in defiance of him. Nor can one any longer defy him, acting thus against his prohibition, and glorifying in this rebellion as if it were a thing holy and very praiseworthy.

As for the sacraments, if we look truly at their nature, we recognize that it is a perverse custom to celebrate them in such a way that the people have nothing but the spectacle, without explanation of the mysteries which are contained in them. For if these are visible words, as Saint Augustine calls them, they must not be merely an exterior spectacle, but doctrine must be joined to them to give them understanding. And so our Lord, in instituting them, expressly demonstrated this, for he says that they were testimonies of the alliance which he made with us, and which he confirmed by his death (Matt. 26:26-29). It is certainly necessary, then, in order to accord them their proper place, that we know and understand what is said in them. Otherwise it would be in vain that our Lord opened his mouth to speak if there were no ears to hear. And this is not a subject for lengthy disputation, for when the matter is judged with a sober disposition, there is no one who will not admit that it is pure trickery to amuse the people with signs whose meaning is not explained to them. Wherefore it is easy to see that one profanes the sacraments of Jesus Christ, administering them in such a manner that the people do not understand the words which are spoken in them. And in fact one sees

Here is the justification for the detailed presentation of the sacraments and their meaning in the Genevan liturgy.

the superstitions which issue from this. For it is commonly agreed that the consecration, as much of the water at baptism as of the bread and the wine in the supper of our Lord, are like a kind of magic; that is to say that when one has breathed on them and pronounced the words, insensible creatures feel the effect, yet people understand nothing.

Now the true consecration is that which is made by the word of faith when it is declared and received, as Saint Augustine says. This is expressly realized in the words of Jesus Christ, for he does not say to the bread that it should become his body, but he directs his word to the company of the faithful, saying, Take, eat, and so forth (Matt. 26:26). If, then, we wish to celebrate the sacrament in the right way, the doctrine signified in the sacrament needs to be declared to us. I know perfectly well that that seems like an outrageous opinion to those who are unaccustomed to it, as is the case with all new things. But it is certainly right, if we are disciples of Jesus Christ, that we prefer his institution to our practice. And what he instituted from the beginning ought not to appear to us like novel opinion.

If that still cannot penetrate everyone's understanding, it will be necessary for us to pray to God that it please him to enlighten the ignorant, to make them understand how much wiser he is than anyone on earth, so that they will learn to be satisfied no longer with their own judgment or with the foolish and maddened wisdom of their blind leaders. Meanwhile, for the use of our church, it seemed well advised to us to have a formulary of prayers and the sacraments published, in order that everyone might know what he should say and do in the Christian assembly. The book will be profitable not only for the people of this church, but also for all those who wish to know what form the faithful should maintain and follow when they gather together in the name of Jesus Christ. We have therefore collected as in a summary the manner of celebrating the sacraments and sanctifying marriage; likewise the prayers and praises which we use. We will speak a little later of the sacraments.

As for the public prayers, there are two kinds: the first are made with the word only, the others with song. And this is not a thing invented a short time ago. For from the first origin of the church, this has been so, as appears from the histories. And even Saint Paul speaks not only of praying aloud, but also of singing (Col. 3:16). And in truth we know from experience that song has great force and vigor to arouse and inflame people's hearts to invoke and praise God with a more vehement and ardent zeal. There must always be concern that the song be neither light nor frivolous, but have gravity and majesty, as Saint Augustine says. And thus there is a great difference between the music which one makes to entertain people at table and in their homes, and the Psalms which are sung in the church in the presence of God and his angels. Now when anyone wishes to judge correctly of the form which is here presented, we hope that he will find it holy and pure, seeing that it is simply directed to the edification of which we have spoken.

And how much more widely the practice of singing may extend! It is even in the homes and in the fields an incentive for us, and, as it were, an organ for praising God and lifting up

Again, Calvin is very sensitive to accusations that he and his fellow Reformers are innovators. Instead, he and his colleagues constantly stress that they are returning to the pure practices of the early church.

The "blind leaders," according to Calvin, are the clergy of the Roman Catholic Church.

Discuss the potential advantages and disadvantages of having a written-down set of liturgies and prayers for use in the "Christian assembly." What assumptions is Calvin working with in order to make this project successful?

our hearts to him, to console us by meditating on his virtue, goodness, wisdom, and justice, something which is more necessary than one can say. For in the first place it is not without cause that the Holy Spirit exhorts us so carefully through the Holy Scriptures to rejoice in God (Phil. 3:1, 4:4), and that all our joy is there, as it were, brought back to its true end. For he knows how much we are inclined to rejoice in vanity. Thus then, as our nature draws us and induces us to look for all manner of demented and vicious rejoicing, so to the contrary our Lord, to distract us and withdraw us from the temptations of the flesh and the world, presents us all means possible to occupy us in that spiritual joy which he recommends to us so much.

Now among the other things which are appropriate for recreating people and giving them pleasure, music is either the first or one of the principal, and we must value it as a gift of God deputed to that use. Wherefore that much more ought we to take care not to abuse it, for fear of fouling and contaminating it, converting it to our condemnation, when it was dedicated to our profit and welfare. If there were no other consideration than this alone, it may indeed move us to moderate the use of music, to make it serve everything virtuous, and that it ought not to give occasion for our giving free rein to licentiousness, or for our making ourselves effeminate in disordered delights, and that it ought not to become an instrument of dissipation or of any obscenity. But there is still more. For there is scarcely anything in the world which is more capable of turning or moving morals this way and that, as Plato prudently considered it. And in fact we experience that it has a secret and almost incredible power to arouse hearts in one way or another.

Wherefore we ought to be the more diligent in regulating it in such a way that it be useful to us and not at all pernicious. For this reason the ancient doctors of the church complain frequently of the fact that the people of their times were addicted to unseemly and obscene songs which, not without reason, they judge and call mortal and satanic poison for corruption of the world. Moreover, in speaking now of music, I understand two parts, that is to say, the letter, or subject and matter; second, the song or the melody. It is true that every evil word (as Saint Paul says in 1 Cor. 15:33) perverts good morals, but when the melody is with it, it pierces the heart that much more strongly and enters into it; just as through a funnel wine is poured into a container, so also venom and corruption are distilled to the depth of the heart by the melody. What is there then to do? It is to have songs not only seemly, but also holy, which will be like spurs to incite us to pray to and praise God, to meditate on his works in order to love, fear, honor, and glorify him. Now what Saint Augustine says is true, that no one is able to sing things worthy of God unless he has received them from him.

Wherefore, when we have looked thoroughly everywhere and searched high and low, we shall find no better songs nor more appropriate to the purpose than the Psalms of David, which the Holy Spirit made and spoke through him. And furthermore, when we sing them, we are certain that God puts the words in our mouths, as if he himself were singing in us

In many ways, Calvin's critique of music's power over human beings can sound very modern, although he was as worried about the power of melody as of text, whereas modern concerns tend to center more on the text of songs rather than the possible corrupting power of a tune.

to exalt his glory. Wherefore Chrysostom exhorts men as well as women and little children to accustom themselves to sing them, in order that this may be, as it were, a meditation for associating themselves with the company of angels. As for the rest, it is necessary for us to remember what Saint Paul says, that spiritual songs can be sung truly only from the heart (Eph. 5:19; Col. 3:16). Now the heart requires intelligence, and in that (says Saint Augustine) lies the difference between human singing and that of the birds. For a linnet, a nightingale, a parrot may sing well, but it will be without understanding. Now the peculiar gift of a person is to sing knowing what he is saying. The heart and the affection must follow after the intelligence, which is impossible unless we have the hymn imprinted on our memory in order never to cease from singing.

For these reasons the present book, even for this cause, in addition to the rest which has been said, ought to be under exceptional consideration by everyone who desires to enjoy himself in seemly fashion and in accordance with God, to look to his salvation and to the profit of his neighbors. And so there is no necessity for it to be particularly recommended by me, seeing that it carries its own value and praise. Only let the world be so well advised that in place of songs in part empty and frivolous, in part stupid and dull, in part obscene and vile, and in consequence evil and harmful, which it has used up to now, it may accustom itself hereafter to singing these divine and celestial hymns with the good King David. Touching the melody, it has seemed best that it be moderated in the manner which we have adopted, to carry gravity and majesty appropriate to the subject, and even to be suitable for singing in church, in accordance with what has been said.

Calvin sets quite a high bar for music to be sung in church. Assess contemporary church music in the light of Calvin's perspective — what might he approve of, and what might he be concerned about?

Geneva, 10 June 1543

Source: John Calvin, Foreword to the Genevan Psalter 1542/43, in *John Calvin: Writings on Pastoral Piety,* ed. Elsie McKee (New York: Paulist Press, 2001), pp. 91-97. McKee reproduced the translation done by Charles Garside in his *The Origins of Calvin's Theology of Music: 1536-1543* (Philadelphia: American Philosophical Society, 1979), pp. 31-33. Garside used the French text presented in *Joannis Calvini Opera Selecta,* ed. P. Barth and D. Scheuner (Munich: Kaiser, 1952), Vol. II, pp. 12-18, and the French text published in the nineteenth-century collected edition of Calvin's works: *Joannis Calvini Opera Quae Supersunt Omnia,* ed. W. Baum, E. Cunitz, and E. Reuss (Braunschweig: Schwetschke and Son, 1867), Vol. VI, cols. 165-72. In both cases, the editors of Calvin's collected works used the French text in the 1545 edition of *La Forme des Prières et Chantz Ecclesiastiques* (Strasbourg: [no printer], 1545), since it is the earliest work that included Calvin's preface.

Polity Documents

Genevan Ecclesiastical Ordinances (1541)

These ordinances regulating the life of the church in Geneva were put together by a committee of magistrates and pastors shortly after Calvin's return to the city from his three-year exile in Strasbourg. The ordinances were adopted by the General Council (all male Genevans of legal age with voting rights) on 20 November 1541. The ordinances were revised in 1561 and 1576, mostly taking into account developments in Geneva over the years, including the creation of the Genevan Academy in 1559 and the increasing number of pastors in the city. The French text of the 1541 ordinances is the one that was placed at the front of the registers of the Genevan Company of Pastors (the minutes of the weekly meetings of the Genevan clergy). Notice how thorough these rules are and how many different facets of worship they address.

On the number, locations, and times of sermons:

On Sundays, the sermon should take place at dawn at Saint Pierre and Saint Gervais and at the usual time at the said Saint Pierre, at la Madeleine, and Saint Gervais.

> "At the usual time" means the regular morning service.

At noon, catechism, or instruction of the little children, should take place in all three churches, namely Saint Pierre, la Madeleine, and Saint Gervais.

At three o'clock, services should also take place in all three parishes.

We should observe parish boundaries as much as possible in terms of sending the children to catechism and receiving the sacraments. Saint Gervais should include the same as before, as should la Madeleine. Saint Pierre should include what was formerly part of Saint-Germain, Sainte-Croix, Notre-Dame-la-neuve, and Saint-Légier.

> How many different worship services (including the catechism service) were to take place on Sundays in Geneva, counting each service in each church separately?

On weekdays, apart from the two scheduled sermons, preaching should take place three times a week at Saint Pierre, namely on Monday, Wednesday, and Friday. The bells for these sermons should ring in sequence, so that at a given hour one sermon would finish before the next one starts somewhere else. If special prayer services are held because of times of trouble, the schedule for Sunday services will be followed.

In order to carry out these responsibilities and others pertaining to ministry, we will need five pastors and three assistants who are also pastors to help and contribute as required.

Geneva thus followed a team-ministry model, in which pastors rotated from pulpit to pulpit.

On the sacraments:

On Baptism:

Baptisms should only be celebrated at sermon time and should only be administered by the pastors or their assistants. A register of the children's names and the names of their parents should be kept, so that if an illegitimate child is presented, the authorities are informed accordingly.

No outsiders should serve as godparents except for those who are faithful and Reformed, given that the others cannot promise the church to teach the children as it should be done.

The pastors had a key role as recorders of births and reporters of illegitimacy to the city authorities, who expended a lot of energy to discover the fathers of these children, to make them pay for the children's upkeep. Those who engaged in sexual activity outside of marriage, especially if it resulted in a child, could expect to face short prison sentences on bread and water, fines, and in serious or repeated cases, banishment from the city.

On the Lord's Supper:

Since the Supper was established by our Lord to have us celebrate it more frequently, and since it was observed in this fashion from the early church up until the devil turned everything upside down, insisting on the Mass instead, we must remedy the error of celebrating the Supper too infrequently. However, for now we have decided and ordered that it is to be administered four times a year, namely at Christmas, Easter, Pentecost, and the first Sunday of September in the autumn.

The pastors are to distribute the bread both reverently and in an orderly fashion. The cup is only to be handed out by the assistants or by the deacons together with the pastors, and therefore there is no need for a multitude of cups.

The tables should be placed close to the pulpit, so that the mystery may be better and more easily explained near the tables.

The Supper should only be celebrated in church until a more favorable time.

On the Sunday prior to the celebration of the Supper, a warning should be issued, so that no child comes to the Supper without first having professed his faith as it will be presented in the catechism. All strangers and newcomers should also be exhorted to present themselves to the church first, so as to be instructed if needed, and so that no one approaches the sacrament risking condemnation.

Genevan Communion services therefore involved movement: everyone went forward to sit around specially set-up tables to receive the Lord's Supper.

On marriage:

Following the customary announcement of the banns, the wedding should take place at the couple's request, either on Sundays or on working days, so long as it happens at the start of the service. However, to honor the sacrament, it would be good to refrain from holding weddings on days when the Lord's Supper is celebrated.

It would be good to introduce singing in church, to better encourage the faithful to pray and praise God.

At the outset, we will teach the little children, and over time, the entire church will follow along.

The need to deal with a wide range of issues is what may explain the jumbling of ideas in this section on marriage. Church authorities didn't always have the time or energy to organize all their ordinances in a strictly coherent fashion. Teaching congregations to sing when they had not previously done so was a significant challenge, given the absence of books and the inability of most worshippers to read music.

On burials:

The dead should be honorably interred in the specified place. We leave it to individuals to decide on the number of accompanying persons and the size of the cortege [procession].

We have also decided and ordered that the bearers swear to their Lordships (the magistrates) that they will prevent all superstitions contrary to the Word of God, that they will not carry bodies for burial at inappropriate times, and that they will report if someone died suddenly, to avoid all potential problems that may occur.

Furthermore, bodies are to be carried for burial no sooner than twelve hours and no later than twenty-four hours after death.

Why the limitations? What might the authorities have been worried about?

The practices to be followed regarding little children:

All citizens and inhabitants must bring or send their children on Sundays at noon to the aforementioned catechism.

A primer is to be prepared, from which the children will be taught. Based on the doctrines they will learn, we will question them about what was said, to see whether they listened attentively and remembered what they learned.

When children have learned sufficiently to do without the catechism, they will have to solemnly recite the summary of its contents. In doing so, they will be essentially professing their Christian faith before the church.

Prior to reaching this point, no child should be admitted to receive the sacrament of the Lord's Supper. Parents are to be warned not to bring their children too soon. For it is a very dangerous thing, both for children and for their fathers, to presume to bring them without

This primer was the Genevan Catechism of 1542.

Only a minority of children actually went to school. Others were apprenticed at a young age or simply worked in their father's business.

good and sufficient instruction. This order should be followed to learn the contents of the instruction.

To prevent any mistakes, all schoolchildren are to assemble at school before noon, and the masters are to bring them in good order according to their parish.

Other children must be sent or brought by their fathers. To minimize confusion, parish boundaries should be observed as much as possible, as noted above in the case of the sacraments.

Schoolboys attended catechism services at church on Sunday afternoons with their classmates, not with their families.

Source: Genevan Ecclesiastical Ordinances, 1541, from Henri Heyer, *1555-1909: L'Eglise de Genève: esquisse historique de son organisation, suivie de ses diverses constitutions, de la liste de ses pasteurs et professeurs et d'une table biographique* (Geneva: A. Jullien, 1909), pp. 265-66, 270-71, 272-73. The translation is by Karin Maag. Heyer transcribed the French text from the original manuscript held in the Archives d'état de Genève, Registres de la Compagnie des Pasteurs, vol. A.

Genevan Consistory Records

The Genevan Consistory, set up after Calvin's return from his exile in Strasbourg in 1541, was a body made up of the Genevan ministers and elders, chaired by a syndic (one of the city government's four leading elected officials), that met on a weekly basis to discuss and adjudicate cases of church discipline. The Consistory did not deal with criminal cases such as theft or murder but instead investigated quarrels, family disputes, marriage and relationship issues, and religious matters. The Consistory had no power to physically punish or fine those who were unwilling to change their ways, though it could refer cases to the city government if it felt the matter was serious enough to warrant such a procedure. The Consistory's main strategy to get Genevans to repent and change their ways was to admonish them during a Consistory meeting and, if that failed, to bar them temporarily from the Lord's Supper until the matter was resolved.

23 March 1542

Robert the pack-saddler

Asked by Monsieur Pertemps why he did not appear and present himself last Thursday when he should have and about his charge and how he had carried out his charge and why he did not present himself and do his duty. Answers that he did what he could and attended the sermons. He could say nothing of his faith. The Consistory is of the opinion that he come every Thursday to show how he has profited and that he come every Thursday before Communion. And that he be given more severe [admonitions] and that . . . [incomplete sentence]. Asked what profit he has made and how he has profited from the sermons since his last

Pertemps was the syndic (one of the chief Genevan magistrates) who chaired the Consistory meetings.

The Consistory had
serious concerns
about admitting to
the Lord's Supper
those who could
not meet the basic
requirements of recit-
ing (in French) the
Lord's Prayer, the Ten
Commandments, and
the Apostles' Creed.

appearance. Says he listened every Sunday and that last Sunday he heard the sermon at St. Peter's and he does not know who preached, or what he said, and that it was at vespers and that
it was Faret [*sic* for Farel] or another, and that he has not been there on Wednesdays. He said
that he preached on the commandments. The Consistory remanded him to present himself
every Thursday from now until Easter, and after Easter until he is fully instructed in the fear
of God, to give an account of how he has profited day by day; otherwise the Council will not be
content with him. The Lord's preachers have given him just admonitions. [vol. I, p. 22]

31 March 1542

Jaques Emyn

Summoned to render an account of his faith. He responded that he had made a little
progress and said the Pater, "Our Father, etc.," and a few words of the creed. The Consistory
advise, having given him proper admonitions, that he find a teacher who will instruct him in
the faith and explain what the words mean and make him understand what concerns God.
And that he be admonished a little later to go every day or more often to the preaching for his
better profit. And that he come close to the pulpit to hear the Word of God better and that
he be refused Holy Communion unless he acquits himself otherwise. And that he be given a
respectable teacher, and if he does not render a better account of his faith before Easter . . .
[incomplete sentence]. [vol. I, p. 26]

Were the Consistory's
expectations realistic?
What challenges
might Emyn have
faced in following
the Consistory's
instructions?

Donne Janne Pertennaz

Asked about her faith and why she has not received Holy Communion and whether she
has heard and gone to Mass every year. And she said her faith and that she believes in one
God and wants to live in God and the holy church and has no other faith. And she frequents
the sermons on Sunday. She recited her Pater in French: "I believe in God the Father, omnipo-
tent, etc." Answered that Our Lord knows our hearts and that she believes as the church believes. Asked what that is. Answers that she does not . . . except as the church believes. Asked
if there is a church in this city. Answers that she knows nothing; she believes that the Word
of God is . . . [incomplete sentence]. And that she wants always to live as a Christian and that
there is only one God. And whether the sacraments of Our Lord are administered. Answers
that it is preached and that Communion is taken, and she believes in Holy Communion as
God said: "This is my body, and do this in my memory." And that where the Word of God is,
God is, and that she conforms to the Word of God and that the Word of God is here. And she

Janne Pertennaz was a
matriarch of a power-
ful Genevan family —
she was the mother of
one of Geneva's four
syndics — and she
clearly had no wish to
adopt the Reformed
faith. Examine this
account and the
next one and assess
the effectiveness
of the Consistory's
approach.

said she wanted to live and die in it, and it has the administration of the sacraments according to the Word of God and nothing else. Asked why she is not satisfied with the Communion celebrated in this city but goes elsewhere. Answers that she goes where it seems good to her. And that there is talk of princes who are not in accord in what they do openly, but they must be obeyed. And that Our Lord will not come here well-clothed or shod and that where His Word is, His body is a word [*sic*]. Our Lord said that ravenous wolves would come, and therefore she does not know who these ravenous wolves are or where there are false prophets and . . . [incomplete sentence]. Remanded as outside the faith and to appear day by day. And she did not want to renounce the Mass. [vol. I, p. 28]

4 April 1542

Donne Janne Pertennaz

Recalled and asked why she displays no efforts to admonish herself and lead herself to the faith. Answers that she has not taken the Host. The said Janne asks if the Holy Scripture has now fully arrived. Lord Calvin admonished her from the Word of God. She said it was true that last Sunday there were some Germans who spoke to her maid, and there was one who came to the said Donne Janne, a respectable German, who asked her [in marriage], saying he wanted her very much. And she told him she was married. And the said German asked how she prayed. She answered that here they do not want you to say the "Virgin Mary, pray for us." She answered that she went nowhere at Christmas because she was ill. Asked what faith she held toward God. Answers that she keeps the faith in good earnest and believes there is one God. Said that the Lord's preachers should know better than she what concerns God, and that she puts all her reliance on God. Said that Our Lord, by the merit of his passion, will pardon her and that she has given her heart to God and that he will guard her from all dangers. And that she will never follow another than God and that she is not a cleric like them and that there is no other God for her than God. She was asked in what manner she takes Holy Communion. Answers that she does not want to be an idolater or hypocrite; she leaves the faith as it is. Said that the Virgin Mary is her advocate. Said the Virgin Mary is a friend of God and that the Virgin Mary is the daughter and mother of Jesus Christ. And she understands that no one will be damned if it pleases God and that she does not know anything about the church. Said her faith is good and she does not know whether the faith of others of others [*sic*] is good. And that she never had another faith than the faith of Jesus Christ and that Our Lady is a gentle woman and that God is our advocate before God the Father and that none can pardon except Our Lord, and that she wants to live in the faith of the holy church, and she said that if the lord syndic was a heretic she would not want to be one.

The Consistory advises that she be made to speak once more to learn her will; afterwards that she be remanded to another Thursday, and depending on what is found that she either be remanded to Friday before the Council or forbidden Communion, so that she will not go elsewhere to worship idols. And that she be admonished to go to the sermons every day. She says she is subject to the Seigneurie of Geneva.

Assess Janne Perten-naz's strategy in responding to the Consistory's repeated questions. What was each side trying to achieve?

Asked if she believes. She believes that everywhere where the Word of God is, she believes in that. Remanded to Thursday to learn first if she is united with us in Holy Communion. That there is only one mediator to God, Jesus Christ; as for the saints, that one should do like them. Secondly whether she does not believe that Jesus Christ is our advocate and whether Jesus Christ is [or] is not in the Holy Communion and that we have no other advocate than Jesus Christ before God the Father. Believes that Jesus Christ is in Heaven; has heard that God sees all and is all. Also always has and always will believe as she has said. Remanded to Thursday to respond firmly without doubt. Answered that she wanted to give for the love of God on Maundy Thursday and that on such a day he made his Communion, and that Our Lord fasted 40 days.

We declare that she cannot be received at Communion and we deprive her of it from now until the Lord touches her heart, and she is declared outside of the church. Answered that in the time when the Jews were expelled from this city, that the time was coming when the Jews would be throughout the city. [vol. I, pp. 30-31]

6 April 1542

Master Robert

This is the same Robert the pack-saddler that appeared in March. Note the Consistory's long-term commitment to get everyone to a minimum level of knowledge of their faith.

Asked how he has advanced in the Christian faith. Answers that he has learned his Pater, which he said, and that he was at the sermon on Sunday and Master Pierre preached and he remembers nothing of the sermon or very [little]. The Consistory orders that he continue the sermons every day and that he not be left alone until he knows all his faith as he should and that he not come to Communion, that he be given sharper admonitions, that he be forbidden Communion until he can recite it well, and that he have a Bible in his house. [vol. I, p. 36]

Franceyse, wife of Claude Bellet

Childcare obligations was one of the standard explanations (or excuses?) given by women for not attending church services.

Asked about the sermons. Answers that she goes on Sundays and that she has a child to watch and cannot go to sermons and that she has to earn a living because her husband has earned nothing since the grape harvest. Said her Pater and confession fairly well. The Consistory admonished her to frequent the sermons. [vol. I, p. 36]

20 April 1542

Monsieur George Poutex, De La Verchiere, and Mychiel Morand, religious from Satigny, appeared

And asked about their duty to God and how they serve the church and why they do not want to read the passion during Communion. Answer that no one gave them the book and they do not have it and do not have a New Testament, and that they are poor. And how they instruct their people in the faith. And they said the Pater, and the confession in a general way. Monsieur George said the Commandments in Latin poorly. Monsieur Verchiere similarly; he said the Commandments well in French. Monsieur Morand said . . . [incomplete sentence] and could not say the Ten Commandments. The preachers gave them proper admonitions that the Council has been advised to admonish them. Admonished whether they have any scruples about the present law of the Reformation. Answer that they have not. All three were enjoined to get books and the Commandments of God and the New Testament, so there will be no more bad reports about them. [vol. I, p. 44]

In other words, they were former Catholic clergy. Not all Catholic clergy left the region when the Reformation was enacted in 1536. Some conformed (more or less) to the new confessional requirements.

2 May 1542

Amyed Darnex of Bourdigny, living in Satigny

Because of a child kept six years without baptism. If he has a child. Answers that he has two sons and two daughters, one daughter about six years old called Claudaz who was baptized last Sunday, and she was still named Claudaz. And he was sorry because a woman had baptized her, and the preacher told them the said baptism had not taken place. And that he did it from ignorance and that the mother died, and the woman who baptized her was named Clauda. The Consistory advises that he be put in prison to learn more from him and that he make a public apology and be admonished. Also it would be good, if there are others, to identify them, and to announce that if there is any child to be baptized it should be brought for baptism, and proclaim these rules, and that he be remanded to Thursday and that he frequent the sermons. Asked if he knows or has heard about any other child at his house who is yet to be baptized. Answers that if he knew of any others he would tell the Seigneurie. And that he frequents the sermons.

Why was little Claudaz only baptized in church at age six? What had happened at her birth, and why did the Consistory discount that?

Jehanete, widow of Jehan de Thouz, Pernete, wife of Claude Darnex of Bourdigny, Mayaz, wife of Jehan Darnex of Bourdigny were asked why the aforesaid girl was kept so long. Answers that the said Amyed told her about it, and she told him that he must baptize her, which he did, and spoke to the preacher about it, and she was godmother of the said Claudaz. Said

It is not clear from the minutes which of the three women listed responded to the Consistory's question.

her Pater in the French tongue and the confession fairly well. They were admonished to frequent the sermons. [vol. I, pp. 55-56]

4 May 1542

Johan Constant from Poitou in France, tailor, about . . .

"Muttering" in this and other cases means that the person was in fact quietly reciting traditional prayers and parts of the Catholic liturgy during the Reformed worship service.

Answers touching muttering at the sermon that he says the passion, and that he can read and understand it in Latin and that he is more attached than he ever was to the gospel and that he knows the Pater in Latin and the Ave Maria and his office of Prime, Terce, etc. The Consistory advises, considering his hypocrisy, that he come every Thursday to give an account of his faith and go every Sunday to catechism and that he be admonished more sharply and that he abstain from the sacraments until he is better informed. [vol. I, p. 60]

11 May 1542

Jana Crosetaz

Continuing Catholic practices in Reformation Geneva could include actions at worship, but also objects — in this case, a rosary or prayer beads.

Touching the rosary that was turned in by François Girin's maid. Says that once at the sermon, and this woman who wore the rosary, and she told her that it would be taken away, and she gave it to the *dizainier*, and she does not know [anything more]. [vol. I, p. 66]

Monsieur Jaques Symo[n]d

Touching the Word of God and the Holy Gospel and frequenting of sermons. Answers the exhortations made to him; answers that he does not despise the Word of God. Said the Pater and confession. Also said that it was proper to pray to God and the Virgin Mary, because he was in great danger from brigands when he called on Our Lord and the Virgin Mary. And is still in this error and asks advice about it and still believes that it is good because of the angelic salutation that descended from Heaven. And he does not understand that it is idolatry, and has received Holy Communion. And he did not understand that it was idolatry to invoke the Virgin Mary, and he was in this error a long time. And he considers the Mass not good and abominable. Asked if he is certain about the holy sacrament of Holy Communion. Answers that he believes as is now believed among us, as is announced to us among us, and the custom of the city. The Consistory gave him proper admonitions. [vol. I, p. 67]

Jana, daughter of Jehan Bovier

And was never married. Acknowledged the rosary and that she carried it in her belt and that she picked it up. And has served masters, and she was brought young to this city. Has served three or four masters, and has always lived in this city. Said her Pater and confession of faith. She does not know whether it is good to pray to the Virgin Mary and does not know whose the said rosary is, but she picked it up and it is not hers, and that she wanted to take it to Decompesio's house to be burned. She was remanded to Monday before the Council, or whenever she will be summoned. Conriousaz, living by the wall, saw her when she found it between the inner and outer doors at St. Peter's at the chief sermon about three weeks ago, and again at the small door of St. Peter's, and they were taken out of her hand while saying the Pater at the morning sermon. Admonished to speak the truth. [vol. I, p. 69]

Among the most persistent features of continued Catholic worship practices in Reformation Geneva was the veneration of the Virgin Mary — why might she have continued to be a reference point for believers?

25 May 1542

Roud Monet

Admonished like the preceding, and also that he criticized the holy sacrament of Holy Communion he last received and that he avoid scandalizing the church. Answers that he has never been found in a place where evil was spoken of the Consistory and that he is not a traitor because he has a trouble in his heart, and that he will not receive Communion this time, because he is troubled in his heart. [vol. I, p. 73]

People in Geneva took to heart the Pauline injunction not to partake of Communion unworthily, but the Consistory did not want people unilaterally deciding for themselves when to take or not to take Communion, especially if a quarrel or personal dispute lay at the heart of the decision. The Consistory wanted to know about any such disputes to make sure they were properly resolved and the quarrelling parties were reconciled to each other.

1 June 1542

Nycolas Baud of Peycier, concerning the official letter of the **castellan** of Peney

Asked whether his wife who was brought to bed of his child which she carried, where it is. Answers that he had a woman come to his house and another woman, and that the child died immediately and that his son carried away the said child dead and it was not baptized. And he carried it to Seyssel, and he says that Our Lord takes all to mercy without being baptized.

Son of the said Nycolas Baud about the answer of the said Nycolas his father concerning the child last mentioned. Answers that his mother was delivered of a son about a month ago, and he took it away and she did not know where he had it, and he took it to Seyssel over the Seyssel Bridge in front of the chapel of the said bridge, in front of the Chapel of Our Lady who does miracles, and it was baptized in the said place and later buried, because Brother Jehan

The castellan (chatelain) was the most senior representative of the Genevan government in the countryside.

The son of Nicolas was following a traditional Catholic practice by bringing the body of his baby brother to a respite chapel, where, it was believed, infants would revive long enough to receive the much-desired baptism, without which they could never get to heaven.

Bourgeoys said so. And that no one commanded him, and if it had been buried he would have dug it up to carry it off. And it was buried there in Seyssel, and he did not have money to have Masses said. And he believes God is a light (?) for all the world and that this was his belief and that he is excitable, and begs mercy from God and the Seigneurie, and claims that he is a cleric.

In the presence of the father strict admonitions were given them. The Consistory advises that they be remanded before the Council. The others are all remanded to next time because of the absence of the elders. [vol. I, pp. 81-82]

10 August 1542

Françoyse, widow of Claude Loup, butcher, called Droblier

Because of frequenting of sermons and other things, swearing and blaspheming God. Answers that the officer Vovrey went to find her at the sermon at St. Gervais. And says the Mass is not good and that she did not go there often except when she had leisure. And goes to the sermon twice a week, and it was last Wednesday, yesterday, and cannot say anything of the sermons that she heard, and does not know how to pray to God except after the preacher. And said the Pater in Latin, and could not say the Credo. She cried much and her hands shook in Consistory before their lordships. Remanded here to Thursday to learn to pray to God and retain what the preachers preach. [vol. I, pp. 106-7]

7 September 1542

Guynome, wife of Loys Meyniez, from Gex

Because of frequenting the sermons and living according to religion, and she hides when she goes to the sermon. Answers that she goes willingly to the sermon and does not live in papistry and has small children that she . . . [incomplete sentence], therefore she cannot go every day, but when she can. And does not know the prayer; her husband is teaching it to her. She said it in Latin, and the Ave Maria in Latin, and every day the Pater and Ave Maria. And that she learn it within two weeks and come give an account [of it] and frequent the sermons, and that she not receive Holy Communion unless she knows it by next Saturday. [vol. I, p. 117]

5 October 1542

Andriaz, widow of Gonyn Genod

Because of children she delivers, that she says the Virgin Mary, invokes the Virgin Mary in aid. Answers that sometimes it escapes her, and she says truly none has power but God, and asks grace, groaning and weeping. And would not want to be other than a respectable woman. She was given proper admonitions to instruct women well in giving birth to children. [vol. I, p. 132]

The Consistory was particularly concerned to make sure that midwives did not engage in Catholic ritual practices at births, whether invoking the Virgin Mary or Saint Anne, the patron saint of pregnant women, or carrying out emergency baptisms, which were deemed invalid by the Reformed church.

26 October 1542

Claude Vuarin, called Macheret, the younger, locksmith

Because of the Word of God and frequenting the sermons and to pray to God. Answers that he was there last Sunday, and other days he cannot go because he must work for himself and his father, who is ill. And he was at St. Gervais Sunday after dinner. And he improved in saying the prayer. And he does not know what the preacher says, he understands nothing, and hopes to be saved by the Commandments and by works. The rest of the sermons is nothing to him, only the prayer and the Commandments. Said that because of some spite he feels against some who have given false testimony against him, that is the reason that has kept him from frequenting the sermons, and he has not said the prayer because of this spite. And that he believes in God, and does not know when he received Communion; about half a year ago. And that he already felt hatred for those who had testified against him, whom he cannot name at this time. The Consistory advises that he be remanded here and that he come in a better frame of mind than he has come here in, and that he name those who have testified against him in order to be reconciled with them. And that he come here next Thursday, and meanwhile commend himself to God. [vol. I, p. 141]

23 November 1542

Messieurs Pierre Falcat and Nycod Moury from Jussy

Asked how long it is since they came to the place. Answer six weeks, and have been to the sermons in the town of Jussy, and do not want to live according to the Reformation. P. Falcat. Pierre answers that he has doubts about the Reformation, because he means to live and die

Both of these men were Catholic priests who held property in Genevan territory but did not want to conform to Reformed worship practices. By 1543, the Genevan city council banished both men from Genevan territory.

in the law of his predecessors and would not want at all to leave the ancient law because of saying the Mass. And his schoolmasters taught him the Mass and he would like to stay with it. Asked whether he would rather follow men than God. Answers as before that he wants to live according to the law under which his father, mother, and master lived. And they want to be good Christians and believe perfectly in God and in Jesus Christ and that Jesus Christ will be the judge of all the world. He would leave Christ in this fashion. And that the Holy Spirit does not inspire him otherwise than it did in the past. And his masters were Magister De Nanto, De Bonnaz, and Magister Corajodi.

Nycod Moury. Answers that he believes in Jesus Christ, and will never renounce the Mass. And that it is said in many places. And he wants to abandon everything that is against Our Lord, and all that is in the Mass is entirely from Holy Scripture. And that there are many respectable people who have said Mass. The Consistory advises that they be given proper admonitions to frequent the sermons and the Word of God. [vol. I, p. 149]

22 February 1543

The widow of Bertheractz, promised wife of Gonrardz de La Palaz

Because of the rosary. Answers it is not so, because she does not mutter anything, and for this someone sent her here. And she frequents the sermons and prays to God as the Council has commanded her, and she says the Pater with good intentions and goes to the sermons and prays to God as she prayed in former times, with good intentions. And she does not keep feasts because she has no calendar, although sometimes when they are together she talks about feasts with the others. And she does not solemnize them and did not fast this Lent and has no scruples about eating meat and does not scandalize others about religion. Remanded to Monday before the Council. [vol. I, pp. 198]

Noble Bartholemie, widow of Richardet, wife of Achard

Because of superstitions and rosaries. Answers that she does not know what this is about and she always keeps the feasts because she does nothing, and she does not know what she said, and she has never said the rosary with her fingers, and someone lent it to her. And she has no images either in her house or elsewhere or blessed things, although she has a St. John that was in their chapel. Monday before the Council and the procurator general. The Consistory decided that she be remanded to the Council with her idol and that someone go with her to investigate her idols, and that two be assigned to visit. [vol. I, p. 199]

15 March 1543

Jaquemetaz, wife of Pernet Guex, shearer

To pray to God; was remanded. Said the prayer and the confession, and that five years ago the law of former times was worth as much as this one, and that since this law came we have gained hardly anything. Indeed it is true that on the eve of Our Lady of Candlemas she went through the city to look for a candle at the apothecaries to give to someone from Mornex, a charcoal-burner, and found one that cost her three *quarts*, and she wants to live according to religion, and can rarely go to the sermon because she has a child, which prevents her. And she heard the sermon at St. Gervais on Sunday. And she pardons Bernarde, who did her an injury. The Consistory: that she be given remonstrances and admonitions to refrain from drunkenness and evil words and that she be punished and guard herself from improper words and that she not keep the feasts again. [vol. I, p. 207]

Notice how many women are called before the Consistory for a wide range of continuing Catholic ritual practices — why so many women?

20 March 1543

Noble Janne Pertennaz

Answers that she is always seen as in former times, and prays to Our Lord; sometimes she says her rosary, and she does not want to be a heretic. She believes that which the holy church believes. And she believes the church of Geneva is good. And she believes in good works. Asked whether Monsieur Calvin is God. The opinion of the Consistory is that she be deprived of the union of Communion and of the church and remanded before the Council and frequent the sermons. Monday, the Council. [vol. I, p. 211]

29 March 1543

Jehan Bennard, host of the Rock

Bennard was an inn-keeper. The Rock (La Roche) was the name of his inn.

Because [of] his child that he had brought to be presented in this city, that [the one] who carried it to be baptized is of the papistry. Answers that the one who carried it was from La Roche and a respectable man and he wanted the said man, named Justz, to be godfather, and he does not know his last name. And that he had his son who was at school in La Roche come to this city. He was not in this city when proclamation was made that such godparents not be sought for children, and if he has erred, it is through ignorance. The Consistory is of the opinion that he be given chastening remonstrances and be well admonished and that he receive the admonition or be remanded before the Council, which will admonish him better, because it is against God and the proclamations, also that it is through ignorance. By resolution he was remanded to Monday before the Council. [vol. I, p. 220]

5 April 1543

Claude Tappugnier, ironmonger

Because of good works. Answers that he believes that he will be saved by the mercy of God and by his good works. He believes that God causes good works and that he does good works by the grace of God. And on praying to the Virgin Mary and praying for the dead, this is his scruple and opinion that he has that the Virgin Mary has the power to pray for us. Of which doubts he was relieved by Monsieur Calvin. Remonstrances. [vol. I, p. 226]

Rolet Viret

Because of the sermons. Answers that he goes to the sermons and knows the Pater but not the Credo and ate meat throughout Lent and did not keep the novena of St. Felix, although the women urged him to do it, which he did not want to do. Said the prayer, and nothing of the confession. And that it was Ayma De Chabloz who urged him to make a novena and give thirteen deniers for a Mass to St. Felix. The opinion of the Consistory is that he strive to learn to pray to the Lord and the catechism. [vol. I, p. 230]

19 April 1543

Mesre, widow of Lambert Aymoz

Because François Conte, she, and Pernete the Adventuress of the Molard met on the Molard. Answers that she did not make the [sign of the] cross, and she had a wax candle, and this was with the consent of those of the house. She and her children go to the sermons and she does not forbid them to go there, and she has not seen anyone make the cross and meant no harm. Sometimes she gets angry at her children when they waste time. Said the prayer, and does not know the confession. She was given admonitions and remonstrances. [vol. I, p. 237]

15 November 1543

Loys Piaget, sheath-maker

Because of the last Holy Communion in the month of September. Answers that he has not received it since Pentecost, and he received it from the hand of Don Jaques de Bonis because he wanted to wait to hear the Passion, and when he saw it was done he asked it of the said Don Jaques who was at the back, and he intended it only in good faith and did not intend any harm. Said the prayer and the confession very poorly. [vol. I, p. 290]

Don Jaques de Bonis, of Saint Gervais

Does not know the reason why he was summoned, and he served at Holy Communion, and he did not have the task of giving it. . . . And he does not remember giving it to anyone except to some children who asked him for it and to a woman named Chamossue. And he had them say the prayer before he gave them the bread, and not the wine. Touching [Regarding] his maid, said that he has had a maid a long time and she is old, and he does not intend to marry, he would rather send her out of the house, and if he were of an age to marry, being sixty years old. He was given remonstrances and admonitions. [vol. I, p. 290]

Jacques de Bonis was a former Catholic priest. It seems some in Geneva preferred to receive the Communion elements from him rather than from one of the pastors.

22 November 1543

Donne Anthoyne Viennesaz

Because of the feasts and papistries, the sermons. Answers that she no longer keeps feasts. On All Saints' Day she came from Bardonnex and could do nothing that day. And she goes to the sermons, although she said sometimes she has to go to dinner when she has been to the sermon in the morning. And she does not despise the Word of God, and she will carry a bell from now on when she goes to the sermon to show that she is going to the sermon. This is in contempt of the Word of God. And she was there last Sunday morning, and she does not know who preached and did not put what he said in her memory. And not this week, and she does not know what they said and did not recognize those who preached. Said that she knows how to pray to the Lord and that she has no advocate but God. She was given firm remonstrances; otherwise she will be remanded to the Council. [vol. I, p. 293]

Here is a case of another prominent woman (the daughter of a former syndic) who appears to have wanted to maintain her Catholic faith in spite of the Consistory's pressure, which she seemed to resist in a spirited way.

29 November 1543

Tevene, widow of Marquet Peronet

Touching the vow she made. Answers that she was very sad when she made it. It was because of her husband, who was ill, and she was badly advised and repents from her heart and begs mercy of God and the Seigneurie and the Company. And she did nothing except what she revealed to the lieutenant, a pound of wax to St. Claude. And now she knows well the fault she committed and is very unhappy about it. And she was at the first sermon at St. Pierre on Sunday, and he produced good words and arguments, and it was a handsome bearded man who preached. Said the prayer, and does not know the confession, and does not pray to the Virgin Mary, and prays to the Lord only and no other. The Consistory, having heard some repentance, [decided] that she be given a term of two weeks to know how to make the confession of her religion. [vol. I, p. 295]

A Catholic shrine to St. Claude was located in Catholic territory right outside Geneva. The Consistory was constantly concerned about the persistent influence of this saint over the cultic practices of Genevans.

5 November 1545

Dardagny

Two people from Dardagny were also called in, and were reprimanded for their superstitions, namely, that a father should not attend his children's baptism: that is a part of witchcraft. They were ordered to put aside this superstition. [vol. II, p. 66]

In other words, in this instance a father did not want to attend his child's baptism, because in Catholic practice, only godparents presented the infant for baptism in church, and fathers did not attend.

3 December 1545

Jehan Dalphin, butcher

Jehan Dalphin, a butcher, appeared and was reprimanded for speaking very dishonorably while selling his meat. He uses lewd and dishonorable words and blasphemes God. When asked to say the prayer [the Lord's Prayer], he does not know how to say it in French, and said it in Latin, along with the Ave Maria, the Credo, the Benedicite, without knowing how to pronounce any of it. He also said grace in Latin and the *Anime Fidelium Defunctorum* and *Requiescant in Pace,* which are horrible and detestable things. When asked if he partakes in the Lord's Supper, he said yes, and said he was around fifty years old.

The decision was made to send him tomorrow before Messieurs [the city council] to deal with the matter, for these are significant issues, and that Messieurs should instruct the teacher at the hospital to teach him to pray. [vol. II, p. 89]

According to Reformed teachings, everyone had to pray in the vernacular, not in Latin, since the Consistory placed a premium on understanding the words of one's prayer.

These are two prayers in Latin for the dead: "For the souls of the faithful departed" and "May they rest in peace."

27 May 1546

The Widow de Ballon

She was reprimanded for being a strong Papist. She answered that she wants to live according to the law of God as declared by the pastors. She was reproached for muttering during the sermons. She replied that regarding the muttering, she was reciting by heart the psalms in Latin as she has done for a long time, thinking she was doing the right thing. She was told that it is wrong to pray to God in this way without understanding what she is saying. [vol. II, p. 230]

5 August 1546

The widow of the innkeeper of the Bear

She was reprimanded for her rebellion and disobedience in that she is still an unbeliever and does not receive the Lord's Supper. She was asked how long it has been since she partook in the Lord's Supper, and she answered that it has not been that long, maybe two years. She was asked why she had stopped partaking, and she answered that it is because she is angry against the one who killed her brother, and she is very stubborn. We had her say the prayer; she said it up to "Forgive us as we forgive those who have sinned against us." And that she prays that Our Lord will forgive her better than she can forgive, and is stubborn. She was asked whether she had not said that she would just as soon have the authorities send Jehan Blancq [the city's executioner] to take her to the scaffold than to make her go to sermons, but she denied this consistently. She was asked whether she had in fact stopped receiving the Lord's Supper for six to seven years, ever since her brother was killed. She answered no, and said that her husband brings it [the bread] to her from church after having received it. [vol. II, p. 267]

12 August 1546

Boniface, wife of Vouvrey

She was interrogated to find out whether it was true that she baptized a child because the minister did not want to give him the name Claude, and gave him the name Abraham, and that she, being in the house when the baptism party returned, said over the child "I baptize you Claude, in the name of the Father and the Son." [vol. II, p. 271]

This revelation would have caused yet more consternation to the Consistory, since this couple was treating the bread of the Lord's Supper like the consecrated hosts of the Catholic Mass. Although she may have thought she was receiving the Lord's Supper, her strategy was not one the Consistory would accept as a genuine partaking of the Lord's Supper.

This case raised several problems for the Consistory. First of all, she was a woman (and women were not supposed to celebrate sacraments or hold any priestly roles). Second, she was engaging in a re-baptism, which was illegal. Third, she was going against the Genevan prohibition on the name Claude. Fourth, she seems to have not used a Trinitarian formula in her baptism, since the Holy Spirit is missing.

12 August 1546

Loys Burdet and his son

They were reprimanded for not going to the sermons, and when he goes, the father crosses himself and makes the sign of the cross. They were asked how many times the Lord's Supper is celebrated each year, and they denied it [*sic*]. The father was reprimanded. He was asked whether anyone remonstrated with him because he crossed himself, and he said that Claude Lollier did so outside St. Gervais. He [Burdet] said he does not think he is doing wrong, and prays for the deceased, and also to the Virgin Mary. And he is very stubborn, and says that if Masses were celebrated in the city, that he would go with the others. We urged him to hand in his rosary. He gave it and threw it down.

It was decided that he be ordered to attend the sermons and that he go to Master Raymond, the pastor of St. Gervais, over the course of two weeks, and come back in two weeks to show what he has learned. We also reprimanded the son, who gave good excuses. He was asked whether his stepmother was not also a Papist. He said yes. [vol. II, p. 273]

26 August 1546

Master Ameyd, the barber

This is the continuation of the case that began with the report of the baptism carried out by Boniface, wife of Vouvrey. Note the Consistory's persistence in dealing with recalcitrant and often confused Genevans.

What did the barber hear the pastor say, and what did he misunderstand?

He was admonished about the child mentioned above. He answered that the child bears the name Claude, the name of his godfather, and that the minister baptized him in the name of Abraham alone and did not baptize him in the name of the Father and the Son and the Holy Spirit. He was asked whether he believes his child was baptized, and he answered as it pleases God. Also that his child's baptism was different than the others, and repeated that the minister said these words: "I baptize you in the name of Abraham." And that he himself was nearby at the time. He was asked whether when other children are baptized, are they not baptized in the same way as his child was, and he answered that he does not know, and it is not his business. He was chastised for calling the child named Abraham by the name Claude. He also said that if they refused to baptize and give the name Claude to his son, that they would have to wait until he was fifteen years old.

Note the Genevans' persistence in continuing their preferred naming practices, regardless of the official rules to the contrary.

It was decided that he should be asked to declare truthfully whether or not he believes that his son was correctly baptized. He answered yes, and always as it pleases God. He was admonished that if the baptism did happen as he alleges, it would not be a valid baptism. He is to be sent to Messieurs tomorrow. [vol. II, p. 279]

31 August 1546

Lucresse, the sister of Lord Curtet

She was admonished for being sent here because she was leaving with money to have masses sung at Annecy by the monks of Saint-Claire, and other admonitions. She was asked to declare any scruples she may have. She answered that her father and mother dedicated her under a different law than the one that is here now, and that she has greater devotion to Saint Claire, but she does not reject the current law. She was asked when the feast of Saint Felix was, and she answered that it was yesterday. She was asked if she ever fasts, and she answered that she fasts when she can. She was asked whether one should pray only to one God, and she answered yes. She was asked whether she prays to Saint Felix, and she replied that she prays to Saint Felix and the other saints who pray for her. She is very stubborn. She was given many lengthy remonstrances.

It was decided that she should go to whichever minister she prefers, and attend sermons daily, and be barred from the Lord's Supper, with solid admonishments. She wanted time to decide which minister to choose to go reconcile herself. She has until tomorrow to decide. [vol. II, p. 285]

Here is another case of a woman (this time from a leading Genevan family) who clearly had no desire to switch to the Reformed faith. Note the Consistory's concern over her use of her own money even if she was spending it on Catholic rites outside of Geneva.

Madame Curtet's ready answers suggest she had no real fear of the Consistory's power to discipline her, perhaps due to her social status.

6 January 1547

Clauda, daughter of Mya Mesaliere

She was told to explain how she received the Lord's Supper. She admitted that it was true that she only took half of it [the bread] in her mouth and put the other part in her hand. She does not want to say why. Her mistress is to be called to reprimand her. [vol. III, p. 4]

Some people retained bread from Communion to use in semi-magical healing practices.

13 January 1547

Pechod, his wife, and their daughter

They were asked to explain why he is angry at Maistre Raymond, the pastor. He said that it was true that when they were at the deathbed of his son-in-law, his wife, who was there, was crying out "Jesus Maria!" and then the said pastor made her leave the room, saying, "Begone, you bad woman with an over-scrupulous conscience!" which the pastor denies saying. He did call her an "evil idolater" but he did not make her leave. Pechod said that if one of the Lord

Note that death-beds could be scenes of conflict over which rituals were appropriate — the reference to Mary seems to have been too much for the pastor in this instance. The family's reaction shows how deep these traditional mourning practices went and how upset they were at the pastor's reaction.

Syndics had said such things to him, he would make an official complaint, and he wants to prove his statement through [the testimony of] reputable folk. He was admonished not to make slanderous statements before God, and that they [the family] had misunderstood what had been said. [vol. III, pp. 9-10]

24 February 1547

La Grande Jeanne

She was reprimanded for still being a Papist. She apologized for not always going to sermons, because she has to take care of various sick people, and that she has learned from various doctors for whom she worked. And she prays to God for them [the sick], that he may have mercy on them. Each day she says the Pater in Latin and the Ave Maria twenty-five times in sets of five, and she says the prayers another five times for the sick that she takes care of, and she admitted this. She was reprimanded for making the sign of the cross when she wants to bleed a patient, which goes to show that she is strongly Papist. She does not know how to pray, nor [does she know the Confession of] Faith in French. She is to return here in three weeks. [vol. III, p. 34]

24 March 1547

Girard Chastellan of Cartigny

He was reprimanded for troubling the church when the pastor of Chancy would not baptize a child because the father was not present. Then the said Girard responded: "Let us go bring him to the pastor of Bernex, who will certainly baptize him and will not refuse." After having asked him repeatedly, he did not want to admit anything except to say that if he had spoken wrongly, he asked God's forgiveness.

Decision: that he be asked again to admit the truth, and, if he is not repentant, he should return here next Thursday, and that the Lord castellan collect information in between times and send it to us, and we will consider the matter further. He admitted having made the statement, and asked God's forgiveness. [vol. III, pp. 51-52]

Traditionally up until the Reformation, fathers did not attend the baptisms of their children. Changing this traditional practice and insisting that fathers be present to make the necessary vows in the presence of the congregation was an uphill struggle for the Consistory.

26 May 1547

Jehan Bresset and his wife from Moëns

He was admonished and asked if he did not say to the minister that he should also baptize his child even if the child was presented by a woman, as he had previously done. He said that the pastor had already done two such baptisms, both for the curial Tombeti and for his brother. Bresset was admonished that even if a woman carried the baby, a man had to make the promises. Then he answered that a woman was as much worth as a man, and that if he [the pastor of Moëns] did not want to baptize the baby, someone else would. He attempted to prove his case.

Decision: he is to bring his witnesses here before next Thursday and is barred from the Lord's Supper. He was also admonished for having said, when the pastor reprimanded him, that God will help the right prevail, meaning that the Duke of Savoy will return. [vol. III, p. 111]

Ameyd Andryon and his daughter Françoyse

He was reprimanded for having promised his daughter to a man from Piedmont, which is a Papist place, and having done so against God and good reason, and against God's commandment. And even if the said girl agreed, it was going against her conscience, wanting to obey her father and mother. He answered that he had gone to Piedmont to sell his goods. There he found a good prospect to whom he gave his goods. He was admonished that this is against God and his commandment. He was admonished because rumor has it that either he or his wife said that Saint Paul talked too much. He denied this.

The father was asked to step outside and the daughter was privately asked for her preference. She answered that the matter cannot be undone for it is done, and that if they have free will over there, they also have the Word of God, just as much as here. She was asked whether she is going into idolatry with no regrets. She answered affirmatively and denied having made any protest. And since she has this one [this fiancé], she does not want another. [vol. III, p. 113]

Notice Françoyse's theologically-based response.

The mother

She was admonished as above. She also answered as above, and that her other son-in-law wanted the girl to be close to him, and that the said prospective husband has helped them a great deal, and has even lent them money. She was rebuked that this was akin to selling their daughter, with many admonishments. [vol. III, p. 113]

11 August 1547

Pauline, wife of de Cherpina, and the wife of Pattu

They were admonished because one day when they attended the birth of a child to a woman called Claudine, they put water on the baby three times and baptized it by their own authority, and it is even being rumored that the said Pauline ordered this to be done. They answered that it was the child's mother who ordered them to do so.

Decision: they should again be admonished to tell the truth, and if they do not want to admit it, the majority felt that if they do not want to tell the truth, they should be sent to Messieurs [the magistrates]. They admit that they gave him the name John. [vol. III, p. 168]

6 October 1547

Estienne Sarpant, from Valromey, shoemaker

Appropriate behavior during church services was expected of all those in attendance.

He was reprimanded because when he goes to sermons, and even one Sunday at Saint Gervais he caused a scandal by sleeping and snoring. [vol. III p. 212]

29 December 1547

The wife of Françoys Chabod

She was admonished because when she went to receive the Lord's Supper, she came late, received Communion in a hurry, and then left without having heard the sermon or having stayed to the end of the service. She made excuses, saying that she has a small child and no wet-nurse. She was admonished to confess her wrongdoing. She said she did not know the pastor who preached, and that she was accompanied by the wife of Grelou and her sister. [vol. III, p. 261]

22 March 1548

Religious rituals surrounding burials were among the most deep-seated faith practices. By way of contrast, see Passevent's reaction to the spare Genevan Reformed funeral rites (see pp. 63-65).

La Bertelotte and la Contesse

They were called in because it is being said that when going to the burial of Chenus, they were praying over the dead, and were throwing dirt for lack of holy water. They were told in

God's name to leave aside these superstitions and to attend faithfully the Word of God to be taught the Christian faith. [vol. IV, p. 20]

12 April 1548

Balthasar Sept

He was called in to be interrogated about certain grimaces and mocking faces that he made one Sunday night when Monsieur Abel, the pastor, was preaching and teaching, saying that we will hear a terrible blast of the trumpet at God's judgment. His [Sept's] grimaces and mocking faces were a cause of great scandal.

He was admonished and told to admit and repent of such an outrage, to confess truthfully and take the reprimand issued by Monsieur Calvin, that it is a disgraceful thing for a young person to mock the Word of God in this way. However, he denied it, saying that he had not meant to mock the pastor or the Word of God, but that he may have laughed, for which he apologizes to God and Messieurs. [vol. IV, p. 45]

Balthasar Sept was a member of a powerful Genevan family — his misbehavior in church may have been due to high spirits, but he (and the majority of his clan) lost few occasions to make the Consistory's life difficult by largely rejecting the Consistory's legitimacy in spiritual and disciplinary oversight.

31 May 1548

Monsieur Cop, minister of the Gospel in Geneva

He stated that last Sunday he was leading the catechism [service] at Saint Pierre, and after the sermon, someone presented himself to have a child baptized, and the godfather wanted to have him called Balthasar. However, he [Cop] did not want to give him that name, since it is prohibited according to the magistrates' ordinances. As a result, there was a great amount of noise and ruckus, insulting the said pastor. The witnesses who were present can testify about the matter, because they slandered him dreadfully, saying that he did not baptize in the name of the Father, the Son, and the Holy Spirit, and other such slanders. He then asked for the witnesses to be called before the Consistory. . . .

See pp. 181-82 for the list of names Genevans could not give their children.

The account of this conflict goes on for several pages. What was the conflict about and what were the main accusations on each side?

The witnesses examined because of the scandal caused last Sunday during the catechism at Saint Pierre against Monsieur Cop:

The first witness: Pierre Franc, a barber-surgeon living in Geneva

He said that it was true that last Sunday he was at the catechism at Saint Pierre and he was present when Monsieur Cop baptized the child. When asked for the name, the godfather wanted to name him Balthasar, and Monsieur Cop refused, saying that the name was prohibited by the magistrates' ordinances. Then a great amount of noise and uproar ensued, because the child's grandfather yelled that he should stop and that they would manage to have him baptized just fine without him, and they created a great disturbance. He also heard the castellan of Jussy say, "We have already put up with too much, and we have let ourselves be over-governed by them." Another man whom he did not know said, "We cannot endure this anymore: we must fight," but he heard nothing else. And he saw and heard when Monsieur Cop baptized the baby in the name of the Father, the Son, and the Holy Spirit, and called him John. He heard nothing else.

The second witness: Lord Jean Du Mast, Lord of l'Isle

He said he was there. He said as reported above. Also that Blecheret and the castellan of Jussy also said as reported above; that the child was named John and baptized by Monsieur Cop in the name of the Father, and the Son, and the Holy Spirit.

The third witness: Monsieur de Cré

He said he heard the disturbance, which was extensive, because instead of honoring the pastors as Saint Paul said, they made a great deal of noise, even the castellan of Jussy and Berthelier.

Both Nicolas Gentil and Philibert Berthelier had official positions in the Genevan government. The former was the Castellan in Jussy, in Geneva's rural hinterland, while the latter served as secretary in Geneva's first court of appeals.

Fourth: Pierre Barrette, inhabitant of Geneva

He said he was present at the baptism and that they wanted to call a child Balthasar, and then Baptiste Sept, who was the godfather, wanted to call him Balthasar, but the pastor told him that this name was not allowed in Messieurs' ordinance, and that he would not give the child that name. And Baptiste said he wanted him to have that name. The other answered no. However, they pestered him, asking him whether he would baptize the baby or not. He answered yes, and baptized him in the name of the Father and the Son and the Holy Spirit and called him John.

He also heard someone he did not know saying that within two weeks, many heads should be cut off and . . . [incomplete sentence].

He also heard André the carpenter, the child's father, say that his child was not baptized and that he had to have the name Balthasar or he would rather spend all his goods and carry the baby for baptism elsewhere, even a hundred leagues away. Also that Monsieur Cop was a thief, and that he had stolen a chalice from his monastery, and that he used to buy manure at Saint Gervais during prayer service times, and that he was a usurer. [vol. IV, pp. 73-75]

[Three more witnesses testified similarly in this case.]

9 August 1548

The pastor of Genthod

He appeared, declaring that last Sunday in the middle of the sermon a woman knelt down and began to pray and then got up to leave. And when the minister chastised her, she answered loudly and scandalously that she wanted to go to her child. And after the sermon, when he warned the lieutenant of the castellan about the matter, the said lieutenant replied mutinously that he [the pastor] was to blame and had caused the scandal, thus publicly supporting the said woman's malice. Thus the pastor called him to the Consistory, also because the lieutenant said he could say much more about the pastor.

The said lieutenant, named Jean Vulliemoz, from Genthod

He said that it was true. He also claimed that the woman in question was forced to tell the pastor that she was going to get her child, because, as he put it, the said minister will not even hear of people moving their legs. He has even often insulted women at church, calling them old crazies.

The said minister

He replied that it was because they usually only laugh during the sermons, and, he declared, this is the reason why the lieutenant hates him, because he [the pastor] once chastised his [the lieutenant's] mother-in-law for this reason.

As a result, the Consistory, knowing the obvious ill-will of the said Vulliemoz, strongly admonished him to encourage good and not evil, and to revere the ministers without allowing or supporting such scandalous doings. If he comes to our attention otherwise, we will complain to Messieurs [the city council], who will know well how to punish him. [vol. 4, p. 109]

Source: *Registers of the Consistory of Geneva in the Time of Calvin: Volume 1: 1542-1544,* ed. Robert Kingdon, Thomas Lambert, and Isabella Watt, trans. M. Wallace McDonald (Grand Rapids: Eerdmans, 2000), and *Registres du Consistoire de Genève au temps de Calvin,* ed. Robert Kingdon et al. (Geneva: Droz, 2001-2007), vols. II-IV. Extracts from volumes II-IV are translated by Karin Maag. The original manuscripts of the Registers of the Genevan Consistory are held in the Archives d'état de Genève, R. Consist. I-IV.

Genevan Council Minutes and Public Announcements

This sequence of edicts and laws concerning worship comes from a four-volume collection of Genevan legal texts. Many of these were recorded in the minutes of the Genevan Small Council, the city's top governing body. Others were "Cries," announcements from the governing authorities of Geneva to the population, read aloud by the town crier. In an age of low literacy, oral public announcements ensured that the population kept abreast of the government's intentions. Consider the amount of repetition from one set of rules to the next and reflect on the key areas of government concern when it came to worship practices. What kind of community were these rules designed to create? How enforceable do you think these rules were? Given that rules are usually put in place to deal with a real or perceived problem, what can you infer about Genevans' worship practices?

Minutes of the Genevan Small Council, 20 January 1541

Geneva's hospital was less a medical center than it was a central location for the provision of social services to orphans, widows, the poor and disabled, etc.

. . . That the preachers are to write down the baptisms and marriages, and the man in charge of the hospital is to record the dead.

Minutes of the Genevan Small Council, 16 July 1542

The authorities of Geneva never lost sight of the fact that many ritual actions and ceremonies had an important administrative component. Why might it have been important to write down the names of those most directly involved in these actions?

The form of the oath taken by preachers and deacons presented before the assembled people.

First, they promise to proclaim the Word of God faithfully and to the edification of the people and to serve in good conscience this church to which God has called me [*sic*], and to be loyal to the magistrates and to maintain their reputation and honor as the truly faithful should, and to display a good example of submission, by obeying the laws and ordinances, issued by the said magistrates; while always retaining the freedom to preach his Word according to the dictates of our office, following his holy commandment.

Minutes of the Small Council, 30 May 1544

The form of the preacher's oath:

I promise and swear that I will serve God faithfully in the ministry to which I am called, purely bringing his Word to edify this church to which he has called me, and that I will not misuse his doctrine to serve my bodily appetites or to please any living man, but I will make use of it with a healthy conscience to serve for his glory and for the good of his people to whom I owe so much.

I also promise and swear to keep the ecclesiastical ordinances as they have been approved by the small, great, and general councils of this city. Insofar as the ordinances charge me with the duty of admonishing those who have fallen short, I will do so faithfully, without giving cause for hatred, favor, vengeance, or any other bodily desire, and in general I will do all that a good and faithful pastor should.

Third, I promise and swear to preserve and maintain the honor and benefit of the magistrates and the city, doing all I can, as far as possible, to keep the people in peace and unity under the leadership of the magistrates, and I will give no support to those who would go against these practices.

Finally, I promise and swear to obey the rules and statutes of the city, and to give a good example of obedience to all others, for my part being subject and obedient to the laws and the magistrates according to the remit of my office, that is without contravening the freedom that we must confess and teach, according to God's commands, and to fulfill the duties of our calling. And thus I promise to serve the magistrates and the people to the extent that in doing so I am in no way prevented from serving God according to my calling.

Minutes of the Small Council, 23 March 1545

It was ordered that in order to provide a good example for the population to attend the sermon, the syndics and council, along with the sautier and fourteen watchmen, should go to the sermon, and that the whole of the small council, the sautier, and the watchmen should sit behind the syndics, and on the other side, the lieutenant, his four assistants, and the secretary should sit, with his officers behind him. And each Sunday, one of the syndics and two of the watchmen, along with two of the court assistants, should attend the sermons at Saint Gervais.

There is a careful balancing act at play here: what challenges might pastors face in trying to obey both God and government?

How might this oath shape a pastor's choice of topic and approach in his sermons?

The sautier was the chief of the Genevan watchmen and was tasked with implementing the Small Council's orders.

The lieutenant was the chief official who oversaw Geneva's law courts.

How might the physical presence of government officials at every worship service affect pastors' sermons?

Minutes of the Small Council, 4 September 1545

Following what the syndic Monsieur Des Ars said about yesterday's Consistory meeting, where the discussion focused on those who do not come to church, so that on prayer days the streets are full of people, and asking that the matter be dealt with, it was decided to make another public announcement about the ordinances. Wednesdays should be just like Sundays until after the sermon, and the assistants and officers of the lieutenant should take it in turns to attend. If they are not available, the current councilors should attend in pairs.

Minutes of the Small Council, 21 November 1547

Here it was ordered that gravediggers be asked to see whether they have come to give the names of the dead to the law court, and if they have not done so, they are to be admonished, and once again the gravediggers are to be ordered to provide the names of the dead to the secretary of the law court, who is ordered to keep this information recorded in a book. And [the names of] those buried at Saint Gervais should be given to the pastors of Saint Gervais, who are also meant to record this.

It is also decided that the pastors must write down [the names of] those they baptize.

Public announcements: Worship — Morals — Behavior, 1 March 1549

Be it known that no one should be so bold or daring as to swear or blaspheme the name of God, under pains of kissing the ground for the first offense, kissing the ground and a three-penny fine for the second offense, a sixty-pence fine and three days on bread and water for the third offense, and being expelled from the city for a year and a day for the fourth offense.

Furthermore, that everyone must come listen to the Word of God, especially on Sundays and on the day of prayer, and on other days when they can do so. Everyone must follow God's Word and live according to it, under pains of civil punishment.

Furthermore, that everyone must send their children to catechism to have them taught, namely, those who are old enough to learn, under pains of a three-penny fine.

Furthermore, that no one is to play around or wander the streets or hang out in taverns during sermon time on Sundays, nor to open shops on prayer days while preaching is taking place, under pains of a five-penny fine.

Getting Genevans to respect the Wednesday prayer and preaching services with the same degree of solemnity as Sunday worship services was an uphill task.

Why the change from 1541? (See p. 174.) Why might the law court records be the best place to record the names of those who had died?

What does this reiterated rule tell you about follow-through?

Cursing seemed to be an endemic problem in Geneva. When more pious Genevans reprimanded those who were cursing and tried to implement the penalties, the result was often a major disagreement or a brawl.

General Council minutes, 16 November 1550

As for feast days, the people, having heard what is being proposed on the subject, unanimously agreed to what the Small Council and Council of 200 have decided, namely, that from now on, Sunday will be the only holiday. Furthermore, that the Lord's Supper will only be celebrated on Sundays. Furthermore, that the Wednesday prayers will no longer be changed to other days.

The exception to the Sunday celebrations of the Lord's Supper up until this point had been the Christmas celebration of the sacrament when Christmas did not fall on a Sunday.

Public announcements: Reminder of the edicts regarding sermon attendance, behavior, etc., 5 July 1555

Our most-feared lord syndics and council of this city of Geneva make it known that though the said most feared lords and superiors have many times issued numerous edicts, prohibitions, orders, and public announcements, according to and based on the Word of God and his holy laws, yet through Satan's cunning and the malice of several ill-intentioned people, these edicts and ways of living good and holy lives have been disdained. Both the magistrates and the Word of God and its ministers have been condemned, mocked, and insulted, and these malicious persons have kept the edicts and mandates from being observed and have prevented the course of justice from flowing freely, so much so that many troubles and major scandals have erupted as a result. Things have gotten so bad that one could justifiably expect God's anger and judgment condemning such ingratitude. However, God, by his singular grace, has healed these troubles to such an extent that the leading authors of such iniquity have been discovered and removed from the places where they previously caused harm. As a result each person should give thanks to God, humble himself, and disarm the divine vengeance by amending his life, following the sermons and preaching of the Word of God, honoring justice and the government, and obeying the holy laws, edicts, and mandates.

Thus our said most-feared lords, wanting from now on to use their power to make this happen and to see to it that the honor of God be maintained and that justice be administered fairly, order and clearly command that all their officers, court officials, citizens, bourgeois, inhabitants, and subjects, of whatever estate, young, old, men, women, lords, masters, and servants, rich or poor, from henceforth attend to the sermons of the Word of God, according to the earlier ordinances. They must honor and respect justice and the magistrates, must live holy and peaceful lives, and must each be obedient, according to his duties, to magistrates, fathers, mothers, lords, and masters. The magistrates prohibit and reject all blasphemy, disrespect for God and his ministers, lascivious talk, worldly songs, drunkenness, dissolute living, excesses, insolent behavior, games, loafing around, slashed clothing, quarrels, ructions,

This date is very important. In 1555, the bulk of Calvin's political opponents in the city were defeated following an abortive riot. This document is evidence of the mindset of Calvin's supporters in the Genevan government.

The "ill-intentioned people" and "malicious persons" were of course Calvin's political opponents, who were native Genevans and objected both to the influence of "foreign" French pastors and to the rising number of French religious refugees.

Notice how worship is used to bolster a particular political outcome.

Slashed clothing, where different-colored fabric was sewn in the rents, was a fashion trend started by mercenary soldiers.

fights, insults, and other activities prohibited by the Holy Commandments and Word of God and by the said edicts and ordinances that were previously issued. . . .

Minutes of the Council of 200, 12 November 1557

Edict and ordinance approved by the Great Council on 12 November 1557, regarding those who turn away from receiving the Lord's Supper.

Because we have previously noticed that some have deliberately abstained from partaking in the Lord's Supper, and even though they were urged to prepare themselves to come to the table, they have disregarded this exhortation; others also, who were excluded from the table, have not come to receive for a long time, either out of disregard or disdain, so that this correction, administered according to the Word of God and our edicts, would become a laughing-stock unless we remedied the situation. We want and require that the following procedure be followed to the letter. That is, if one notices that someone is abstaining from the Holy Communion of the faithful, the Consistory should summon that person, if needed, according to its mandate, and as has previously been practiced. If the abstention is due to enmity, the person will be urged to reconcile with their opponent, or if there is some other impediment, it should be addressed appropriately. If the person is not immediately receptive to the admonition, they should be given time to think about the matter. But if he continues to be stubborn, so much so that another six months go by without him coming to receive, then he should be sent before the magistrates (except if he asks forgiveness for his wrongdoing and is ready to amend his conduct) and be banished from the city for a year, for being incorrigible. However, even if he recognizes his mistake in having rejected the Consistory's admonitions, he should be punished at the magistrates' discretion and sent away to repair the scandal he will have caused by his open rebellion.

Similarly, if, following the exhortations, someone promises to receive the Lord's Supper and then fails to follow through, he is to be summoned to be confronted with his hypocrisy and pretense. And if he is convicted of having misled and blocked the Consistory for a second time, he should receive the same punishment as indicated above.

If someone is barred from the Supper for one time only because of a scandal he caused, if he chooses to absent himself for longer out of anger or for other reasons, if he is summoned to the Consistory and refuses to submit, he should be dealt with as above.

If someone, due to hardening of heart or stubborn clinging to his errors, or for having been found unworthy of Holy Communion and barred from it, and instead of humbling himself, shows contempt for church order and does not come freely to the Consistory to admit his fault, so that he abstains from the Lord's Supper for six months, he should be summoned and urged to submit. If he persists until the end of the year without amending his conduct on the basis of the admonitions received, he should also be banished for a year as incorrigible,

This text raises an important pastoral question: How should one handle a member of the congregation who unilaterally decides not to take Communion?

In other words, people noticed when their neighbor did not come forward to receive Communion, and such a unilateral decision was dangerous because it broke community.

unless he prevents this by apologizing to the magistrates and recognizing his error in the Consistory, so that he can be admitted to communion.

If any stubborn or rebellious person should challenge the ban, the minister's role is to send him away, since he is not allowed to receive him at the table. However, all this should be done in a moderate fashion, so that no one is harmed by excessive rigor and that the corrections are only medicines to bring sinners to submit to the Lord.

And all this should be done in such a way that the pastors have no civil jurisdiction and . . . the Consistory should not challenge the authority of the magistrates or ordinary justice, so that civil power remains intact. Even in cases where punishment is necessary or opposing parties have to be compelled [to reconcile], the ministers together with the Consistory, having heard both sides and given admonitions or verbal correction as needed, should give a full report to the Council, who will decide on actions and judgments based on their report, according to the gravity of the case.

Imagine the scene. Would this strategy be workable in practice?

This ordinance will apply both to the city and to the villages that are under the magistrates' authority.

Public announcements for the lands of Saint-Victor and for the Chapter lands, 18 April 1560

Be it known from our magnificent, powerful, and most-feared lords the magistrates of Geneva, lords of the lands and jurisdiction of the Chapter, and also from their castellan in the said jurisdiction, their deputy and commissioner:

These were territories formerly controlled by the Genevan Catholic church but secularized at the Reformation and taken over by the Genevan government. The Chapter referred to the governing body of clergy of Geneva's cathedral when the city had been Catholic.

1) That each and every one, subject and inhabitant in the said jurisdiction, is to come hear the Word of God, especially on Sundays and on other days when preaching takes place in the said jurisdiction, apart from those who remain to watch over the house and cattle. These [people] in turn must come and others remain in their place to watch over the said houses and cattle, so that everyone gets to come, and they must behave and conform to it [the Word of God], under pains of a ten-pence fine each time.

2) Catechism — Also, that each person should send their children, menservants, and maidservants to the catechism held in the jurisdiction so that they can be taught, especially those of an age and aptitude for learning, under pains of a three-pence fine for non-compliance.

3) Being present for the start and end of preaching services, etc. — Also, that everyone must be present by the last sound of the bell at the start of the prayer, both for sermons and catechism, and no one is to leave before the prayers are done, except in cases of legitimate need, under pains of the same fine as above.

4) Paying heed — Also, that during and throughout the said sermons and catechism,

everyone must pay close attention and not engage in any dissolute or scandalous behavior, under pains of being punished according to the seriousness of the offense.

5) Attending catechism [*sic*: the content of this heading has nothing to do with catechism attendance specifically] — Also, that all those who accompany an infant to baptism or attend a wedding must remain and listen to the sermon without leaving the church except for legitimate reasons, until the said baptism or wedding is completed, under pains of a three-penny fine. . . .

11) Baptisms are to be done locally — Also, no one is to have children baptized or get married except by the preachers assigned and commissioned in the said jurisdiction, or to carry out any kind of Papist works or ceremonies, under pains of being chastised and punished according to the seriousness of the offense.

12) On loafing around — Also, no one is to loaf around during sermon time, under pains of a non-negotiable five-pence fine for each person contravening this ordinance. . . .

19) No sale of beverages during sermon time — Also, all tavern-keepers (male or female) living in the said territory are not to be so daring or bold as to provide drinks to anyone coming or going during sermon time or at suspicious times, under pains of a five-pence fine for the first time, ten-pence fine the second time, and a sixty-pence fine for the third occurrence.

20) On prayers before and after meals — Also, that all the said innkeepers and all others in the jurisdiction should pray to God before the meal and give thanks to God after the said meal, under pains of a five-pence fine for each time they fail to do so, and of being punished for their rebellion.

Given that the Genevan rural territories were nestled right up against the Catholic lands of Savoy, it was hard to prevent people in the Genevan territories from slipping off to Catholic ceremonies.

See the catechism prayers on pp. 85-87 for this purpose.

In your opinion, how enforceable was this rule?

Among the favorite Genevan pastimes that took people away from worship was target shooting, which often took place outside the city walls.

Public announcement: Games are prohibited on Communion days, 6 April 1562

Be it known . . . that everyone, of whatever estate, quality, and status, is prohibited from playing any kind of game next Sunday or from henceforth on any day when the Lord's Supper is to be celebrated. Games are banned, whether played in the streets, in the public squares of this city, or anywhere else inside or outside the city. Instead each person is to spend the day reflecting on God's grace towards us. All this under pains of a sixty-pence fine and of being chastised and punished as rebels.

Public announcement: Sermons – Feasts, 28 July 1564

Be it known from our most-honored lords, syndics, and Council of this city. Given that we see God's chastisement of some of the neighboring nations and peoples, and this chastisement is coming close to us, everyone is to devote themselves even more earnestly to prayer and supplications, both at home and in private and in public, and especially to gather together on the day of prayer, namely, on Wednesdays, more diligently than usual, to obtain God's mercy and grace. Furthermore, in order to be more ready to implore God's aid, everyone is to abstain from banquets and excesses on that day, humbling themselves before God in sobriety and fasting, so that he may be pleased to turn away his wrath from us and perpetuate his grace and blessings on this poor republic, by being its protector, as he has done up until now.

Both private and corporate prayer were closely tied to contemporary threats and calamities.

_____

Source: Genevan City Ordinances: From *Les Sources du droit du canton de Genève*, ed. Emile Rivoire and Victor van Berchem (Aarau: H. R. Sauerländer, 1927-1935), Volume II, pp. 364, 392-93, 470, 474, 514, 526-27, 540; Volume III, pp. 24-25, 50-51, 116-18, 129-30, 157-58. The translation is by Karin Maag. The original manuscripts of these various ordinances are held in the Archives d'état de Genève.

Extract of the Ordinance Established by the Small Council Regarding the Selection of Baptismal Names (1546)

This text established a list of names that could not be given to children at baptism. The controversy over baptismal names had flared up earlier in 1546. See the extracts of the Consistory records for the same year to find out more about how families reacted when they were not allowed to give their children names that the pastors felt were too closely linked to Catholic beliefs. As you read this text, reflect on how parents might have reacted to these rules, bearing in mind that it was a common early modern practice to name children after older relatives, and that in the 1540s, older relatives would all have been baptized before the Reformation came to Geneva. Their own names may well have been on this list.

Notice that the government is issuing rules about names given at baptism — the Genevan church was a state church, and hence the government regularly put its weight behind rules and laws dealing with church-related matters.

[The magistrates] first of all prohibit giving the names of the idols [saints] who ruled in the land, such as Suaire, Claude, Mama, and others, because there may still be elements of superstition and also because it is a reminder of the idolatry from which God was pleased to deliver this land by his grace. Also included are the names of those known as the [three] kings, both because this is an erroneous practice and because some have put misplaced confidence in them.

According to legend, the names of these kings were Gaspard (or Caspar), Melchior, and Balthasar.

Also the name of offices, because these only belong to those to whom such a charge is given and who are called by God, such as Baptist, Angel, Evangelist, and other similar ones.

Also the names belonging to God alone or to our Lord Jesus Christ, such as God the Son, Spirit, Emmanuel, Savior, Jesus.

Also badly chosen names or ones whose absurdity can lead to mockery, such as All-Saints, Cross, Sunday, Epiphany, Sepulcher, Christmas, Easter, Pentecost; and Christian, because that name is common to all.

The legislation was so thorough that even names that sounded awkward or ridiculous, rather than too Catholic, were prohibited.

Also double names and others that sound clumsy, like Gonin, Mermet, Sermet, and Allemand.

Also distorted names such as Tyvan or Tevette instead of Estienne, or Monet instead of Simon.

Source: Ordinance on the Selection of Baptismal Names (1546) from *Registres de la Compagnie des Pasteurs de Genève au temps de Calvin,* ed. R. Kingdon and J.-F. Bergier (Geneva: Droz, 1964), Volume I, p. 29. The translation is by Karin Maag. The original manuscript of the Registers of the Company of Pastors for this period is held by the Archives d'état de Genève, Registres de la compagnie des pasteurs de Genève, Vol. B1.

Ordinances for the Supervision of Churches in the Country (1547)

These ordinances were issued six years after the Ecclesiastical Ordinances of 1541. It is instructive to compare the two sets. The ordinances for rural churches put much more emphasis on fines, whereas the 1541 ordinances for the city made no mention of penalties. Why the difference?

February 3, 1547

Ordinances for the Supervision of the Churches dependent on the Seigneury of Geneva [the Genevan government], which it is advised be put in force, subject to the complete discretion of their Lordships

Sermons

Why would the regulations for attendance at weekday services be more flexible than those for Sunday attendance?

1. Everyone in each house is to come on Sundays, unless it be necessary to leave someone behind to take care of children or animals, under penalty of 3 sous.

2. If there be preaching any weekday, arranged with due notice, those who are able to go and have no legitimate excuse are to attend, at least one from each house, under penalty as above.

Notice the Genevan authorities' concern for the religious instruction of people across the social spectrum. What evidence have you seen in the Consistory records that show this same concern even for servants?

3. Those who have man or maid servants are to bring them or have them conveyed when possible, so that they do not live like cattle without instruction.

4. Everyone is to be present at Sermon [the entire service] when the prayer is begun, under penalty as above, unless he absent himself for legitimate reason.

5. Everyone is to pay attention during Sermon, and there is to be no disorder or scandal.

6. No one is to leave or go out from the church until the prayer be made at the end of the Sermon, under penalty as above, unless he have legitimate cause.

Catechism

1. Because each preacher has two parishes, Catechism is to take place each fortnight. Those who have children are to bring them, with the rest of their household who have not been to Sermon, as above.

2. The same attention, honest and regular, is to be given to Catechism as has been said for Sermon.

Penalties

1. Those who fail in their duty of coming are to be admonished by the **Guardians,** both themselves and their family.

2. If after intimation they continue to default, they are to be fined three groats, for each time. Of this one third will be applied to the Guardians; the other two-thirds will be applied to the poor of the parish, and put into the funds of the church for distribution according to need as it becomes known.

3. If anyone come after the Sermon has begun, he is to be admonished, and if after this is done he does not amend, for each fault he is to be fined three sous, which will be applied as above.

4. If during Sermon anyone make any disturbance or scandal, he is to be reported to the Consistory to be cautioned, in order that procedure be in proportion to the fault: that is, if by carelessness, he is to be well told off; if it happen[ed] by intended malice or rebelliousness, he is to be reported to their Lordships to be punished appropriately.

The Guardians were officials appointed by Geneva to watch over the behavior of the inhabitants of the countryside.

The groat, or denier, was a Genevan coin of lesser value than the sou. Does the planned distribution of the proceeds of the fines raise any red flags for you?

By Whom Fines Are to Be Exacted

1. The local lord, in conjunction with the Ministers and the Guardians, is to oblige the delinquents to pay the fines they have incurred, when they will not pay of their own free will. Legitimate excuses are to be admitted, but this is to be done without any formal procedure.

2. If there be any so rebellious that, despite the above fines, they do not at all amend, they are to be reported to the Consistory with advice to the effect that their Lordships punish them according to the seriousness of their obstinacy.

3. Fathers are to be responsible for their children, and, if there be a penalty, it is to be exacted from them.

Clearly the Genevans did not intend to be lax about these matters. What can you infer about relations between Geneva's urban world and rural areas in this period? How much support did the Reformation have in the countryside if everything had to be enforced by fines?

Of Baptism

1. Baptism is to be administered any day, provided that there be Sermon along with it. The Ministers are always to exhort the people to link it up with the Catechism.

2. Children are to be brought at the beginning of Catechism or Sermon.

3. Fathers are to be present, unless they have legitimate excuse of which cognizance will be taken by the Consistory.

4. No godfather is to be admitted for presenting a child unless he is of an age to make such a promise; that is, he must have passed fifteen years, be of the same confession as ourselves, and be duly instructed.

5. As to names, let their Lordships' ordinances be careful both to avoid all superstition and idolatry and to remove from the Church of God everything foolish and indecent.

6. If midwives usurp the office of Baptism, they are to be reproved or chastised according to the measure of fault found, since no commission is given them in this matter, under penalty of being put on bread and water for three days and fined ten sous; and all who consent to their action or conceal it will be liable to the same penalty.

Here is the practical outworking of Calvin's strong opposition to baptism by women.

Of the Supper

1. No one is to be received at the Supper unless he first have made confession of his faith. That is to say, he must declare before the Minister that he desires to live according to the reformation of the gospel, and that he knows the Creed, the Lord's Prayer, and the Commandments of God.

2. Those who wish to receive the Supper are to come at the beginning of the Service; those who come at the end are not to be received.

3. Other impediments are to be within the cognizance of the Consistory, to deal with them in accordance with what has been ordained.

4. All are to remain until the end, unless there be a legitimate excuse which is recognized as above.

Why were those who came late not admitted? What crucial part of the service had they missed?

Of Times of Meeting at Church

Buildings are to remain shut for the rest of the time, in order that no one outside the hours may enter for superstitious reasons. If anyone be found making any particular devotion inside or nearby, he is to be admonished: if it appear to be a superstition which he will not amend, he is to be chastised.

What sort of superstitions might the Genevan authorities be concerned about? What do these rules tell us about the Genevan Reformed understanding of the church building as sacred space?

Faults Contravening the Reformation besides Those Already Mentioned

1. Those found to have any paternosters or idols for adoration are to be brought before the Consistory, and, besides the punishment imposed on them there, they are to be brought before their Lordships.

2. Those who have been on pilgrimages or voyages the same.

3. Those who observe the papistical feasts or fastings are to be admonished only, unless they are obstinate in their rebellion.

4. Those who have attended Mass, besides admonition, are to be brought before their Lordships.

5. In such cases, their Lordships will have the right of chastising by means of prison or otherwise, or of punishing by extraordinary fines, at their discretion.

6. In the case of fines, they are to apply some small portion of them to the Guardians, if the delict [fault or wrongdoing] was notified by them.

Paternosters were Catholic prayer books and "idols" refers to images of saints or of the Virgin Mary.

Why might those who observe Catholic fasts or feasts be treated more leniently than those who have images or go on pilgrimages?

_____

Source: Ordinances for the Supervision of Churches in the Country, 1547, from *Calvin: Theological Treatises*, ed. J. K. S. Reid (Philadelphia: Westminster Press, 1954), pp. 77-80. Reid translated the text from the French version published in the nineteenth-century collected edition of Calvin's works: *Joannis Calvini Opera Quae Supersunt Omnia*, ed. W. Baum, E. Cunitz, and E. Reuss (Braunschweig: Schwetschke and Son, 1872), Vol. X, cols. 52-55. The editors of the *Opera* based their text on the original manuscripts held in the Archives d'état de Genève, Pièces historiques nos. 1384 and 1395.

Statutes of the Genevan Academy (1559)

The Genevan Academy was established in 1559, and rapidly became a reference point for students and future pastors from across Reformed Europe. Both Calvin and his successor, Theodore Beza, taught biblical exegesis in the Academy, and Beza became the school's first rector. The Academy was modeled on other Reformed centers of learning at the time, including the Lausanne Academy and the Strasbourg Gymnasium Illustre. The institution had two parts: a lower level that corresponded to a middle school or high school, and an upper level that provided university-level instruction in the humanities, Greek, Hebrew, and theology. All instruction throughout the Academy was in Latin, and only boys and young men were admitted. Girls in Geneva only had access to vernacular education.

In Geneva, school attendance included mandatory church services. In church the schoolboys sat not with their families but with their peers. This practice was part of the close integration of religious instruction provided in church and at school — nothing was left to chance.

The regents (all male) taught the classes in the lower level of the Genevan Academy that corresponded roughly to a middle-school/high-school level of instruction.

The principal and **regents** must divide all the pupils into four groups, not according to their classes, but according to their neighborhoods, and must make a list of each group, giving one list to each regent. Thus the pupils must come to church in their own group, and be seated in a specific place in each church assigned to them by the magistrates. No one else should be allowed to sit here.

All the pupils must come to church in good time, to the Wednesday morning service and to the two Sunday services, one in the morning and one in the afternoon, and to the catechism service. They are to sit in their seats and listen to the sermon attentively and with reverence. In each church, one of the regents should be there in good time, so as to oversee his group. If necessary, after the sermon he should read out the list of pupils and take note of those who were absent or failed to listen attentively to the Word of God. These pupils, if found to be at fault, will be punished publicly the next day in school according to the seriousness of their offense. . . .

See the prayers from the Genevan Catechism on pp. 85-87.

The pupils should begin each day in their classrooms with the prayer specially written for them in the catechism. Each one should in turn recite it devoutly. . . . After the morning classes, each one in turn should recite in each class the Lord's Prayer and a brief prayer of thanksgiving. . . . The pupils should return to the college both in winter and in summer at 11 o'clock and then should practice singing the Psalms until noon. From noon to one they should be taught for an hour, and then should have a snack, followed by prayers, followed by writing exercises or homework. Then they should have two more hours of class, and then gather at the sound of the bell in the assembly room. . . . Finally, three pupils each day in class order should recite in French the Lord's Prayer, the Creed, and the Ten Commandments. After this, the principal should dismiss them, blessing them in God's name.

Note the centrality of Psalm singing: the schoolboys were meant to teach the rest of the congregation over time how to sing the Psalms.

On Wednesday, as stated above, they are to attend the morning sermon. . . . On Saturday . . . from three to four . . . they should recite the passages that will be dealt with on the following day in the Catechism session, and the regents should explain the meaning to them in a clear and understandable way, according to their level. . . .

Having read this text, and knowing that the boys in this school (no girls were admitted) ranged in age from about eight to about sixteen, how likely is it that these statutes achieved their desired effect? What would be most difficult to implement?

On Sundays, they should listen to the sermons, meditate on them, and take notes on them. During the week before the celebration of the Lord's Supper, one of the ministers of the Word of God should give a short talk about the Lord's Supper in the assembly room, exhorting his hearers to fear God and maintain peace among themselves.

Source: *Worship in Medieval and Early Modern Europe: Change and Continuity in Religious Practice,* ed. Karin Maag and John D. Witvliet (Notre Dame: University of Notre Dame Press, 2004), pp. 117-18. This translation from the French is by Karin Maag, from the text of the statutes published in *Le Livre du Recteur de l'académie de Genève,* ed. Sven and Suzanne Stelling-Michaud (Geneva: Droz, 1959-1980), Vol. I, pp. 68-69. The editors of the Livre du Recteur based their text on the manuscript of the Livre du Recteur, held by the Bibliothèque publique et universitaire de Genève, Ms. Fr. 151.

PART THREE

ASSISTING THE INVESTIGATION

Why Study Geneva's Worship?
Suggestions for Devotional Use

The following are suggestions for devotional use that correspond with specific sections of the book.

The Context of the Worshiping Community: Sixteenth-Century Geneva

- Think back to the various places of worship you have attended during your lifetime. How close were these places of worship to your home? Did you worship in your neighborhood or across town? How has the location of your place of worship relative to your home affected your sense of where God is present and at work in your community?
- Notice the walls that surround Geneva in so many of the images in this section. Walls can protect, but they can also exclude and divide. Think about the presence of walls in your own personal experience of faith: these can be mental walls as well as physical ones. Have these walls kept you safe? Have they hemmed you in?
- The Genevan Reformation took place in an era of religious conflict. Compare the Reformation era to today. Do you sense that there is still religious conflict that touches you today? How do you deal with it in the light of your faith?

People and Artifacts

- Looking at the images of wedding processions and baptismal gatherings, think back to these moments in your life. If you have been baptized, what do you remember or what have you been told about your baptism? What family members were there, and what role did they play? In what ways has your baptism been meaningful in your subsequent life of faith?
- Think about weddings you have attended (including your own, if applicable). The image included here seems to focus more on the celebration of family and friends than on the actual church service. Is that true for you too when you think back to weddings you have attended? How much focus has God received in these events?

Worship Setting and Space

- Picture yourself attending a Reformation-era service in one of the Genevan or French churches portrayed in this section. What would church services be like? What would you see and hear? What would people around you be doing? Where would your focus be?
- Look carefully at the images in this section, and think about the interior of places of worship you have attended. Are there any images of any kind in the sanctuary? How would you feel about worshiping in a sanctuary with lots of religious images versus none at all? Which setting do you feel is more conducive to devotion, and why?

Descriptions of Worship

- Many of Calvin's letters in this section were to churches that were experiencing persecution or that were definitely a confessional minority in their communities. Imagine that you were part of one of these churches. How would you sustain your own personal faith and the faith of your fellow congregants under pressure or persecution from people whose understanding of the Christian faith was different from your own?
- André Ryff wrote about his experiences of household worship in Reformation-era Geneva. Describe your own devotional practices at home. What could you do to deepen them?

Orders of Service and Texts

- Use the prayers from the Genevan Catechism over the course of a day, praying them at the times of day indicated in the text. How does using these prayers affect your awareness of God's presence with you throughout your day?
- Add the singing of a Psalm to your daily devotional practice over the course of a week. How does singing the Psalm — compared to simply reading it — shape your devotional life?

Sermons and Theology of Worship Documents

- Consider carefully what Calvin says in his foreword to the Genevan Psalter about the use of music in worship and reflect on his insights in the light of your own experience of music as an aid to devotion. What music brings you closer to God?

- Re-read Calvin's sermon on 2 Samuel 6. In what ways does this sermon deepen your awareness of what it means to worship God?
- Read over what Calvin writes in his commentary on Paul's letter to the Corinthians about the Lord's Supper, and reflect on your church's celebration of that sacrament. What do you usually think about during that part of the service? How does what Calvin has to say deepen your own participation in the sacrament?

Polity Documents

- Especially when you were young, did you ever feel like you were made to participate in worship and devotional practices whether you wanted to or not? Reflect on that training, and on the impact (positive or negative) it has had on your faith in the short term and the long term.
- Many of the documents in this section focus on accountability, albeit perhaps in a stricter and more structured way than we are used to today. What use have you made of accountability partners in your life of faith? How would having an accountability partner help you in your commitment to follow Christ?

Why Study Geneva's Worship?
Discussion Questions for Small Groups

The following are discussion questions for each section of this book.

General Introduction and Timeline

- What challenges did Geneva face in moving from Catholicism to Protestantism?
- What surprised you most about Geneva from the early sixteenth century to 1564? Why?

The Context of the Worshiping Community: Sixteenth-Century Geneva

- Imagine what it might have been like to live in sixteenth-century Geneva. In what ways did their urban world look different than a similar-size city today? What similarities do you see?
- What might it be like to worship in an uncertain and sometimes dangerous political situation, with external enemies poised to attack? What can we learn from Geneva's experiences about how to worship in such circumstances?

People and Artifacts

- The first image in this section shows a vessel used for Communion wine. What does this container tell you about how the Lord's Supper was celebrated in Geneva? How does that compare with present-day Communion rituals?
- What do these images tell you about worship practices in early modern Reformed communities? What did people seem to value?
- How do the images of practices surrounding weddings and baptisms compare with those of today? What similarities and differences do you see?

Worship Setting and Space

- As you consider these images, imagine yourself at worship in these churches. What strikes you most? How does the set-up and use of liturgical space in these sixteenth-century churches compare to present-day places of worship?
- Discuss the presence or absence of images in churches you know well. Think broadly about images. Include banners, crosses, stained-glass windows, and so on. Do these contribute to or detract from the worship experience?
- Was the Reformers' decision to eliminate images from the worship space ultimately counter-productive? What were the consequences and implications of their decision?

Descriptions of Worship

- Calvin was consulted about many different worship-related issues. Evaluate his counsel. How realistic were his responses? What might have happened if congregations had tried to implement the advice he sent?
- What did you learn about the impact of worship in early modern Geneva from reading the eye-witness accounts by Charles Perrot, André Ryff, and the anonymous author of the *Passevent*? What changes seem to have been most difficult for people to accept? What changes were seemingly welcomed?
- Taken together, what do these documents tell you about the outcomes of the Genevan Reformation in terms of moving people's hearts and minds away from Catholic practices and toward a new way of worship?

Orders of Service and Texts

- As you read through these liturgies, compare their structure and key points with the liturgies and orders of service you are familiar with. What is the same, and what is different about these Genevan documents?
- Compare the use and place of music in worship in Calvin's Geneva with music in today's churches. What aspects of the Genevan practice are worth retaining for today?
- What do the prayers included in the Genevan catechism tell us about personal devotional practices expected in Genevan households? How do these devotional practices compare with today's approach to personal prayer?

Sermons and *Theology of Worship Documents*

- Calvin had a great deal to say about how to worship and how not to worship. What practices did he reject, and why? Which practices and attitudes of worship did he recommend? Were his arguments always fully coherent and persuasive?
- Examine Calvin's use of Scripture in his *Institutes*, his commentaries, and his sermon. How does Calvin approach Scripture, and does he always give equal weight to its teachings?
- How do the form and content of Calvin's sermon and commentaries compare to sermons you have heard and biblical commentaries you have read?
- Compare Calvin's teachings on baptism, on images, and on the singing of Psalms with the images in the two previous sections and with the Psalter documents in the "Order of Service and Texts" section. From what you can tell, based on your analysis, were his teachings consistently applied?

Polity Documents

- Compare the documents in this section with the eyewitness accounts in the "Descriptions of Worship" section. What problems tend to resurface again and again? Why might these problems be so prevalent in the Genevan population?
- Consider the response of the Genevan Consistory and that of the Genevan government to worship-related misbehavior or ignorance. How effective did their response seem to be? Are there other approaches you could think of that they should have tried to use instead?
- Given these ordinances and records, articulate in your own words what the Genevan expectations were for the population at worship. Why did it seem so hard to get the population to fulfill these expectations? Were the Genevan church and state authorities unrealistic?
- What is your reaction to the Genevan ordinances and Consistory cases in this section? If these documents make you uncomfortable, try to explain why.

Why Study Geneva's Worship? A Guide for Different Disciplines and Areas of Interest

Christianity

If you are interested in Christianity as a religion generally, then Reformation-era Geneva is helpful for understanding the following:

- the challenges inherent in moving a community from one confessional perspective (Roman Catholicism in this instance) to a different one (Reformed Christianity);
- the range of confessional views and preferences present in the territory even after the Reformation was officially implemented;
- the strategic decisions made by church and state authorities to work together to achieve common goals but also the problems that could emerge as a result of this combined effort.

Here are discussion questions based on these general religious issues:

- What factors may have made it difficult or even impossible for Calvin's vision of a Reformed community at worship to be realized in early modern Geneva?
- What were the main reasons for the continuing confessional diversity in Geneva even after Reformed Protestantism became the official Genevan faith?
- What impact (positive or negative) did the government authorities have in the implementation of the Reformed faith in Geneva?

Christian Worship

If you are interested in worship generally, then Reformation-era Geneva is helpful for understanding the following:

- how scriptural passages can be interpreted to support certain forms of worship and reject others;

- how prayer can be incorporated into both communal worship and private devotional practices;
- how the Psalms can be used to shape the devotional life of the church in its singing;
- how liturgies can link theological instruction and communal understandings about the role and value of these church rituals;
- how the reform of worship touches all aspects of church life, not simply liturgies and sacraments.

Here are discussion questions based on these general worship issues:

- In what ways should worship leaders turn to Scripture as a key resource in shaping not only the content but also the theology of worship?
- How can Reformation Geneva's example help shape worshiping communities' approaches to the Book of Psalms?
- How effective was the theological instruction provided by Calvin and others in transforming the mind-set and practices of Genevans at worship?
- Should a church make use of images in worship? Why or why not?
- How might worship be broadened to be understood as much more than simply the regular weekly worship gathering, and how might that expanded notion of worship change even what is done during the regular weekly gathering of the community of believers?

Evangelism and Discipleship

If you are interested in evangelism and discipleship, then Reformation-era Geneva is helpful for understanding the following:

- how churches can turn to each other for mentoring and advice, particularly regarding worship questions;
- how education both in church and in school can be used as a tool for evangelism and discipleship.

Here are discussion questions based on these evangelism and discipleship issues:

- In what ways did Geneva serve as a reference point for the wider Reformed Church, and how did Genevan advice take into account the differing circumstances of Reformed Christians in framing answers? What can we learn from these encounters about the importance of the local context in evangelism and discipleship?

- What were the take-home messages provided by Genevan religious instruction? How effective did they seem to be in helping to foster discipleship?

Spirituality

If you are interested in spirituality, then Reformation-era Geneva is helpful for understanding the following:

- the impact of a pared-down liturgy and unadorned worship space on Reformed devotion;
- the use of sung Psalms and prayers both in church and at home as means to foster spirituality.

Here are discussion questions based on these spirituality issues:

- What impact did the Genevans' move from a largely visual corporate faith focused on the celebration of the Mass to a largely aural corporate faith focused on preaching have on people's spirituality?
- Would a more pared-down liturgy held in a more unadorned worship space, as in Reformation-era Geneva, tend to foster spirituality or hamper its development?

Preaching

If you are interested in preaching, then Reformation-era Geneva is helpful for understanding the following:

- how Scripture was presented and interpreted in sermons;
- how sermons were used as teaching tools, and how congregations were meant to receive these sermons.

Here are discussion questions based on these preaching issues:

- Is the practice of preaching sequentially through entire books of the Bible over several weeks or months worth retaining or reviving? Why or why not?
- Should more be done in churches today to help people remember and retain the content of sermons? What are possible strategies to achieve this goal?

Glossary of Names

People

Theodore Beza (1519-1605) French Reformed theologian and scholar. After finishing a degree in civil law and moving to Paris, Beza developed an interest in Reformed theology. His Reformed faith forced him to flee Catholic France. He went first to Lausanne and then to Geneva, where he eventually became the first rector of the Genevan Academy. He was acknowledged as Calvin's heir in Geneva, as he was elected moderator of the Company of Pastors after Calvin's death in 1564. He also became one of the chief advisors to the French Reformed churches.

Martin Bucer (1491-1551) Originally a friar of the Dominican order, Bucer was influenced early on by Luther and was excommunicated by the Catholic Church in 1523. Bucer played a crucial role in establishing the Reformation in the free imperial city of Strasbourg. Calvin was strongly influenced by Bucer and by the liturgy of the Strasbourg church during his three-year stay in the city from 1539 to 1541. When Strasbourg fell to the Holy Roman Emperor, after the emperor's success against the Schmalkaldic League (1546-1547), Bucer emigrated to England. He died there in 1551.

Heinrich Bullinger (1504-1575) Swiss reformer and Reformed theologian. Bullinger was most influenced by the doctrines of Huldrych Zwingli, the prominent Swiss Reformer and theologian. After Zwingli's death in 1531, Bullinger replaced Zwingli as Antistes (the chief pastor of the church) in Zurich. Bullinger preserved the city's Reformed status and worked to ensure strong links between the government and the church. He was the primary author of the Second Helvetic Confession, adopted in 1566, one of the most recognized confessions of the Reformed faith.

John Calvin (1509-1564) French reformer and theologian best known for his work in Geneva from 1541 until his death in 1564. Calvin's systematic theology, allied to his skills in establishing and organizing the Genevan church, strengthened his position in the city and made him a reference point for the wider Reformed Church. Alongside his extensive biblical commentaries and published sermons, Calvin wrote and revised his *Institutes of the Christian Religion,* first published in 1536, and played a leading role in the foundation of the Academy of Geneva in 1559.

Antoine Cathelan (sixteenth century) French Franciscan and anti-Protestant pamphleteer.

Antoine Cathelan is one possible author of the polemical work *Passevent Parisien,* published in 1556, which details Reformed Protestant practices from the point of view of a shocked Catholic. In spite of its polemical perspective, the *Passevent Parisien* is a rare and valuable eyewitness account of sixteenth-century Geneva.

Reymond Chauvet (?-1570) Chauvet was born in St. Celli, which became a part of modern-day France in 1790. He first met Calvin in Strasbourg in 1535. He spent time as a prisoner in Beaucaire, France, in 1544. In 1545 he became the pastor of Saint Gervais Church in Geneva until his death in 1570.

Artus Désiré (early 1500s-ca. 1580) Catholic, anti-Protestant pamphleteer. In his lifetime he published about twenty works ranging from anti-Protestant polemics to social commentaries. Désiré is one possible author of the polemical *Passevent Parisien,* published in 1556, which criticized the practices and faith of the Reformed Genevan church, offering a rare look into Genevan worship.

Guillaume Farel (1489-1565) French Reformer. Farel was one of the main leaders who brought Geneva to the Reformation. In 1536 he urged Calvin to join him in his efforts. Both Farel and Calvin were banished from Geneva in 1538 due to controversy between the pastors and the government over worship and church discipline. After his banishment Farel became the pastor of Neuchâtel until his death twenty-seven years later. Farel is considered a pioneer of the French Reformation because of his charismatic preaching and popular writings on Reformation doctrines.

Clément Marot (ca. 1496-1544) French poet and versifier of French metrical psalms. A noted French humanist, Marot repeatedly shifted between Catholicism and the Reformed faith. His enduring contribution to Reformed worship was his versification of fifty Psalms in French. These, alongside Theodore Beza's versifications, formed the core of the Genevan Psalter.

Sebastian Münster (1480-1552) Sixteenth-century German Hebraist, theologian, and critical interpreter of biblical texts. Münster converted to Protestantism in 1524 and taught Hebrew at the University of Heidelberg and later at the University of Basel, publishing numerous dictionaries focusing on Hebraic studies. In the process, he collaborated with Elijah Levita, a prominent Jewish grammarian. He was very interested in scriptural studies and published many works that included Jewish scholarship as a reference. Münster's work provoked accusations of Judaizing, and these accusations eventually drove him from his exegetical work toward the study of geography and cartography until his death in 1552.

Charles Perrot (1541-1608) Originally a monk, Perrot accepted the Reformation and became pastor at Moens and Genthod in the Genevan countryside in 1564. In 1568 he became a pastor in the city of Geneva and was later the rector at the Academy of Geneva from 1570 to 1572 and again from 1588 until 1596. He also served the Academy as professor of theology starting in 1598 until his death in 1608.

Denis Raguenier (?-ca. 1560) French religious refugee from Bar-sur-Seine. Raguenier was living in Geneva when he was asked by the deacons to be Calvin's stenographer. He was able to use his skills in shorthand to record accurately Calvin's many sermons. During his tenure he recorded over 2,000 of them. His efforts allowed for an increase in publications of Calvin's sermons and serve as valuable records of Calvin's theology. Raguenier served as Calvin's stenographer until his death around 1560.

Pierre Viret (1511-1571) Reformer and church leader. Born in Orbe, near Lausanne, Viret adopted Protestantism during his studies in Paris in the late 1520s. He worked alongside Guillaume Farel to spread the Reformation message in the Pays de Vaud and Geneva, surviving two assassination attempts in the process. From 1536 to 1559, he served as the chief pastor of Lausanne. He later served in Geneva and ended his career as a pastor in Béarn, in southwestern France. A noted preacher and popularizer of the Reformation message, Viret played a key role in promoting and establishing the Reformed faith, alongside his close friends and colleagues Guillaume Farel and John Calvin.

Places

Geneva Now a city (and canton) in modern-day Switzerland, Geneva was historically an ecclesiastical state ruled by a prince-bishop. As the Reformation began in the early sixteenth century, the elected councils and the four top city officials known as syndics started to assume more power in Geneva in an effort to rid themselves of the control of their bishop and of their overlord, the Duke of Savoy. Geneva's Reformation was first propagated by Guillaume Farel, who recruited a young John Calvin to help in his efforts. The two were expelled in 1538, but Calvin returned in 1541, and with the support of the city government he set up ecclesiastical ordinances to govern the Reformed church and city. The Reformation that took place in Geneva gave the city a considerable reputation and a prominent role in the formation of the Reformed movement across Europe.

Saint Gervais Church Notable church in Geneva. The Temple de Saint-Gervais was built in the fifteenth century on the foundations of a tenth-century Romanesque church.

Saint Pierre Cathedral Famous Genevan cathedral built in the Romanesque and Gothic styles on the upper reaches of Geneva's old city. The construction of Saint Pierre started in the twelfth century.

Strasbourg Located on the west bank of the Rhine River in the greater Alsatian region, Strasbourg was historically a free imperial city of the Holy Roman Empire. The Reformation came to Strasbourg in 1521 through the work of Reformers including Matthias Zell,

Wolfgang Capito, Caspar Hedio, and Martin Bucer. For most of the sixteenth century, Strasbourg's chief pastor was Johannes Marbach, a strong Lutheran. Controversy developed in the city when Marbach and his colleagues clashed with the leadership of the Strasbourg academy. Marbach felt that the academy, under the oversight of rector Johannes Sturm, was too Calvinist in its leanings. Sturm and the academy triumphed temporarily, but Marbach's successor, Johann Pappus, was able to reverse the tide, and in 1581 Sturm was dismissed from the academy. Lutheranism once again became a powerful force in Strasbourg. Pappus also developed a new church order that codified the procedures that had become customary during Marbach's time in Strasbourg. This order was officially recognized in 1598, and in the process Strasbourg officially became Lutheran.

Temple de la Madeleine Notable church in Geneva. The Temple de la Madeleine was built in the fifteenth century on the ruins of religious buildings dating back to the fifth century.

Glossary of Terms

Absolution A theological term for forgiveness granted by God through words spoken by a priest in the sacrament of penance or confession.

Banns The announcement of the names of the prospective bride and groom, read from the pulpit over the course of several weeks so that those with objections could let the pastor know if there were any impediments to the wedding, such as a prior engagement or marriage.

Carmelites Members of the Roman Catholic Order of the Brothers of the Blessed Virgin Mary of Mount Carmel, founded in the late twelfth or early thirteenth century.

Castellan (or *châtelain*) The most senior representative of the Genevan government in the countryside.

Catechesis The teaching of converts or children so that they may learn the basics of the Christian faith.

Catechism The summary of Christian doctrine taught in Geneva during weekly Sunday-afternoon church services, intended primarily for children, servants, and those new to the Reformed faith. The question-and-answer format was intended to aid memorization. John Calvin published two catechisms in Geneva: his 1538 version was intended for the use of pastors, and his 1541/42 version for the general population.

Chasuble A liturgical vestment worn during church services by clergy in the Catholic, Anglican, and Lutheran traditions.

Chrism Anointing with holy oil (see the Form for the Celebration of Baptism).

Christening The Christian sacrament and ceremony during which an infant or an adult convert is baptized and named.

Cloister This term refers specifically to a sheltered walkway between buildings or around the perimeter of a garden or an enclosure in a monastery or nunnery. The term can also be used more generally as a synonym for a monastery or nunnery.

Consistory An ecclesiastical council that oversees spiritual matters in individual congregations in the Reformed Christian faith. The Genevan Consistory, established in 1542, included all the pastors of the city and twelve lay elders from the city councils (appointed by their fellow councilors) and was presided over by one of the city's four top government officials, known as syndics. The Genevan Consistory met weekly and dealt with any and all matters of faith and life in the city, including marital issues, family and neighbor quarrels, unorthodoxy and persisting in Catholic practices, and so on. The Consistory had no power to inflict physical punishment or imprisonment; its only sanctions were verbal admonitions and suspensions from the Lord's Supper, though it could refer recalcitrant parishioners to the city government for further and more forceful action.

Council of Constance An ecumenical council held in the southern German city of Constance from 1414 to 1418. The council ended the "Three Popes Controversy," which had divided Catholics' allegiance between three different claimants to the Papacy.

Council of Frankfurt An ecumenical council called by Charlemagne in 794. The council condemned Adoptionism, which suggested that Jesus was adopted as the Son of God at the time of his baptism. The council also revoked the decrees regarding icons made during the Second Council of Nicaea in 787.

Council of Nicaea (The Second Council of Nicaea) An ecumenical council held in in 787, in which the use of icons was restored.

Council of Trent A Catholic church council held from 1545 to 1563. The council worked to cleanse the church from corruption highlighted by Protestant critics, but at the same time it reiterated foundational Catholic doctrines, such as belief in Purgatory, transubstantiation, the role of the Virgin Mary and the saints as mediators, and so on.

Guardians Lower-level officials appointed by the Genevan city government to provide a measure of law and order and behavior oversight in the Genevan countryside.

Iconoclasm The destruction of religious images.

Lent Forty-day season of the church year that falls between Ash Wednesday and Easter. Lent was traditionally a season of penance and prayer.

Manicheanism A gnostic religion originating from the teachings of the prophet Mani (AD 216-274). Manicheanism stressed dualism between the spiritual and the physical, the spirit and the body, and between good and evil.

Paternosters Catholic prayer books, usually including a number of key prayers in Latin, such as the Lord's Prayer (*Pater Noster*) and the Hail Mary (*Ave Maria*), as well as portions of the Psalms and liturgies. By extension, the term refers to rote prayers recited in Latin, including the Lord's Prayer.

Regents Male Latin schoolteachers in Geneva whose instruction was at a middle-school or high-school level.

Reliquary A specially made container for relics, which were usually objects associated with or actual physical parts (e.g., bones) of holy persons such as saints, the Virgin Mary, or Christ.

Satrap A high-ranking government official of ancient Persia.

Suggestions for Further Study

Read these books and articles:

Beeke, Joel R. "Calvin and Preaching: The Power of the Word." In *Calvin: Theologian and Reformer*, edited by Joel R. Beeke and Garry J. Williams, 137-67. Grand Rapids: Reformation Heritage Books, 2010.

Cammenga, Ronald L. "Calvin's Reformation of Public Worship." *Protestant Reformed Theological Journal* 44, no. 1 (2010): 3-26.

Grosse, Christian. "Places of Sanctification: The Liturgical Sacrality of Genevan Reformed Churches, 1535-1566." In *Sacred Space in Early Modern Europe*, edited by Will Coster and Andrew Spicer, 60-80. Cambridge: Cambridge University Press, 2005.

Hyde, Daniel R. "According to the Custom of the Ancient Church? Examining the Roots of John Calvin's Liturgy." *Puritan Reformed Journal* 1, no. 2 (2009): 189–211.

Johnson, Terry L. "Calvin the Liturgist." In *Tributes to John Calvin: A Celebration of His Quincentenary*, edited by David W. Hall, 118-52. Phillipsburg, N.J.: P&R Publishing, 2010.

Kingdon, Robert M. "The Genevan Revolution in Public Worship." *Princeton Seminary Bulletin* 20, no. 3 (1999): 264–80.

———. "Nostalgia for Catholic Rituals in Calvin's Geneva." In *Grenzgänge der Theologie. Professor Alexandre Ganoczy zum 75. Geburtstag*, edited by Otmar Meuffels and Jürgen Bründl, 209-20. Münster: LIT, 2004.

Lambert, Thomas A. "Preaching, Praying, and Policing the Reform in Sixteenth-Century Geneva." Ph.D. dissertation, University of Wisconsin-Madison, 1998.

Luth, Jan Roelof. "Where Do Genevan Psalms Come From?" *Reformed Music Journal* 5, no. 2 (1993): 33-43.

Maag, Karin, and John D. Witvliet, editors. *Worship in Medieval and Early Modern Europe: Change and Continuity in Religious Practice*. Notre Dame: University of Notre Dame Press, 2004.

McKee, Elsie Anne. "Context, Contours, Contents: Towards a Description of the Reformed Teaching on Worship." *Princeton Seminary Bulletin* 16, no. 2 (1995): 172-201.

Naphy, William. *Calvin and the Consolidation of the Genevan Reformation*. Manchester: Manchester University Press, 1994.

Old, Hughes Oliphant. "Calvin's Theology of Worship." In *Give Praise to God: A Vision for*

Reforming Worship, edited by Philip Graham Ryken et al., 412-35. Phillipsburg: P&R Publishing, 2003.

Spierling, Karen E. *Infant Baptism in Reformation Geneva: The Shaping of a Community, 1536-1564*. Louisville: Westminster John Knox Press, 2009.

Visit these Web sites:

Virtual Tour of Geneva, Saint Pierre Cathedral
http://www.360cities.net/virtual-tour/geneva-switzerland?view=simple

Saint Pierre Photos
http://www.sacred-destinations.com/switzerland/geneva-cathedral/photos

Genevan Psalter Resources Center (with music files for each Psalm)
http://www.genevan psalter.com/

International Museum of the Reformation, Geneva
http://www.musee-reforme.ch/enresai

Works Cited

Anonymous. *Passevent Parisien respondant à Pasquin Romain. De la vie de ceux qui sont allez demourer à Genève, et se disent vivre selon la réformation de l'Évangile: faict en forme de Dialogue.* Reprint of the third edition published in 1556. Paris: Isidore Liseux, 1875.

La Bible, qui est toute la saincte Escriture, contenant le vieil & le nouveau Testament, autrement, la vieille & la nouvelle alliance. Geneva: François Estienne, 1567.

Calvin, John. *Calvin's Commentaries: The First Epistle of Paul the Apostle to the Corinthians.* Translated by John W. Fraser, edited by David W. Torrance and Thomas F. Torrance. Grand Rapids: Eerdmans, 1960.

——. *Calvin's Commentaries: The Epistle of Paul the Apostle to the Hebrews and The First and Second Epistles of St Peter.* Translated by William B. Johnston, edited by David W. Torrance and Thomas F. Torrance. Grand Rapids: Eerdmans, 1963.

——. *Calvin's Commentaries: The Gospel according to St. John 1-10.* Translated by T. H. L. Parker, edited by David W. Torrance and Thomas F. Torrance. Grand Rapids: Eerdmans, 1961.

——. *Calvin's Ecclesiastical Advice.* Translated by Mary D. Beaty and Benjamin Wirt Farley. Louisville: Westminster/John Knox Press, 1991.

——. *Commentaires de M. Jean Calvin sur le livre des Pseaumes.* [Geneva]: Conrad Badius, 1561.

——. *Epistolae et Responsa.* Geneva: Pierre de Saint-André, 1575.

——. *La Forme des Prieres et Chantz Ecclesiastiques.* Facsimile of the original 1542 Genevan edition. Edited by Pierre Pidoux. Kassel: Barenreiter, 1959.

——. *Institution de la religion Chrestienne. Nouvellement mise en quatre Livres: & distinguée par Chapitres, en ordre & methode bien propre: Augmentee aussi de tel accroissement, qu'on la peut presque estimer un livre nouveau.* Geneva: Jean Crespin, 1560.

——. *Joannis Calvini Opera Quae Supersunt Omnia.* Edited by W. Baum, E. Cunitz, and E. Reuss. 59 vols. Braunschweig: Schwetschke and Son, 1863-1900.

——. *Joannis Calvini Opera Selecta.* Edited by P. Barth and D. Scheuner. 5 vols. Munich: Kaiser, 1952.

——. *Sermons on 2 Samuel: Chapters 1-13.* Translated by Douglas Kelly. Edinburgh: The Banner of Truth Trust, 1992.

————. *Supplementa Calviniana*, Volume I. Edited by Hans Rückert. Neukirchener Verlag, 1961.

Doumergue, Emile. *La Genève Calviniste*. Lausanne: Bridel, 1905.

Duke, A. C., Gillian Lewis, and Andrew Pettegree. *Calvinism in Europe, 1540-1610: A Collection of Documents*. Manchester: Manchester University Press, 1992.

Fatio, Olivier. *Understanding the Reformation*. Geneva: International Museum of the Reformation, 2005.

Gautier, Adolphe. "Un jeune Bâlois à Genève au XVIe siècle." In *Mémoires et documents publiés par la société d'histoire et d'archéologie de Genève* 17 (1872): 412-16.

Heyer, Henri. *1555-1909: L'Eglise de Genève: esquisse historique de son organisation, suivie de ses diverses constitutions, de la liste de ses pasteurs et professeurs et d'une table biographique*. Geneva: A. Jullien, 1909.

Kingdon, R., and J.-F. Bergier, editors. *Registres de la Compagnie des Pasteurs de Genève au temps de Calvin*. Geneva: Droz, 1964.

Kingdon, R., T. Lambert, and I. Watt, editors. *Registers of the Consistory of Geneva in the Time of Calvin: Volume 1: 1542-1544*. Grand Rapids: Eerdmans, 2000.

Kingdon, R., T. Lambert, and I. Watt, editors. *Registres du Consistoire de Genève au temps de Calvin*. Volumes II-IV. Geneva: Droz, 2001-2007.

Lambert, Thomas A. "Preaching, Praying, and Policing the Reform in Sixteenth-Century Geneva." Ph.D. dissertation, University of Wisconsin-Madison, 1998.

Maag, Karin, and John D. Witvliet, editors. *Worship in Medieval and Early Modern Europe*. Notre Dame: University of Notre Dame Press, 2004.

McKee, Elsie, editor. *John Calvin: Writings on Pastoral Piety*. New York: Paulist Press, 2001.

Naphy, W. G. *Calvin and the Consolidation of the Genevan Reformation*. Manchester: Manchester University Press, 1994.

Reid, J. K. S., editor. *Calvin: Theological Treatises*. Philadelphia: Westminster Press, 1954.

Rivoire, Emile, and Victor van Berchem, editors. *Les Sources du droit du canton de Genève*. 4 vols. Aarau: H. R. Sauerländer, 1927-1935.

Spierling, Karen E. *Infant Baptism in Reformation Geneva: The Shaping of a Community, 1536-1564*. Louisville: Westminster John Knox Press, 2009.

Spon, Isaac [sic for Jacques]. *The History of the City and State of Geneva from Its First Foundation to This present Time*. London: Bernard White, 1687.

Van den Berg, M. A., W. J. Eradus, and Sjaak Verboom. *Van Noyon tot Genève: tien woonplaatsen van Calvijn in beeld*. Bunnik: De Banier, 2009.

Vischer, Lukas, Lukas Schenker, Rudolf Dellsperger, and Olivier Fatio, editors. *Histoire du Christianisme en Suisse: une perspective œcuménique*. Geneva: Editions Labor et Fides, 1995.

Index

Baptism, 4, 14, 19, 25, 26, 27, 31, 35, 54, 58, 59, 62, 67, 70, 72, 78, 79, 80, 81, 101, 102, 107, 145, 149, 155, 161, 164, 165, 166, 168, 169, 170, 171-73, 174, 176, 180, 181, 184, 189, 192, 194

Baptisms: emergency, 19, 27, 157, 184; private, 58, 59, 165, 170

Basel, 4, 17, 27, 31, 36, 66

Bern, 4, 7, 13, 16, 27, 37, 46

Berthelier, Philibert (the elder), 6

Berthelier, Philibert (the younger), 172

Beza, Theodore, 11, 29, 62, 90, 92, 143, 185

Bullinger, Heinrich, 46

Calvin, Idelette (de Bure), 9

Calvin, John, 5, 6, 8, 9, 10, 11, 13, 17, 18, 19, 21, 22, 25, 27, 28, 29, 30, 33, 40, 42, 48, 49, 50, 61, 62, 64, 78, 87, 88, 89, 90, 107, 108. 143, 148, 153, 171, 185, 193, 195; commentaries of, 18, 113-38, 191, 194; correspondence of, 18, 29, 48-60, 190; *Institutes of the Christian Religion*, 10, 28, 108-13, 194; sermons of, 18, 21, 96-106, 194

Catechizing, 68, 69, 70, 71, 72, 150

Catholic feast days, 19, 160, 161, 162, 163, 167

Catholic worship practices, 29, 32, 53, 54, 55, 105, 112, 120, 121, 124, 125, 127, 132, 136, 162, 163, 166, 170-71, 180, 184, 185, 193

Catholicism, 18, 20, 25, 108, 192, 195

Chauvet, Reymond, 32

Confession/penance, 14, 48, 73, 74, 135

Confirmation, 14

Cop, Michel, 25, 171-73

Courault, Antoine, 8

Deacons, 14, 62, 82, 149, 174

Elders, 14, 17, 20, 25, 32, 68, 70, 106, 111, 151, 158

Erasmus, Desiderius, 6, 131

Farel, Guillaume, 7, 8, 32, 61, 82, 152

Forme des Prieres, 9, 13, 27, 73-85, 89, 90, 91

France, 3, 6, 8, 9, 10, 11, 12, 14, 16, 17, 21, 22, 35, 39, 45, 51, 52, 57, 60, 96, 132, 143, 156

Fribourg, 6, 7

Froment, Antoine, 7

Funerals, 31, 64, 150, 176

Geneva, church of: and bishop of Geneva, 3, 6, 8, 25; catechism of, 9, 13, 20, 25, 28, 67, 85-88, 149, 150, 162, 186, 190, 193; catechism service in, 25, 26, 69, 78, 150, 151, 156, 171, 176, 179, 183, 184; and church buildings, 20, 29, 31, 38, 39, 41, 42, 43, 44, 63, 148, 157, 175, 184; church discipline in, 8, 13, 151-74, 178, 179, 194; and the Company of Pastors, 9, 31, 32, 55, 148; consistory of, 9, 17, 20, 21, 25, 31, 32, 41, 63, 64, 68, 70, 71, 151-74, 176, 178, 179, 181, 183, 184, 194; ecclesiastical ordinances of, 9, 13, 20, 27, 51, 82, 148-51, 175, 182; Genevan Academy of, 10, 30, 66, 148, 185-86; and *Hôpital general*, 8, 164, 174; and household worship, 19, 66, 190, 193; Sunday worship in, 20, 29, 67, 68, 73, 148, 175, 176, 182, 186; weekday worship in, 29, 68, 148-49, 176, 181, 182, 186

Geneva, city of, 3, 4, 5, 8, 9, 10, 11, 12, 13, 15, 16, 17, 19, 20, 21, 22, 25, 26, 27, 28, 30, 32, 35, 36, 37, 38, 39, 40, 41, 44, 46, 48, 61, 62, 96, 107, 113, 143, 189, 192, 195, 196, 197; and Council of Two Hundred, 8, 175, 177, 178; and General Council, 4, 6, 8, 148, 175; and Small Council, 31, 32, 174, 175, 177, 181; and Syndics, 3, 32, 151, 153, 168, 175, 176, 177, 180

Godparents, 26, 35, 70, 80, 149, 161, 166, 172, 184

Iconoclasm, 29, 46, 139

Images, 4, 13, 18, 29, 30, 31, 46, 47, 54, 55, 59, 60, 63, 99, 100, 122, 139, 140-42, 160, 185, 190, 193, 194, 196

Last rites/extreme unction, 14

Lausanne, 27, 62, 185

Liturgical space/church interiors, 30, 32, 63, 110, 184, 190, 193, 197

Liturgy, 4, 13, 14, 15, 18, 27, 28, 29, 30, 48, 63, 64, 66, 73-84, 89, 94, 144, 156, 193, 197

Lord's Supper/Communion, 4, 14, 19, 30, 31, 34, 48, 54, 56, 57, 65, 66, 67, 68, 70, 72, 75, 76, 77, 101, 102, 107, 125-36, 145, 149, 150, 151, 152, 153, 154, 155, 157, 158, 159, 161, 163, 164, 165, 167, 169, 170, 177, 178, 179, 180, 184, 186, 191, 192

Lord's Supper/Communion for the sick, 49

Luther, Martin, 4, 6, 7, 9

Lyon, 3, 30, 45, 63

Marot, Clément, 21, 29, 90, 92, 143

Marriage/weddings, 14, 31, 41, 63-64, 67, 71, 82, 82, 83, 84, 125, 150, 169, 174, 180, 189, 192

Mary (Virgin), 20, 28, 55, 63, 141, 153, 156, 157, 159, 162, 166

Mass, 4, 7, 8, 14, 20, 30, 34, 43, 64, 101, 112, 127, 132, 136, 149, 152, 153, 156, 158, 160, 162, 166, 167, 185, 197

Netherlands, the, 3, 7, 11, 12, 33, 46, 143

Neuchâtel, 14, 32, 61

Ordination, 14, 50, 51, 52

Perrot, Charles, 17, 21, 31, 66-72, 82, 193

Prayers/praying, 20, 21, 28, 32, 54, 57, 63, 64, 66, 69-70, 71, 74, 75, 76, 77, 80, 84, 85, 86, 87, 88, 93, 94, 102, 103, 104, 108-13, 114, 115, 118, 119, 120, 123, 126, 138, 143, 144, 145, 152, 154, 156, 157, 158, 159, 161, 162, 164, 165, 168, 173, 176, 180, 181, 182, 190, 193, 196, 197

Preaching/sermons, 21, 28, 30, 32, 43, 50, 51, 52, 53, 57, 61, 64, 65, 69, 71, 74, 78, 82, 96-106, 144, 151-52, 154, 156, 158, 159, 160, 161, 163, 165, 166, 167, 168, 170, 171, 173, 177, 179, 180, 182, 183, 184, 186, 197

Psalm-singing, 20, 21, 29, 32, 63, 67, 74, 76, 90, 91, 92, 94, 95, 104, 105, 111, 112, 143-47, 150, 186, 190, 194, 196, 197

Ryff, André, 17, 19, 31, 66, 190, 193

Sadoleto, Jacopo, cardinal, 13

Savoy, Duchy of, 3, 8, 12, 16, 20, 37, 180

Savoy, Duke of, 3, 6, 12, 25, 169

Strasbourg, 5, 8, 9, 21, 27, 29, 78, 89, 148, 151, 185

Viret, Pierre, 61, 62

Zurich, 4, 6, 7, 13, 27, 46

Zwingli, Huldrych, 6, 7

CPSIA information can be obtained
at www.ICGtesting.com
Printed in the USA
LVHW022002090122
708132LV00006B/380

9 780802 871473